Mastering Jenkins

From Basics to Expert Proficiency

Contents

Introduction

Jenkins is an integral part of modern software development practices, playing a pivotal role in the implementation of Continuous Integration and Continuous Delivery (CI/CD). This book, "Mastering Jenkins: From Basics to Expert Proficiency," is meticulously designed to guide readers from the foundational concepts to advanced techniques, equipping them with the skills required to proficiently use Jenkins in real-world scenarios.

Jenkins, an open-source automation server, has evolved significantly since its inception. Initially developed as a fork of the Hudson project, Jenkins has emerged as the de facto standard for CI/CD automation. Its robust architecture, flexibility, and extensibility make it an indispensable tool for development teams of all sizes.

This book is structured to provide a comprehensive understanding of Jenkins. We begin with an introduction to Jenkins, covering its history, evolution, and role in CI/CD pipelines. We delve deep into the Jenkins architecture, key features, and the various editions and distributions available. Readers will become familiar with the essential terminology and system requirements, setting a solid foundation for the subsequent chapters.

Setting up Jenkins effectively is crucial for maximizing its potential. We guide readers through the installation process on different operating systems, including Windows, macOS, and Linux, as well as running Jenkins in Docker. The initial setup and configuration, including security settings, user management, and plugin installation, are thoroughly covered to ensure a smooth and secure start.

Jenkins Pipelines, a powerful feature for defining complex workflows, are explored in detail. Readers will learn the differences between scripted and declarative pipelines, how to set up and manage pipelines as code, and the best practices for designing efficient and maintainable pipelines. The use of the Blue Ocean interface for visualizing pipeline stages is also addressed.

Automated testing is a cornerstone of CI/CD, and Jenkins excels in this area. This book covers the setup and execution of various types of automated tests, including unit tests, integration tests, and end-to-end tests. The integration of popular test frameworks and the systematic handling of test results and failures are meticulously discussed.

The chapters on Continuous Integration and Continuous Delivery elucidate how Jenkins facilitates these practices. From integrating version control systems, automating builds, managing dependencies, to deploying applications and release management, readers gain a comprehensive understanding of how to effectively implement CI/CD pipelines using Jenkins.

Managing Jenkins involves a wide array of tasks, from configuration and monitoring to managing nodes, plugins, and credentials. We provide detailed instructions and best practices for efficient Jenkins management, ensuring that the system remains robust, secure, and performant.

Security is paramount in any CI/CD environment. This book dedicates a chapter to Jenkins security, covering authentication, authorization, role-based access control, SSL setups, and best practices to safeguard the Jenkins environment.

Integration with other tools is another critical aspect of Jenkins. Detailed guidance on integrating Jenkins with version control systems, build tools, containerization tools, testing frameworks, monitoring tools, cloud services, and issue tracking systems is provided. This ensures that Jenkins can seamlessly fit into a diverse range of technology stacks.

Finally, we explore advanced Jenkins features, including using the Jenkins DSL, implementing shared libraries, setting up multi-branch pipelines, customizing the Jenkins UI, creating custom plugins, and optimizing Jenkins for performance and scalability. These advanced topics equip readers with the knowledge to handle sophisticated CI/CD requirements and scale Jenkins to meet the demands of large, complex projects.

"Mastering Jenkins: From Basics to Expert Proficiency" is designed to be a comprehensive reference for both beginners and experienced users. With detailed explanations, step-by-step instructions, and best practices, this book aims to empower readers to leverage Jenkins to its fullest potential, thereby enhancing the efficiency and effectiveness of their software development processes.

Chapter 1

Introduction to Jenkins

This chapter provides a foundational understanding of Jenkins, including its definition, historical background, and evolution in the context of software development. It explores the role Jenkins plays in continuous integration and continuous delivery (CI/CD), outlines its architecture, and highlights key features that make it essential for automation. The chapter also covers the different editions and distributions of Jenkins, introduces basic terminology, explains system requirements, and discusses the advantages and limitations of using Jenkins in various development environments.

1.1 What is Jenkins?

Jenkins is an open-source automation server extensively employed for continuous integration (CI) and continuous delivery (CD) processes in software development. It orchestrates the automation of various developmental stages, ensuring that the code developed by multiple contributors is integrated smoothly and deployed efficiently. Jenkins achieves this through its vast array of plugins, which extend its capabilities to accommodate various tasks and tools commonly used in modern software development pipelines.

Developed initially as Hudson by Kohsuke Kawaguchi in 2004, Jenkins emerged as a separate entity following a fork in 2011. Since then, it has grown to become a cornerstone of DevOps practices, providing a robust platform for automating repetitive tasks, thus reducing manual efforts and minimizing the potential for human error.

A critical aspect that defines Jenkins is its capacity to monitor the execution of repeated jobs, such as building a software project or running pre-defined tests. By continuously integrating new code changes and running automated tests, Jenkins helps maintain a stable codebase and facilitates early detection of defects.

For those working in environments with multiple developers, Jenkins offers a consistent and repeatable build process. Each developer can have their code changes integrated, tested, and validated systematically, ensuring consistency across development cycles. This capability becomes even more critical when dealing with complex projects where code dependencies and integration challenges are prevalent.

The system's modular architecture allows it to be highly extensible. Jenkins can integrate seamlessly with various version control systems (VCS) such as Git, Subversion, and Mercurial. Moreover, it supports numerous build tools including Maven, Gradle, and Ant, making it adaptable to different development approaches such as continuous delivery, continuous deployment, and agile methodologies.

Jenkins operates primarily through jobs or projects. These jobs can be configured to execute various tasks such as pulling the latest code from a version control repository, compiling the code, running tests, and deploying the artifacts to a staging or production environment. An example of a simple Jenkins pipeline configuration, defined in a Jenkinsfile, might look like this:

```
pipeline {
    agent any
    stages {
        stage('Build') {
            steps {
                // Command to build the project
                sh 'mvn clean package'
            }
        }
        stage('Test') {
            steps {
                // Command to run tests
                sh 'mvn test'
            }
        }
        stage('Deploy') {
            steps {
                // Command to deploy the application
                sh 'scp target/myapp.jar user@server:/path/to/deploy'
            }
        }
    }
```

```
}
```

In the example above, the pipeline block defines a series of stages for building, testing, and deploying the project. The agent any directive indicates that the stages can run on any available Jenkins agent. Each stage contains specific steps executed sequentially, using shell commands (sh) to perform tasks like building with Maven, running tests, and copying files to a server.

Jenkins also supports distributed builds, where the workload can be delegated to multiple nodes, enhancing performance and enabling scalable automation. By setting up multiple agents, either on several physical machines or virtual environments, Jenkins can parallelize the execution of jobs. This parallelism is especially beneficial for large-scale projects with extensive test suites or complex build processes.

Furthermore, Jenkins' web-based interface provides an intuitive platform for managing and monitoring various jobs. Users can view job status, history, and console outputs, making it easier to diagnose issues and track the progress of ongoing activities. Jenkins' interface also supports customizable views and dashboards, which can be tailored to display relevant job metrics and key performance indicators.

Consider the following command to trigger a Jenkins job using the Jenkins REST API:

```
curl -X POST http://JENKINS_URL/job/JOB_NAME/build --user USER:TOKEN
```

In this command, http://JENKINS_URL/job/JOB_NAME/build specifies the job to trigger, with USER:TOKEN being the credentials used for authentication. This capability allows developers to integrate Jenkins job executions into other systems and scripts, further enhancing automation potential.

Jenkins' ecosystem includes various community-contributed plugins that augment its functionality. These plugins cover a wide array of needs, from source code management integrators to build notifiers and deployment pipelines. The Plugin Manager, accessible through Jenkins' interface, simplifies the process of installing and configuring these plugins.

Its enduring popularity is not only a testament to its effectiveness but also to the vibrant community that continuously maintains and enhances it. This collaborative effort ensures that Jenkins remains at the cutting edge of automation technologies, with regular updates and new plugins being made available to address emerging needs and challenges.

Jenkins' role as an automation server in CI/CD pipelines is indispensable for modern software practices. Its flexibility, extensive plugin ecosystem, and robust features make it an essential tool for achieving streamlined, error-free, and efficient software development and deployment processes. Through consistent integration, testing, and deployment, Jenkins contributes significantly to maintaining high development standards and accelerating the delivery of high-quality software products.

1.2 History and Evolution of Jenkins

Jenkins, originally developed under the name Hudson, emerged as a response to the challenges faced by software developers in managing and automating the continuous integration process. The inception of this tool dates back to 2004, when Kohsuke Kawaguchi, a software developer at Sun Microsystems, began the project as an internal tool to make his own job of running tests and builds more efficient.

The initial release of Hudson occurred in 2005. Its purpose was to act as an automation server that could handle the building, testing, and deployment of software applications, ensuring that these processes were conducted in a consistent and controlled manner. Hudson quickly gained traction due to its user-friendly interface, extensibility, and the capability of easing the burden on development teams by automating repeated tasks.

The project's popularity grew rapidly within the software development community, and its adoption spread across many organizations, both large and small. A watershed moment for the project came in 2008 when Hudson reached the milestone of 1,000 installs. This testified not only to its utility but also to the community's trust in the software.

In 2010, a rift between Hudson's developers and Oracle, which acquired Sun Microsystems, led to a crucial fork in the project. Oracle's control over the project and the associated trademark prompted the majority of the core developers, including Kawaguchi, to fork Hudson into what is now known as Jenkins. This decision was driven by the need for a more open, community-led governance model that could better support and sustain the tool's development and usage in the spirit of open-source software.

In February 2011, the rename to Jenkins was officially announced, and the Jenkins project remained under the governance of the Software Freedom Conservancy to ensure the community's needs were the guiding force behind the project's evolution. This pivotal moment in the history of Jenkins marked the true beginning of continuous growth and evolution independent of corporate dominance.

From its inception, Jenkins has evolved significantly. Initially focused on build automation, Jenkins has expanded to become the face of Continuous Integration (CI) and Continuous Delivery (CD). The extensive plugin infrastructure is one of its most significant evolutions. The Jenkins ecosystem consists of a rich collection of plugins that extend its functionality to support various aspects of software development lifecycle automation. Jenkins plugins facilitate integration with a plethora of tools and platforms, spanning version control systems, build tools, testing frameworks, deployment services, and more.

Jenkins 2.0, released in April 2016, marked a new chapter by delivering new features aimed at simplifying CI/CD for new and experienced users alike. One of the central features introduced in Jenkins 2.0 was Pipelines as Code. The Pipeline DSL (Domain-Specific Language) enabled developers to script their build, test, and deployment workflows using the Groovy-based Jenkinsfile format. This transition advocated the shift from freestyle projects to pipeline-based projects, promoting the "pipeline-as-code" paradigm that enhances visibility, code review, and version control of Jenkins jobs.

The LTS (Long-Term Support) releases ensure stability and reliability, catering to production environments where stability is paramount. Jenkins' LTS releases receive rigorous testing and come with backported fixes, offering a balance between the cutting-edge and reliable performance.

The Jenkins community has been a driving force in its evolution, contributing to an ever-expanding repository of plugins, improving core functionality, and advocating best practices for CI/CD. Today, the Jenkins project is administered by the Continuous Delivery Foundation (CDF), which provides a neutral home for the project and its community, ensuring openness and collaboration continue to thrive.

Overall, the evolutionary journey of Jenkins reflects the broader shifts in software development practices—from simple build automation towards comprehensive continuous integration, continuous delivery, and DevOps adoption. By continuously adapting to the industry's needs and embracing community contributions, Jenkins has cemented its place as an indispensable tool in modern software development, facilitating the shift toward automated, continuous delivery pipelines, and agile methodologies.

1.3 The Role of Jenkins in CI/CD

Jenkins has become a cornerstone tool in the implementation of Continuous Integration (CI) and Continuous Delivery (CD) practices within modern software development workflows. These practices are essential for improving code quality, reducing time to market, and ensuring that applications are always in a deployable state. This section delves into the fundamental role Jenkins plays in orchestrating CI/CD pipelines, providing a detailed examination of its functionalities and impact on the software development lifecycle.

At the heart of CI/CD is the automation of repetitive tasks, which Jenkins excels at by scheduling and triggering the execution of scripts and processes according to predefined criteria. Jenkins supports a diverse range of plugins that extend its capabilities, allowing it to integrate seamlessly with various tools and technologies across the software development ecosystem.

Continuous Integration (CI)

Continuous Integration refers to the practice of frequently integrating code changes into a shared repository. This practice is designed to detect integration issues early by automatically building and testing code upon each code commit. Jenkins automates the CI process by:

- **Source Code Management (SCM) Integration:** Jenkins connects with various SCM tools such as Git, Subversion, and Mercurial. It listens for changes in the repository and triggers jobs to pull the latest code.
- **Build Automation:** Jenkins integrates with build tools such as Maven, Gradle, and Ant to automate the compilation, packaging, and assembly of code. This ensures that each commit leads to a new build, which can be evaluated for quality.
- **Automated Testing:** Jenkins executes automated tests (unit, integration, and functional tests) to validate the new code. Integration with testing frameworks such as JUnit, TestNG, and Selenium allows comprehensive testing coverage.

- **Notifications and Feedback:** Jenkins sends immediate feedback to developers through emails, dashboards, and other channels. This feedback loop ensures that errors are flagged and addressed promptly.

By automating these tasks, Jenkins helps maintain a consistent and reliable CI process. The main advantage of continuous integration is the early detection of defects, which minimizes the risk of integration problems spiraling into more significant issues.

Continuous Delivery (CD)

Continuous Delivery extends the principles of CI by ensuring that the software is always releasable to production. CD encompasses the practices that allow code changes to be automatically tested and prepared for release to production. Jenkins facilitates CD by managing the deployment pipeline, which includes several critical stages:

- **Build Deployment:** Jenkins can deploy the successfully built artifacts to various environments (development, staging, production). This deployment can involve copying files, running container orchestrations, or even managing VM instances.
- **Environment Provisioning:** Integration with infrastructure as code (IaC) tools such as Terraform, Ansible, and Docker allows Jenkins to dynamically provision and configure environments tailored for testing and production.
- **Release Automation:** Jenkins automates the tasks needed to release software to end-users, such as versioning, tagging releases, and ensuring proper package distributions.
- **Post-deployment Testing:** After deployment, Jenkins can orchestrate post-deployment tests to verify that the application works as expected in the target environment. Integration with performance testing tools like Apache JMeter and load testing services adds further validation.

Continuous Delivery aims to shorten the time between writing a code change and the change being deployed in production without compromising on quality and stability. Jenkins's powerful orchestration capabilities make CD practical by managing the complexity and providing visibility into every stage of the deployment pipeline.

Integration with Other Tools

Jenkins enhances the CI/CD process by seamlessly integrating with a multitude of other tools. Some of these integrations include:

- **Configuration Management:** Tools like Chef, Puppet, and Salt-Stack help Jenkins manage and configure software rocesses and infrastructure, paving the way for consistent and repeatable deployments.
- **Artifact Repositories:** Jenkins can publish built artifacts to repositories like Nexus, Artifactory, or Docker Hub, ensuring traceability and version control of deployed applications.
- **Monitoring and Logging:** Integrations with monitoring tools like Prometheus, Grafana, and ELK stack enable Jenkins to monitor the health of deployments and collect logs for analysis and troubleshooting.
- **Notification and Collaboration:** Jenkins integrates with collaboration tools such as Slack, Microsoft Teams, and email systems to keep all stakeholders informed about the build and release status.

Pipeline as Code

One of Jenkins's most powerful features for managing CI/CD pipelines is the Pipeline as Code. This approach uses a Jenkinsfile—a script written in Groovy—to define the entire CI/CD pipeline. The Jenkinsfile is stored in the source code repository, providing a version-controlled, human-readable blueprint of the pipeline. Here is a simple example of a Jenkinsfile:

```
pipeline {
    agent any

    stages {
        stage('Build') {
            steps {
                echo 'Building...'
                sh 'make'
            }
        }
        stage('Test') {
            steps {
                echo 'Testing...'
                sh 'make test'
            }
        }
        stage('Deploy') {
            steps {
                echo 'Deploying...'
                sh 'make deploy'
            }
```

```
            }
        }

        post {
            success {
                echo 'Pipeline completed successfully!'
            }
            failure {
                echo 'Pipeline failed.'
            }
        }
    }
```

The concise nature of Jenkinsfiles promotes the consistent and reproducible definition of pipelines, further integrating Jenkins deeply into the software development workflow.

In essence, Jenkins serves as the backbone of CI/CD, offering an extensive array of functionalities designed to optimize and accelerate the development pipeline. By automating necessary tasks and integrating with numerous tools, Jenkins not only increases efficiency but also enhances the quality and consistency of software products.

1.4 Jenkins Architecture

Jenkins' architecture is designed to be highly modular and extensible, making it capable of scaling and adapting to various project needs. The core of Jenkins is based on a master-slave architecture, which allows it to distribute workloads efficiently across multiple nodes. This distributed model enhances Jenkins' capability to handle a vast number of build projects simultaneously, distributing the workload to ensure optimal performance and resource utilization.

The main components of Jenkins architecture are the Jenkins Master, Jenkins Slaves (or agents), the Build Executor, and the Job Configuration. Each of these components plays a significant role in ensuring that Jenkins operates smoothly and efficiently.

Jenkins Master

The Jenkins Master is the central control unit of the Jenkins environment. It is responsible for several key tasks:

- Scheduling build jobs.
- Dispatching builds to the Jenkins Slaves (agents) for actual execution.

- Monitoring the state of all the Jenkins Slavery nodes.
- Recording and presenting the build results.
- Providing the application's user interface, serving HTTP requests.

Additionally, the Master node houses all the configurations associated with the builds, including job configurations, build logs, and artifacts. It also manages plugins and system configurations.

Jenkins Slaves (Agents)

Jenkins Slaves, or agents, are Java executables that run on remote machines. They are responsible for executing build jobs that the Master assigns to them. A Jenkins environment can include one or more Slaves, which can run on various operating systems, thereby allowing for a diverse and flexible build environment. The connection between the Master and the Slave can be established via HTTP or SSH protocols.

Key aspects of Jenkins Slaves include:

- Slaves can run on a variety of platforms, including Linux, Windows, and macOS.
- Each Slave can run a specific job or a set of jobs based on the configuration.
- Slaves can be temporarily disabled (taken offline) when not needed, to save resources.
- The communication between Master and Slave is secured via encryption.

Build Executor

Each Jenkins Slave node has one or more Build Executors. These executors are the actual agents that carry out the build tasks assigned by the Master. A Build Executor can be thought of as a single-threaded entity that runs one job at a time. The number of executors can be configured based on the hardware capacity of the Slavery node. Increasing the number of executors increases the parallel processing capability but may lead to resource contention if not managed properly.

Job Configuration

Job Configuration in Jenkins defines what a build will do. This includes:

- Source code management (SCM) configurations, specifying where the source code resides (e.g., Git repository).
- Build triggers that define how a build is initiated (manually, scheduled, after a push to SCM, etc.).
- Build steps that detail the actions taken to compile the code, run tests, etc.
- Post-build actions like archiving artifacts, sending notifications, or deploying applications.
- Plugins integration that adds additional functionalities or steps to the job.

Jenkins jobs can be configured through the web interface or using configuration files to script the setup of complex build pipelines.

Plugins and Extensibility

A key part of Jenkins' architecture is its plugin system. Jenkins is designed to be highly extensible, and this extensibility is primarily achieved through plugins. Plugins in Jenkins offer numerous functionalities, such as:

- Integrating different SCM systems like Git, Subversion, Mercurial, etc.
- Adding additional build steps or post-build actions.
- Enhancing UI functionalities or providing new visualizations.
- Communicating with third-party tools like Slack, JIRA, or Docker.

The plugin framework supports both developing new plugins and integrating existing tools into Jenkins. The community-contributed plugin ecosystem ensures Jenkins remains flexible and up-to-date with the latest development practices and tools.

Here's an example of what a simple Jenkins job script might look like:

```
pipeline {
    agent any
    stages {
        stage('Checkout') {
            steps {
                git 'https://github.com/example/repo.git'
            }
        }
```

```
        stage('Build') {
            steps {
                sh './build.sh'
            }
        }
        stage('Test') {
            steps {
                sh './run-tests.sh'
            }
        }
        stage('Deploy') {
            steps {
                sh './deploy.sh'
            }
        }
    }
    post {
        always {
            archiveArtifacts artifacts: '**/target/*.jar', allowEmptyArchive: true
            mail to: 'team@example.com',
                subject: "Job '${env.JOB_NAME}' (${env.BUILD_NUMBER})
                    completed",
                body: "Job '${env.JOB_NAME}' (${env.BUILD_NUMBER})
                    completed successfully. Check the build logs at ${env.
                    BUILD_URL}."
        }
    }
}
```

Visualization and Monitoring

Efficient build monitoring and visualization play crucial roles in Jenkins architecture. Critical data visualization elements include:

- Build History and Console Output: These features allow developers and DevOps engineers to track the progress and outcomes of builds.
- Dashboard Views: Customizable dashboards in Jenkins provide overviews of project statuses, recent builds, and other crucial metrics.
- Notifications: Jenkins can be configured to send build status notifications via various channels like email, Slack, or other messaging platforms.
- Logs and Metrics: Logs provide detailed insights into build processes, while metrics can be consumed by monitoring tools like Prometheus for performance tracking.

Ensuring Jenkins is properly monitored entails leveraging existing plugins for logging and monitoring or integrating customized solutions as needed for specific project requirements.

The underlying architecture of Jenkins, with its modular design and extensible components, offers a robust framework for managing continuous integration and continuous delivery pipelines efficiently and reliably.

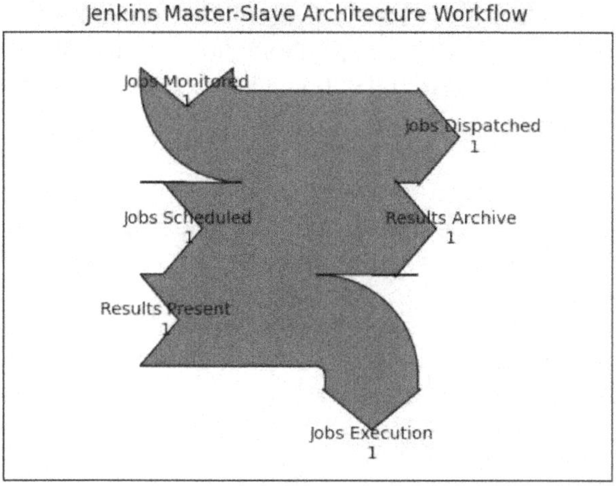

1.5 Key Features of Jenkins

Jenkins possesses a plethora of features that have established it as a cornerstone in CI/CD pipelines, offering flexibility, extensibility, and ease of use. This section will delve into some of the most notable features that distinguish Jenkins as a preeminent automation server.

1. **Open-Source Nature**: Jenkins is free and open-source, affording organizations the benefit of cost-effective automation. The open-source model also ensures continuous improvement and regular updates driven by a robust community of contributors and users. This contributes to the overall reliability and security of the platform.

2. **Extensible Plugin Architecture**: One of Jenkins' most powerful features is its extensive plugin ecosystem. With over 1,500 plugins available, users can customize Jenkins to meet specific requirements. Plugins cover a wide array of functionalities such as source code management (SCM), build tools, user interface customization, notifications,

and more. Here is a simple example that demonstrates how to install a plugin via the Jenkins Script Console:

```
Jenkins.instance.updateCenter.getPlugin("git").deploy()
```

3. Easy Installation and Configuration: Jenkins installation is straightforward, supporting various platforms including Windows, macOS, and numerous Unix-based systems. The initial setup is guided, requiring minimal manual configuration. An example of installing Jenkins on a Unix-based system using Docker is provided below:

```
docker run -p 8080:8080 -p 50000:50000 jenkins/jenkins:lts
```

4. Distributed Builds: Jenkins can distribute build and test loads across multiple machines, thus optimizing build processes by leveraging parallelism. This distributed approach not only expedites the CI/CD process but also enhances resource utilization and scalability. Configuration for distributed builds involves setting up a master node and multiple agent nodes. An example snippet for adding a new agent node through the Jenkins UI is as follows:

```
Jenkins.instance.addNode(new DumbSlave("agent-node", "Agent Node Description",
  "/home/jenkins", "1", Node.Mode.NORMAL, "label",
  new JNLPLauncher(), RetentionStrategy.INSTANCE, new ArrayList()))
```

5. Pipeline as Code: Jenkins Pipelines uses a 'Pipeline as Code' approach, enabling users to define build processes with a domain-specific language (DSL) based on Groovy. Pipelines can be version-controlled alongside application code. This promotes best practices for continuous integration and delivery. Below is an excerpt of a simple declarative pipeline script:

```
pipeline {
    agent any
    stages {
        stage('Build') {
            steps {
                echo 'Building...'
                sh 'make'
            }
        }
        stage('Test') {
            steps {
                echo 'Testing...'
                sh 'make test'
            }
        }
        stage('Deploy') {
            steps {
                echo 'Deploying...'
                sh 'make deploy'
            }
```

```
      }
    }
}
```

6. Rich Set of Integration Points: Jenkins integrates seamlessly with numerous third-party tools across the software development lifecycle. These integrations extend to SCM systems like Git and Subversion, build tools such as Maven and Gradle, and containerization platforms including Docker and Kubernetes, among others. This interoperability streamlines the integration process, facilitating cohesive workflows.

7. Robust Monitoring and Management: Jenkins provides extensive logging and monitoring capabilities. Users can configure and view detailed build logs, system logs, and monitor system health via the Jenkins Dashboard. Furthermore, Jenkins supports integration with various monitoring tools, ensuring proactive management of the automation server. Below is a command to fetch Jenkins system logs:

```
tail -f /var/log/jenkins/jenkins.log
```

8. Security: Jenkins offers a comprehensive security suite, including role-based access control (RBAC), matrix-based permissions, project-based security, and support for various authentication mechanisms such as LDAP, SAML, and OAuth. This ensures that access is restricted and managed appropriately, thereby safeguarding project and build information.

9. Community and Documentation: The vast Jenkins user community contributes to extensive documentation, forums, and user groups, which serve as valuable resources for troubleshooting, best practices, and knowledge sharing. This community support underpins the continual advancement and refinement of Jenkins features.

As evidenced by these features, Jenkins excels in providing a versatile and robust platform for CI/CD pipelines, catering to diverse project needs and facilitating efficient software development workflows.

1.6 Jenkins Editions and Distributions

The Jenkins software ecosystem is versatile and adaptive, manifesting in various editions and distributions, each tailored to distinct use cases, ranging from beginner use to enterprise-level deployments. This section provides a comprehensive examination of the primary Jenkins editions and their respective distributions, elucidating their unique characteristics, capabilities, and deployment scenarios.

Jenkins Open Source: Widely referred to simply as Jenkins, this is the free, community-supported edition. The open-source nature of Jenkins allows for continuous contributions and enhancements from a vast global community of developers. This edition is ideal for small to medium-sized projects where budget constraints may preclude the use of commercial solutions. It embodies a rich repository of plugins that extends Jenkins' core functionality, offering vast customization possibilities to tailor the CI/CD pipelines according to specific requirements.

Characteristics of Jenkins Open Source:

- **Cost:** Free and open-source.
- **Support:** Community-driven support through forums, mailing lists, and public issue trackers.
- **Updates:** Rapid release cycle with continuous integration of new features and fixes.
- **Plugins:** Access to an extensive library of over 1,500 plugins.
- **Flexibility:** High flexibility and customizable to meet a wide range of CI/CD pipeline configurations.

Jenkins Cloud-Native: This edition embodies the principles of cloud-native applications, designed to run efficiently on modern cloud platforms. Examples include Jenkins X, a variant that focuses on Kubernetes as the deployment environment. This integration supports dynamic scaling and resource optimization, leveraging Kubernetes services like Helm charts and Jenkins X pipelines for automating the CI/CD processes.

Characteristics of Jenkins Cloud-Native:

- **Deployment:** Seamless integration with Kubernetes and other cloud environments.
- **Scalability:** Auto-scaling capabilities to meet fluctuating demands.
- **Containerization:** Docker-based deployments offering improved isolation and resource usage.

- **Resource Efficiency:** Optimized for cloud resource management, reducing operational overhead.
- **Developer Focused:** CI/CD pipelines simplified for workflows common in cloud-native development.

Jenkins Enterprise: Targeted at large organizations requiring robust, enterprise-grade support, Jenkins Enterprise is a commercial distribution offered by CloudBees, the company behind Jenkins. It offers additional features such as advanced security, performance optimizations, and professional support, aiming to fulfill stringent enterprise requirements.

Characteristics of Jenkins Enterprise:

- **Premium Support:** Access to professional support services and dedicated customer resources.
- **Enhanced Security:** Advanced security features like role-based access control (RBAC) and compliance with industry standards.
- **Performance:** Optimized for higher performance with features designed to enhance scalability and reliability in large deployments.
- **Analytics:** Integrated analytics and monitoring tools to track performance metrics and usage statistics.
- **Integrations:** Seamless integration with other enterprise tools and platforms, including those for IT service management (ITSM) and enterprise resource planning (ERP).

Jenkins Evergreen: Developed to simplify Jenkins for users who may not require highly customizable pipelines, Jenkins Evergreen presents a simplified, opinionated distribution. The focus is on minimizing configuration overhead, offering easy-to-setup CI/CD workflows. This edition is particularly suitable for users new to Jenkins who need reliable CI/CD automation with a minimal setup hurdle.

Characteristics of Jenkins Evergreen:

- **User-Friendly:** Simplified configuration and user interface, designed to streamline setup.
- **Automatic Updates:** Automatically updates to the latest stable version, including plugins, reducing maintenance effort.

- **Standardization:** Provides a more predictable and controlled environment with predefined configurations.
- **Minimal Configuration:** Pre-configured best practices to reduce the need for intricate setup and customization.
- **Stability:** Emphasis on stable and reliable operation with automated error detection and recovery.

Comparison and Deployment Considerations:

When selecting the appropriate Jenkins edition, several factors should be considered:

- The **size and complexity** of the project or organization.
- The **level of customization** and flexibility required in CI/CD pipeline configurations.
- **Budget constraints** and availability of resources for maintenance and support.
- **Deployment environment**, including cloud versus on-premises installations.
- **Security and compliance** requirements, especially for regulated industries.

The diverse offerings within the Jenkins ecosystem ensure that there is a suitable solution for developers at varying stages of their CI/CD maturity, from small startups to large, complex enterprises. Each edition and distribution aligns with specific operational and organizational needs, enabling optimal CI/CD pipeline management tailored to unique project requisites.

1.7 Basic Terminology in Jenkins

In order to effectively utilize Jenkins, it is paramount to have a firm understanding of the terminology associated with this powerful automation tool. The following terms are fundamental to grasping the core concepts and functionality within Jenkins:

Job: A job in Jenkins, also referred to as a project, is a runnable task that is configured for execution within Jenkins. This definition encompasses a wide array of tasks, such as building a project from a version control system, running test cases, deploying applications, and more. Each job is defined with specific build steps and post-build actions that determine its behavior.

Build: A build is an instance of executing a Jenkins job. Each build is identified by a build number and contains the results of running the job at a particular point in time. Builds can be triggered manually by users, scheduled to run at defined intervals, or initiated by external events such as commits to a version control repository.

Node: In Jenkins, a node refers to any machine—be it physical, virtual, or cloud-based—that is part of the Jenkins environment and capable of executing pipelines or jobs. The master node controls Jenkins itself, while subordinate worker nodes (agents) perform the distributed tasks. Nodes facilitate scalable and efficient build execution across different environments.

Pipeline: Jenkins pipelines are a suite of plugins that aid in implementing and integrating continuous delivery pipelines using domain-specific language (DSL). It allows complex build workflows to be defined as code and managed as any other piece of software. Pipelines can be viewed as an orchestration of jobs with prescribed stages and steps.

Stage: Stages within a Jenkins pipeline are used to delineate different segments of the pipeline process. For example, stages might include "Build," "Test," "Deploy," etc. They provide high-level structure to the pipeline and help visualize the pipeline's progression.

Step: Steps are the individual tasks or commands within a stage of a Jenkins pipeline. Each step performs a specific action, such as checking out code, running a shell script, or executing a test. The configuration of steps in each stage determines the detailed behavior of the pipeline.

Executor: Executors are computational resources provided by nodes for running builds. Each node has a specified number of executors, which defines how many concurrent builds it can handle. Optimizing the number of executors per node is crucial for efficient resource utilization in a Jenkins environment.

SCM (Source Code Management): SCM refers to the tools and practices used to manage code repositories. Jenkins integrates seamlessly with many SCM systems such as Git, Subversion, and Mercurial. This integration is essential for automating the triggering of builds based on repository changes.

Workspace: A workspace is a directory on the node where Jenkins executes a job or pipeline. It's essentially where all the files related to a project are stored temporarily while a job runs. Each job build has its own workspace isolated from others.

Artifact: Artifacts in Jenkins are files generated by a build, representing compiled binaries, documentation, or any outputs. These artifacts are archived and can be used by other builds or deployed directly as part of the release process.

Trigger: Triggers are events or conditions that start a Jenkins job. Types of triggers include manual triggers initiated by users, scheduled triggers (Cron jobs), SCM changes, and webhooks from other systems. Triggers ensure that jobs run automatically in response to changes or specific schedules.

Plugin: Plugins extend the functionality of Jenkins by adding new features or integrating with other tools. Jenkins has a highly modular architecture with a vast ecosystem of plugins available to enhance its capabilities. Common plugin categories include build tools, SCM integrations, UI improvements, and more.

View: Views in Jenkins are filters that allow users to see jobs and builds that match certain criteria. Views help organize and manage numerous jobs, providing customized perspectives based on project requirements or user preferences.

Slave (Agent): A slave, also known as an agent, is a node configured to offload jobs from the master node, enabling distributed builds across multiple machines. Slaves help scale Jenkins by leveraging additional computational resources to accommodate increased workloads.

```
pipeline {
    agent any
    stages {
        stage('Build') {
            steps {
                echo 'Building...'
                // Insert build steps
            }
        }
        stage('Test') {
            steps {
                echo 'Testing...'
                // Insert test steps
            }
        }
        stage('Deploy') {
```

```
                steps {
                    echo 'Deploying...'
                    // Insert deploy steps
                }
            }
        }
}
```

The concepts and terminologies discussed here form the backbone of Jenkins operations. Understanding and leveraging these terms will facilitate effective use and configurations, leading to more efficient CI/CD processes and better software delivery outcomes.

1.8 System Requirements and Compatibility

To ensure optimal performance and stability in Jenkins, it is imperative to understand the system requirements and compatibility considerations essential for deploying Jenkins effectively. This section details the necessary specifications and compatibility checkpoints to facilitate a smooth Jenkins installation and operation.

Hardware Requirements

The hardware requirements for Jenkins depend significantly on the scale and nature of automation tasks. Below are the baseline recommendations:

- **CPU**: At a minimum, a dual-core processor is recommended. For large-scale operations involving numerous builds and complex pipeline executions, a quad-core or more processor is advisable.
- **Memory**: Jenkins requires a minimum of 1 GB of RAM for basic operations. However, for a more stable environment, especially in scenarios with multiple jobs running concurrently, 4 GB or more is recommended.
- **Disk Space**: A minimum of 1 GB of free disk space is needed for Jenkins' installation. Additional disk space is essential for build logs, build artifacts, and plugin storage. It is prudent to allocate at least 50 GB for a moderate-scale setup.

Operating Systems

Jenkins is compatible with various operating systems. The primary OS families include:

- **Windows**: Jenkins runs seamlessly on Windows 10, Windows Server 2016 and newer versions. Installing Jenkins as a Windows service can enhance its management and integration.
- **Linux**: Popular distributions such as Ubuntu 16.04 and above, CentOS 7 and above, Red Hat Enterprise Linux (RHEL) 7 and newer are fully supported. Jenkins is often preferred on Linux systems due to kernel-level performance and stability.
- **macOS**: Jenkins supports macOS (10.13 High Sierra and newer). macOS might be less commonly used in production deployments but is suitable for development and testing purposes.

Java Development Kit (JDK)

Jenkins runs on Java and requires a Java Development Kit (JDK) to function. Specific considerations include:

- **JDK Version**: Jenkins requires Java 8 or Java 11 (LTS). As Java versions evolve, it is essential to ensure compatibility with the specific Jenkins version in use.
- **Choosing the Right JDK**: For security and stability, using an LTS (Long Term Support) version of JDK, such as AdoptOpenJDK or Oracle JDK, is recommended. Configure the JAVA_HOME environment variable to point to the JDK installation directory.

Web Browser Compatibility

Jenkins' web-based interface supports a range of modern web browsers, including:

- **Google Chrome**: Version 71 and later.
- **Mozilla Firefox**: Version 65 and later.
- **Microsoft Edge**: Version 42 and later.
- **Safari**: Version 12 and later.

To prevent compatibility issues, ensure that the web browser is updated to the latest stable version.

Database Management Systems (DBMS)

While Jenkins primarily uses its embedded H2 database, for extensive usage, external Database Management Systems (DBMS) are supported:

- **MySQL**: Version 5.7 and newer.
- **PostgreSQL**: Version 9.4 and newer.
- **Oracle Database**: It supports Oracle DB, though specific version compatibility should be cross-verified.

External databases are advantageous for large-scale CI environments, providing better performance and management.

Integrations and Plugins Compatibility

Jenkins thrives on its extensibility through plugins. To maintain a smooth operation:

- **Plugin Versions**: Ensure compatibility between the Jenkins core version and the plugins by regularly updating both. Plugin version information and compatibility details can be verified from the Jenkins Plugin Index.
- **Third-Party Integrations**: When integrating with third-party tools (e.g., Git, Maven), ensure you adhere to the recommended versions and configurations as documented by the plugin or tool.

Network Requirements

Network infrastructure determines the efficiency of Jenkins operations, especially in a distributed environment:

- **Bandwidth**: Adequate bandwidth is necessary for transferring build artifacts, SCM (Source Code Management) operations, and general HTTP traffic. Consider a minimum of 100 Mbps for small setups, scaling upwards for larger environments.
- **Latency**: Low latency ensures quicker response times. Optimize the network environment to minimize delays, especially when using distributed build slaves.
- **Firewall and Ports**: Jenkins employs port 8080 as the default HTTP port. Ensure that firewalls are configured to allow traffic through this port or a custom port if changed. Additionally, secure connections should be facilitated using HTTPS.

Backup and Security

Maintaining backups and strong security measures are crucial:

- **Backup**: Regular backups of the Jenkins home directory, where build configurations, job definitions, and plugins reside, are vital. Tools like the Jenkins ThinBackup plugin can automate this process.
- **Security**: Enable and configure Jenkins security features, such as user authentication, authorization, and securing Jenkins through HTTPS. Regularly update Jenkins and plugins to mitigate security vulnerabilities.

Comprehending and implementing these system requirements and compatibility checks ensures that Jenkins operates robustly and optimally, paving the way for efficient CI/CD pipelines.

1.9 Who Uses Jenkins?

Jenkins is utilized by a diverse range of users, including individual developers, small teams, large enterprises, and organizations across different sectors. The widespread adoption of Jenkins can be attributed to its robustness, flexibility, and extensive plugin ecosystem. Understanding the typical users and their use cases helps in grasping the versatility and value Jenkins adds to software development practices.

Individual Developers: Individual developers often use Jenkins to automate repetitive tasks in their development workflow. By setting up Jenkins on a local machine or a small server, they can automate the building, testing, and deployment of their code. This automation frees up time for more complex tasks, reduces human error, and ensures that the code is consistently tested before integration. For instance, a single developer working on an open-source project can utilize Jenkins to automatically run unit tests and generate documentation with each commit.

Small Development Teams: Small teams, usually comprising a handful of developers, benefit significantly from Jenkins' capabilities in continuous integration and continuous delivery (CI/CD). Jenkins enables these teams to maintain a shared code base where all changes are automatically built and tested. This setup ensures that integration issues are caught early, reducing the overhead of manual testing and integration. For example, a small startup developing a web application can use Jenkins to continuously deploy updates to a staging environment, ensuring that every change is validated through automated tests before being approved for production.

Large Enterprises: Large organizations deploy Jenkins to manage complex, large-scale CI/CD pipelines involving multiple software projects and teams. Jenkins' scalability and ability to integrate with various development tools make it an ideal choice for enterprises aiming to streamline their software delivery processes. Corporations in sectors like finance, healthcare, and retail use Jenkins to maintain high standards of code quality, security, and compliance. In such environments, Jenkins is often integrated with tools for code analysis, security scanning, and artifact management, forming a comprehensive DevOps toolkit.

Open Source Projects: Many open-source projects rely on Jenkins for their CI infrastructure. Jenkins' open-source nature aligns well with the ethos of open-source communities, promoting innovation and collaboration. By utilizing Jenkins, open-source projects ensure that contributions from developers around the world are automatically built and tested, maintaining the stability and reliability of the project. For example, prominent open-source projects such as Apache, Mozilla, and Kubernetes use Jenkins to manage their CI pipelines, handle contributions, and build release versions.

Educational Institutions: Educational institutions and research organizations also leverage Jenkins to facilitate learning and development in software engineering. Jenkins can be set up in classrooms and laboratories to teach CI/CD practices, providing students with hands-on experience in modern software development techniques. Additionally, research projects that involve software development can use Jenkins to automate and streamline the development workflow, from building research prototypes to deploying experimental setups.

Sectors and Industries: Jenkins' versatility allows it to be used across various sectors and industries, each with specific requirements and challenges:

- **Technology**: Tech companies, from startups to tech giants, adopt Jenkins to achieve rapid and reliable software delivery. The ability to quickly iterate and continuously deliver new features is a competitive advantage in the tech industry.

- **Finance**: Financial institutions use Jenkins to ensure that their software systems are always up to date, secure, and compliant with regulatory standards. Jenkins helps in automating complex workflows that include extensive testing and validation processes.
- **Healthcare**: In the healthcare sector, Jenkins is used to maintain and deploy software systems that require high reliability and compliance with healthcare regulations. Automated testing ensures that changes do not introduce errors that could affect patient safety.
- **Retail**: Retail companies use Jenkins to manage their e-commerce platforms and backend systems. Automated CI/CD pipelines ensure that new features and fixes are deployed quickly without disrupting the shopping experience.
- **Government and Public Sector**: Government agencies deploy Jenkins to modernize their IT infrastructure and implement DevOps practices. Jenkins helps in automating the deployment of public services, ensuring reliability and scalability.

To illustrate Jenkins' versatility and real-world application, consider the following example of a Jenkins pipeline used by a technology company:

```
pipeline {
    agent any
    stages {
        stage('Build') {
            steps {
                echo 'Building...'
                sh 'mvn clean package'
            }
        }
        stage('Test') {
            steps {
                echo 'Testing...'
                sh 'mvn test'
            }
        }
        stage('Deploy') {
            steps {
                echo 'Deploying...'
                sh 'scp target/*.jar user@server:/path/to/deploy'
            }
        }
    }
    post {
        success {
            echo 'Pipeline completed successfully!'
        }
        failure {
            echo 'Pipeline failed.'
        }
```

```
    }
}
```

This pipeline automates the build, test, and deployment stages of a typical Java project using Maven. Each stage contains specific steps that define the actions to be carried out. The 'post' section defines actions to be executed based on the outcome of the pipeline, ensuring that appropriate feedback is provided.

The output of a successful pipeline execution is displayed as follows:

```
Building...
[Test] ...
... (build logs)
Tests run: 25, Failures: 0, Errors: 0, Skipped: 0
[Test] ...
... (test logs)
Deploying...
... (deploy logs)
Pipeline completed successfully!
```

Jenkins' flexibility allows configuration of similar pipelines for different languages, tools, and deployment environments, making it a valuable asset across various use cases and sectors.

1.10 Advantages and Limitations of Jenkins

The adoption of Jenkins in modern software development pipelines underscores its numerous advantages, which span across automation, integration, and efficient project management. However, it is essential to also understand its limitations to maximize its benefits and mitigate potential challenges. This section delves deeply into the comprehensive assessment of both advantages and limitations of using Jenkins within a CI/CD setup.

Advantages of Jenkins:

- **Open Source and Cost-efficient:** Jenkins is an open-source tool, which means it is free to use and benefits from community contributions. This makes it a cost-effective solution for both small and large organizations.

- **Extensibility through Plugins:** The Jenkins ecosystem boasts over a thousand plugins that extend its functionality to cover virtually any need in the CI/CD pipeline. This extensive plugin support allows developers to integrate Jenkins with a wide array of tools including version control systems like Git, build tools like Maven and Gradle, and testing frameworks like JUnit and Selenium.

- **Ease of Installation and Configuration:** Jenkins can be installed and configured easily on various operating systems such as Windows, macOS, and Linux. Its web-based management interface simplifies the setup process, allowing users to start using Jenkins with minimal initial learning curve.
- **Support for Various Languages and Technologies:** Jenkins is not limited to a specific set of programming languages or technologies. It supports any software stack, making it a versatile tool for developers working with diverse technologies.
- **Continuous Integration and Continuous Delivery:** Jenkins provides robust support for CI/CD, enabling rapid and frequent integration of code changes, automated testing, and deployment. This leads to faster development cycles and early detection of integration issues.
- **Scalability and Distributed Builds:** Jenkins supports distributed builds, allowing workload to be distributed across multiple machines. This scalability ensures that Jenkins can handle projects of varied sizes without compromising performance.
- **Active Community and Documentation:** Jenkins has a strong and active community that provides support, shares plugins, and contributes to its development. Furthermore, extensive official documentation and numerous tutorials are available, making it easier for newcomers to get up to speed.
- **Customizable Build Pipelines:** With the introduction of Jenkins Pipeline, users can define build steps using the Groovy-based DSL. This makes it possible to create complex, multi-step deployment pipelines in a more modular and reusable manner.

Limitations of Jenkins:

- **Complex Setup for Large Projects:** While Jenkins is easy to set up initially, configuring it for large, multifaceted projects can become complex. Managing numerous plugins and ensuring compatibility between them requires meticulous planning and ongoing maintenance.

- **Plugin Compatibility Issues:** The rich plugin ecosystem is both a strength and a potential weakness. Plugins are developed by independent contributors and may not always be up to date or compatible with each other or with the core Jenkins. This can lead to issues that affect the stability and reliability of the CI/CD pipeline.

- **Resource Intensive:** Jenkins can consume significant system resources, especially when running multiple jobs concurrently or executing complex build processes. Ensuring the server has adequate resources is crucial for maintaining optimal performance.

- **Steep Learning Curve for Advanced Features:** Although basic usage of Jenkins is straightforward, mastering its advanced features, especially the Pipeline as Code, can present a steep learning curve. Users need to be familiar with Groovy scripting and the intricacies of the Jenkins Pipeline syntax.

- **User Interface and User Experience:** Jenkins' web interface, while functional, is often criticized for being less intuitive and visually appealing compared to modern CI/CD tools. Navigating through the interface to configure jobs can be cumbersome, particularly for new users.

- **Security Concerns:** As an open-source tool with numerous plugins, Jenkins can be vulnerable to security threats if not properly configured and maintained. Regular updates and strict access controls are necessary to mitigate these risks.

- **Dependency on Continuous Internet Connection:** For Jenkins to reach external repositories and third-party services, a continuous internet connection is required. Any interruption in connectivity can disrupt the CI/CD pipeline.

- **Maintenance Overhead:** Regular updates and plugin management are necessary to ensure Jenkins' smooth operation. This ongoing maintenance can be time-consuming and requires dedicated effort to keep up with the latest changes and improvements.

The effective utilization of Jenkins depends on a clear understanding of these advantages and limitations. By leveraging its strengths and addressing its weaknesses, teams can optimize their CI/CD processes to achieve seamless and efficient software delivery.

Chapter 2

Setting Up Jenkins

This chapter details the process of setting up Jenkins, covering system requirements, installation on various operating systems, and running Jenkins in Docker. It provides instructions for initial setup and configuration, including managing the Jenkins home directory, setting up global security, and configuring user accounts and roles. Additionally, the chapter discusses installing and managing plugins, configuring external tools and integrations, and strategies for backup and restore to ensure a secure and efficient Jenkins environment.

2.1 System Requirements and Preparations

Understanding and meeting the system requirements is crucial for the successful installation and optimal performance of Jenkins. This section outlines the hardware and software prerequisites you must consider before setting up Jenkins on your server or local machine.

Hardware Requirements: The hardware resources required by Jenkins vary depending on the scale and complexity of the jobs you plan to run. Here are some general guidelines:

- **CPU:** Jenkins can run on virtually any modern CPU, but for optimal performance, a multi-core processor is recommended. For small setups, a dual-core CPU should suffice, whereas for larger installations managing hundreds of jobs, at least a quad-core processor or better is advisable.

- **Memory:** Jenkins itself is not very memory-intensive; however, the jobs it manages can be. A minimum of 1 GB of RAM is recommended for small installations, but for larger installations, especially those running many concurrent jobs, 4 GB of RAM or more is preferred.
- **Storage:** Jenkins builds, archives, and logs can consume significant disk space over time. Ensure you have ample storage, with at least 10 GB available for Jenkins and its dependencies. The exact requirement will depend on the duration and number of builds you intend to keep. It is advisable to use SSDs over HDDs for better I/O performance.

Software Requirements: Jenkins is a Java-based application, which implies that it is compatible with both Unix-based and Windows operating systems. The following software components are required:

- **Java Development Kit (JDK):** Jenkins requires a Java Development Kit (JDK) to be installed. Jenkins recommends JDK 8 or JDK 11. Ensure that the JDK version you use is supported by Jenkins. Check the compatibility matrix on the Jenkins website for the most current information.
- **Operating System:**
  - *Linux:* Most distributions like Ubuntu, CentOS, and Debian are supported. Ensure your system is updated to the latest version for security and compatibility.
  - *Windows:* Jenkins runs on any modern version of Windows. However, Windows Server versions like 2016 and 2019 are recommended for production environments.
  - *macOS:* Jenkins runs on macOS versions 10.9 (Mavericks) or later. Ensure your macOS is updated to leverage the latest security enhancements.
- **Web Browser:** Since Jenkins is accessed through a web interface, having a modern web browser is necessary. Supported browsers include recent versions of Chrome, Firefox, Safari, and Edge.

Preparations: Before proceeding with the installation, certain preparations are essential to ensure a smooth setup:

- **Environment Variables:** Set the JAVA_HOME environment variable to the path where the JDK is installed. This can be done by adding the following line to your environment configuration file (e.g., .bashrc for Linux):

```
export JAVA_HOME=/path/to/jdk
export PATH=$PATH:$JAVA_HOME/bin
```

  For Windows, set the environment variable via the System Properties or using the command line:

```
setx JAVA_HOME "C:\Path\To\JDK"
setx PATH "%PATH%;%JAVA_HOME%\bin"
```

- **Network Configuration:** Ensure that the system where Jenkins is installed has a stable network connection, as Jenkins will need to fetch updates and plugins from the internet. If the system is behind a firewall, configure the necessary proxy settings.

- **User Permissions:** The user account that runs Jenkins should have adequate permissions to access the system resources necessary for Jenkins operations, including read/write access to the directories where Jenkins will be installed and where it will store its data. It is generally recommended to run Jenkins under a dedicated user account for better security and manageability.

- **System Updates:** Ensure your system is updated with the latest patches and updates. Running outdated software increases the risk of security vulnerabilities and compatibility issues. On a Linux system, this can be done using:

```
sudo apt-get update && sudo apt-get upgrade
```

  For Windows, use the Windows Update utility. For macOS, use the Software Update tool available in System Preferences.

Being thorough about the system requirements and preparation steps paves the way for a smooth Jenkins installation and operation, minimizing the likelihood of encountering issues later. Proper planning and resource allocation are critical, especially for larger, more complex Jenkins environments.

2.2 Installing Jenkins on Windows

To effectively install Jenkins on a Windows operating system, adequate preparation and attention to detail are essential. The process entails downloading the necessary files, verifying system requirements, and correctly configuring the application to ensure optimum performance. Below are the steps to guide through this process.

First, confirm that your Windows system meets the minimum system requirements for Jenkins. Ensure you have:

- Windows 10 or a newer version
- At least 256MB of RAM (512MB or more recommended)
- 1GB of drive space for Jenkins and much more for projects
- A recent Java Development Kit (JDK) - JDK 8 or later versions

Downloading Jenkins

To download the Jenkins executable, follow these steps:

1. Open your web browser and navigate to the official Jenkins download page at https://www.jenkins.io/download/.
2. Under the **Windows** section, click on the link to download the MSI-based installer for Jenkins.

Executing the Installer

Upon downloading the installer, proceed with the following steps to execute it:

1. Locate the downloaded Jenkins.msi file in your system's Downloads folder or the directory you configured for downloaded files.
2. Double-click the Jenkins.msi file to start the installation process.
3. Upon launching the installer, the Jenkins Setup Wizard appears. Click **Next** to continue.
4. Read and accept the license agreement by checking the corresponding box and clicking **Next**.

5. Choose the installation folder. The default directory is acceptable for most cases. However, if you prefer a different directory, click **Change** and specify your desired path. Click **Next**.
6. Opt to install the suggested plugins for a standard setup by selecting **Install suggested plugins**. This selection simplifies the initial setup by including commonly used plugins.
7. Allow the installation process to complete. This may take a few minutes, depending on your system's performance.
8. Once installation is complete, click **Finish** to exit the Setup Wizard.

Starting Jenkins

Post installation, Jenkins needs to be started:

1. Jenkins runs as a service on Windows, and it starts automatically by default. Verify this by searching for services.msc in the Windows search bar and opening the Services manager.
2. In the Services manager, locate the Jenkins service. Its status should be marked as **Started**.
3. If Jenkins did not start automatically, right-click on the Jenkins service and select **Start**.

Accessing Jenkins

To access your Jenkins instance:

1. Open a web browser.
2. Enter http://localhost:8080 in the address bar. This address points to your Jenkins server on the default port 8080.

Initial Configuration

Upon accessing Jenkins for the first time:

1. You will be prompted to unlock Jenkins. Locate the initialAdminPassword file:

```
C:\Program Files (x86)\Jenkins\secrets\initialAdminPassword
```

2. Open this file and copy the password contained within it.
3. Paste the password into the **Administrator password** field on the Jenkins web page and click **Continue**.
4. Proceed through the configuration steps, which include setting up an initial admin user, instance configuration, and installation of recommended plugins.

Configuring Jenkins as a Windows Service

Jenkins runs as a Windows service by default, making it more manageable. Adjust configurations if necessary:

1. Open the Services manager by searching for services.msc.
2. Locate the Jenkins service and right-click on it. Select **Properties**.
3. In the **General** tab, configure the startup type to **Automatic** to ensure Jenkins starts with the system.
4. Adjust user permissions under the **Log On** tab if needed, ensuring that Jenkins runs under a user account with adequate permissions.

Should there be a need to reinstall or repair Jenkins at any point, merely re-running the Jenkins.msi installer and following the prompts will suffice. Performing a fresh configuration may occasionally be necessary if drastic changes to your OS or system files occur.

By adhering to these meticulous steps and ensuring settings are precisely configured, Jenkins can be effectively dispensed on a Windows operating system, providing a robust and flexible environment conducive to building and integrating software projects.

2.3 Installing Jenkins on macOS

To install Jenkins on macOS, a reliable method involves using the Homebrew package manager, which simplifies both the installation and management of software packages. Before proceeding, ensure that Homebrew is installed and updated on your system. Here is the detailed step-by-step guide:

First, verify that Homebrew is installed on your macOS by running:

```
brew --version
```

If the above command returns a version number, Homebrew is already installed. If not, you can install Homebrew by executing the following command in your Terminal:

```
/bin/bash -c "$(curl -fsSL https://raw.githubusercontent.com/Homebrew/install/
    HEAD/install.sh)"
```

After installing Homebrew or confirming its installation, it is good practice to update the Homebrew packages to ensure the latest versions are used. Execute:

```
brew update
```

Next, you need to install Jenkins. Homebrew provides a simplified method to install Jenkins along with its dependencies:

```
brew install jenkins-lts
```

The jenkins-lts formula installs the latest Long-Term Support (LTS) version of Jenkins, which is recommended for production use due to its stability and reliability.

Once installed, Jenkins can be started as a service. To start Jenkins immediately:

```
brew services start jenkins-lts
```

This command launches Jenkins using the built-in launchctl, ensuring that Jenkins starts automatically after each reboot. If you prefer to run Jenkins manually, you can start it with:

```
jenkins-lts
```

After starting Jenkins, you can access the Jenkins interface via a web browser. By default, Jenkins runs on port 8080. Open your browser and navigate to:

```
http://localhost:8080
```

The first time Jenkins starts, it creates an initialAdminPassword file at /usr/local/var/jenkins_home/secrets/initialAdminPassword. To unlock Jenkins, you need to extract the administrator password from this file:

```
cat /usr/local/var/jenkins_home/secrets/initialAdminPassword
```

Copy the password displayed and paste it into the setup wizard's prompt in your web browser. After entering the password, the setup wizard guides you through installing recommended plugins.

The next step in the setup involves creating the first administrator user. Provide the necessary details such as username, password, and full name to create your initial admin account.

At this stage, you can make further configurations in Jenkins according to your needs. However, it is essential to ensure that Jenkins has been set up correctly by running a test job. To do this, perform the following steps:

1. Navigate to the Jenkins dashboard and click on "New Item." 2. Enter a name for the job and select "Freestyle project," then click "OK." 3. Configure the job, setting up simple build steps, for instance, echoing "Hello, Jenkins!". 4. Save the configuration and click "Build Now" to run the job. 5. Monitor the job's execution, ensuring it completes successfully.

Additional configurations might be required based on your Jenkins use case, including integrating with version control systems, customizing the security realm, or setting up build agents. To maintain the integrity and performance of Jenkins, remember to periodically update Homebrew and Jenkins by performing:

```
brew update && brew upgrade jenkins-lts
```

Periodic updates ensure that you utilize the latest security patches and feature enhancements.

This completes the installation and initial setup of Jenkins on macOS using Homebrew, positioning you to leverage Jenkins for continuous integration and delivery tasks.

In the following sections, the process for setting up Jenkins in different environments, such as Windows and Docker, will be detailed, providing a holistic understanding of Jenkins setup across various platforms.

2.4 Installing Jenkins on Linux

To install Jenkins on a Linux-based system, follow the procedure detailed below, which includes steps for updating the repository, installing Java, and setting up Jenkins. Ensuring that the system meets the aforementioned prerequisites is crucial for a smooth installation process.

First, update your system packages to their latest versions using the package manager. On Debian-based systems like Ubuntu, this can be done with the following commands:

```
sudo apt-get update
sudo apt-get upgrade
```

For Red Hat-based distributions like CentOS, use:

```
sudo yum update
```

Next, Jenkins requires Java to run. We will install OpenJDK, which is the free and open-source implementation of the Java Platform, Standard Edition. To install OpenJDK on a Debian-based system, execute the following:

```
sudo apt-get install openjdk-11-jdk
```

For Red Hat-based systems, use:

```
sudo yum install java-11-openjdk-devel
```

Verify the Java installation:

```
java -version
```

The output should indicate that Java has been installed correctly:

```
openjdk version "11.0.11" 2021-04-20
OpenJDK Runtime Environment (build 11.0.11+9-Ubuntu-0ubuntu2.20.04)
OpenJDK 64-Bit Server VM (build 11.0.11+9-Ubuntu-0ubuntu2.20.04, mixed mode, sharing)
```

Now, import the GPG key for the Jenkins repository and add the Jenkins repository to your system. For Debian-based systems, use:

```
wget -q -O - https://pkg.jenkins.io/debian/jenkins.io.key | sudo apt-key add -
sudo sh -c 'echo deb http://pkg.jenkins.io/debian-stable binary/ > /etc/apt/sources.list
    .d/jenkins.list'
```

Update the package index again:

```
sudo apt-get update
```

To install Jenkins, run the following command:

```
sudo apt-get install jenkins
```

For Red Hat-based systems, use these commands to add the Jenkins repository and install Jenkins:

```
sudo wget -O /etc/yum.repos.d/jenkins.repo https://pkg.jenkins.io/redhat-stable/
    jenkins.repo
sudo rpm --import https://pkg.jenkins.io/redhat-stable/jenkins.io.key
sudo yum install jenkins
```

After installing Jenkins, start the Jenkins service and enable it to start on boot:

```
sudo systemctl start jenkins
sudo systemctl enable jenkins
```

To check the status of the Jenkins service:

```
systemctl status jenkins
```

The output should indicate that Jenkins is active and running:

```
jenkins.service - LSB: Start Jenkins at boot time
 Loaded: loaded (/etc/init.d/jenkins; generated)
 Active: active (running) since Wed 2021-05-12 14:47:20 UTC; 2min 53s ago
   Docs: man:systemd-sysv-generator(8)
  Tasks: 2 (limit: 1152)
 Memory: 435.6M
 CGroup: /system.slice/jenkins.service
         6063 /usr/bin/java -Djava.awt.headless=true -jar /usr/share/jenkins/jenkins.war
```

To access Jenkins, open a web browser and navigate to http://your_server_ip_or_domain:8080. You will see the Jenkins setup wizard.

Retrieve the initial admin password, which is stored in the log file of Jenkins. Use the following command:

```
sudo cat /var/lib/jenkins/secrets/initialAdminPassword
```

Enter this password in the setup wizard to unlock Jenkins.

With Jenkins installed and running, the next steps involve customization and configuration to suit your specific development and CI/CD requirements.

2.5 Running Jenkins in Docker

Setting up Jenkins in a Docker environment simplifies the deployment process and provides a scalable infrastructure. Docker allows Jenkins to run in isolated containers, ensuring consistent environments across different systems. This section will guide you through the steps to run Jenkins in Docker, addressing the prerequisites, installation steps, volume management, network configuration, and verification processes.

Prerequisites:

To run Jenkins in Docker, ensure that the following prerequisites are met:

- Docker Engine: Ensure that Docker Engine is installed on the host machine. You can download and install Docker from the official Docker website.
- Sufficient Storage and Memory: The host machine should have enough storage space and memory to accommodate the Jenkins container and its operations.

Installation Steps:

1. Pull the Jenkins Docker Image:

   To begin, pull the official Jenkins Docker image from the Docker repository. Open a terminal and run:

   ```
   docker pull jenkins/jenkins:lts
   ```

   The jenkins/jenkins:lts tag ensures that you are using the Long-Term Support (LTS) version of Jenkins, which is recommended for production environments.

2. Create a Jenkins Docker Container:

   Next, create and run a Docker container using the pulled Jenkins image. Execute the following command:

   ```
   docker run -d -p 8080:8080 -p 50000:50000 --name jenkins-master jenkins/
       jenkins:lts
   ```

   This command performs the following actions:

   - -d: Runs the container in detached mode.

- -p 8080:8080: Maps port 8080 on the host machine to port 8080 on the container, allowing access to the Jenkins web interface.
- -p 50000:50000: Maps port 50000 on the host machine to port 50000 on the container, enabling communication with build agents.
- –name jenkins-master: Assigns the name jenkins-master to the container for easier identification.

Volume Management:

To preserve Jenkins data and configurations, it's crucial to manage volumes effectively. Volumes allow data to persist across container restarts and upgrades. The following steps illustrate how to set up Docker volumes for Jenkins:

1. Create a Docker Volume:

   Create a named volume for Jenkins data storage:

   ```
   docker volume create jenkins-data
   ```

2. Run Jenkins with Persistent Storage:

   Modify the docker run command to use the created volume:

   ```
   docker run -d -p 8080:8080 -p 50000:50000 --name jenkins-master -v jenkins-
        data:/var/jenkins\_home jenkins/jenkins:lts
   ```

   The -v jenkins-data:/var/jenkins_home option mounts the jenkins-data volume to the /var/jenkins_home directory within the container, ensuring that Jenkins data is stored persistently.

Network Configuration:

Configuring network settings is essential for Jenkins to interact with other services and agents. Docker supports several network modes, but for simplicity, we will use the default bridge network.

```
docker network ls
```

Use the above command to list available Docker networks. By default, Docker creates a bridge network, which is typically sufficient for most setups.

To create a user-defined bridge network:

```
docker network create jenkins-network
```

Now, run the Jenkins container within this network:

```
docker run -d -p 8080:8080 -p 50000:50000 --name jenkins-master --network jenkins-
    network -v jenkins-data:/var/jenkins\_home jenkins/jenkins:lts
```

This setup helps isolate Jenkins from other containers not part of the jenkins-network, enhancing security and configuration management.

Verifying Jenkins Deployment:

After launching the Jenkins container, verify the deployment by following these steps:

1. Check Container Logs:

   To ensure Jenkins is running correctly, examine the container logs:

   ```
   docker logs jenkins-master
   ```

2. Access Jenkins Web Interface:

   Open a web browser and navigate to http://<DockerHostIP>:8080. Replace <DockerHostIP> with the IP address of the host machine running Docker. For example, if the Docker host IP is 192.168.0.10, enter http://192.168.0.10:8080 in the browser.

3. Unlock Jenkins:

   The initial setup wizard prompts for an administrator password. Retrieve the password from the container logs:

   ```
   docker exec jenkins-master cat /var/jenkins\_home/secrets/
       initialAdminPassword
   ```

   Enter the password in the setup wizard to proceed with configuring Jenkins.

Running Jenkins in Docker offers a robust and scalable solution for continuous integration and continuous delivery (CI/CD) workflows. With the detailed steps provided, users can effectively deploy and manage Jenkins within Docker containers, leveraging Docker's isolation and portability benefits.

2.6 Initial Setup and Configuration

Upon installing Jenkins, it is crucial to perform the initial setup and configuration to ensure that the system operates optimally. This section will guide you through the various steps needed to get a freshly installed Jenkins instance ready for use.

When Jenkins is started for the first time, a configuration wizard initializes, walking you through essential aspects of the setup. This juncture is where you begin by unlocking Jenkins.

Unlocking Jenkins

Navigate to your Jenkins instance in a web browser (the default address is http://localhost:8080). Jenkins will present a page prompting you to unlock it using a password stored in a specified file on your local system. This is how Jenkins ensures the initial connection is secure.

Locate the password file on your machine. For a Debian-based Linux or macOS installation, the location is typically:

```
/var/lib/jenkins/secrets/initialAdminPassword
```

For Windows, it might be located at:

```
C:\Program Files (x86)\Jenkins\secrets\initialAdminPassword
```

Copy the password from the file and paste it into the administrator password field on the Jenkins webpage. Click **Continue** to proceed.

Customized vs. Suggested Plugins

After unlocking Jenkins, the setup wizard presents two options for plugin installation: *Install suggested plugins* and *Select plugins to install*.

Choosing **Install suggested plugins** provides a quick setup with plugins commonly used in Jenkins environments. This is the recommended option for beginners and utilities the system effectively out-of-the-box.

Selecting **Select plugins to install** allows you to tailor the plugin installation according to specific requirements. Use this option when you have particular needs or wish to opt out of plugins you will not use, thereby keeping the system lean.

Creating the First Admin User

In the subsequent step, Jenkins asks for the creation of the first Administrator user. This involves setting up a username, password, full name, and email address:

```
Username: <user>
Password: <password>
Full Name: <full name>
Email Address: <email>
```

This account has full control over Jenkins and is essential for managing global system settings, plugins, and other user accounts.

Instance Configuration

Following the creation of the admin user, Jenkins prompts for instance configuration. This includes setting the Jenkins URL, which is the address through which users will access Jenkins. By default, this is set to the URL Jenkins was initially accessed from, but you can change this if necessary. It is crucial to ensure this URL is accessible to your intended user base.

Validating Configuration

Once the basic configuration is complete, the setup wizard will perform a validation check. This ensures that Jenkins is correctly configured and operational. Any issues found will be highlighted, and it's essential to address them before proceeding.

Additional Configuration

Beyond the setup wizard, several configurations should be fine-tuned:

1. **Email Notification**: Ensure Jenkins is configured to send out email notifications. Navigate to **Manage Jenkins** → **Configure System** and locate the **Jenkins Location** section. Here, set the **System Admin e-mail address** and configure the SMTP server settings under **E-mail Notification**.

```
SMTP server: smtp.example.com
Default user e-mail suffix: @example.com
```

For a more secure setup, configure SMTP authentication and, optionally, TLS:

```
SMTP Authentication: Yes
   User Name: <SMTP User>
   Password: <SMTP Password>
Use SSL: Yes
Use TLS: Yes
```

2. **Security Realm and Authorization**: Configure the **Security Realm** to manage user authentication. Jenkins supports several types including Jenkins' own user database, LDAP, and more.

Next, set up the authorization strategy under **Manage Jenkins** → **Con-**

figure Global Security. Opt for *Role-based strategy* or any other suitable method, such as *Matrix-based security*, to finely control permissions for users and groups.

3. **Tools and Environment Configuration**: Set up necessary tools like JDK, Git, Maven, etc., under **Manage Jenkins** → **Global Tool Configuration**. This ensures Jenkins jobs have access to required tools.

```
JDK:
    Name: JDK8
    JAVA_HOME: /usr/lib/jvm/java-8-openjdk-amd64
Git:
    Name: Default
    Path to Git executable: /usr/bin/git
Maven:
    Name: Maven3
    MAVEN_HOME: /usr/share/maven
```

4. **Backup Configuration**: Ensure routine backups of Jenkins configurations and data by setting up backup plugins. Navigate to **Manage Plugins** and install suitable plugins like 'ThinBackup' or 'Periodic Backup'. Configure these plugins via their respective settings found typically under **Manage Jenkins** → **Configure System**.

Testing Your Setup

To confirm that your Jenkins setup is functional, create a simple freestyle project. Go to **New Item**, name your project, and choose **Freestyle project**. Add a simple build step such as:

```
echo "Hello, Jenkins!"
```

Build the project and ensure it runs successfully. The console output should display:

```
Started by user <user>
Building in workspace <workspace directory>
Hello, Jenkins!
Finished: SUCCESS
```

Completing these steps ensures the basics of Jenkins' configuration are correctly set, paving the way for a smooth integration into your continuous integration and continuous deployment pipelines.

2.7 Jenkins Home Directory and File Structure

The Jenkins home directory is a crucial component that houses essential configurations, job configurations, plugins, user content, and logs required for Jenkins operation. Understanding the layout and content of this directory allows for effective management, troubleshooting, and backup of Jenkins.

Upon Jenkins startup, it sets a default home directory path, which is /var/lib/jenkins on most Unix systems and C:\ProgramData\Jenkinsjenkins on Windows. However, this location can be altered through the JENKINS_HOME environment variable or configuration settings.

Key Directories and Files in JENKINS_HOME:

- config.xml: This file contains the primary configuration for the Jenkins system, including system-wide settings that affect Jenkins' overall behavior.
- jobs/: This directory contains subdirectories for each Jenkins job. Every job's configuration and runtime data are maintained within its respective subdirectory.
- plugins/: This directory contains the installed plugins. Each plugin is stored as a .hpi or .jpi file, representing the plugin archives, and may have corresponding folders for its data within the same directory.
- users/: The subdirectories in this folder represent user profiles and credentials.
- secrets/: This folder holds sensitive information like security tokens and encrypted passwords. It is critical to ensure this directory is securely managed and backed up properly.
- nodes/: This directory manages Jenkins agent machines, storing configuration data and status information about the connected agents.
- war/: This directory typically contains the Jenkins war file, which is an executable web application archive vital for Jenkins' operation.

- logs/: This directory includes various log files such as Jenkins logs, plugin logs, and build logs, facilitating the troubleshooting of issues.
- workspace/: Active job workspaces reside here. Each job has a unique subdirectory where all builds and file operations are performed during job execution.
- builds/: This directory stores historical build data, including build status, console output, and other relevant build information. Specific job-related builds are kept in subdirectories named based on job identifiers.
- queue/: This folder manages tasks that are queued for execution. It is pivotal for the scheduling of jobs.
- fingerprints/: This directory contains fingerprint records for tracking files used across multiple jobs or builds, enhancing traceability and aiding in artifact management.

Example structure of JENKINS_HOME **directory:**

```
JENKINS_HOME/
|-- config.xml
|-- jobs
| |-- job1
| | '-- config.xml
| |-- job2
| '-- config.xml
|-- plugins
| |-- plugin1.hpi
| |-- plugin2.hpi
|-- users
| |-- user1
| '-- config.xml
|-- secrets
| |-- master.key
|-- nodes
| |-- agent1
| '-- config.xml
|-- war
| |-- jenkins.war
|-- logs
| |-- jenkins.log
| |-- pluginA.log
|-- workspace
| |-- job1
| | '-- build temp files
|-- builds
| |-- job1
| |-- build1
| | '-- build.xml
| |-- build2
| '-- build.xml
|-- queue
```

```
| |-- queue.xml
|-- fingerprints
| |-- fileFingerprint.xml
```

Anticipated Usage and Maintenance:

1. Backing Up JENKINS_HOME: Regular backups of the home directory are critical. Focus should be on preserving configurations (config.xml), job definitions (jobs/), user credentials (users/), and sensitive keys (secrets/).

2. Disaster Recovery: A precise restoration from backups can be achieved by copying backed-up data into a fresh JENKINS_HOME directory on a new Jenkins instance.

3. Security Best Practices: Securely manage access permissions, especially for sensitive directories such as secrets/ and users/.

Proper understanding and management of the JENKINS_HOME directory are prerequisites for configuring a resilient and efficient Jenkins instance, ensuring continuous integration and continuous delivery processes remain robust.

2.8 Configuring Global Security

Configuring global security in Jenkins is critical to safeguard your CI/CD pipeline from internal and external threats. This section focuses on the integral security settings that Jenkins administrators should configure to ensure a secure environment.

Jenkins provides a robust set of security controls and options, typically accessible via the Jenkins dashboard under *Manage Jenkins → Configure Global Security*. Ensuring these settings are appropriately configured is pivotal for maintaining security throughout the pipeline.

Enabling Security

By default, Jenkins operates in an unsecured mode upon initial setup. To enable security, you need to navigate to the specified security configuration option.

- Open Jenkins in a web browser.
- Navigate to *Manage Jenkins*.
- Click on *Configure Global Security*.

- Check the *Enable Security* box.

Choosing an Authentication Method

Authentication in Jenkins can be managed through various methods such as Jenkins' own user database, an external LDAP (Lightweight Directory Access Protocol) server, Active Directory, or through centralized authentication services like SSO (Single Sign-On) systems. Common choices include:

- **Jenkins' Own User Database**: Allows Jenkins to store user information directly, suitable for small teams or for standalone Jenkins setups.
- **LDAP**: Integrates Jenkins with corporate user directories, allowing LDAP credentials to be validated through the existing user database.
- **Active Directory**: Ensures users can authenticate using Windows domain credentials.
- **Security Realm Plugins**: Plugins like Google Login Plugin, GitHub Authentication Plugin, allowing use of third-party authentication mechanisms.

To configure Jenkins to use an LDAP server:

```
# Ensure the LDAP plugin is installed
Manage Jenkins -> Manage Plugins -> Available -> LDAP plugin

# Configure LDAP for authentication
Manage Jenkins -> Configure Global Security -> LDAP
# Enter LDAP server details:
Server: ldap://ldap.example.com
Root DN: dc=example,dc=com
User search base: ou=People
User search filter: uid={0}
Group search base: ou=Groups
```

Authorization Strategy

Authorization determines what authenticated users can do and view within Jenkins. Jenkins supports several authorization strategies:

- **Logged-in Users Can Do Anything**: Any logged-in user has full control over Jenkins.
- **Legacy Mode**: A historical mode, mainly used for backward compatibility.

- **Matrix-based Security**: Provides fine-grained control over permissions, allowing setting permissions for individual users and groups across different jobs and nodes.
- **Role-based Authorization**: Enabled through the Role Strategy Plugin, allowing administrators to define roles with specific permissions and assign these roles to users or groups.

Configuring matrix-based security:

```
# Enable Matrix-based security
Manage Jenkins -> Configure Global Security -> Matrix-based security

# Define permissions by checking the appropriate boxes for each user/group
# Example:
Anonymous | NoRead | NoWrite
Authenticated | Overall/Read | Overall/Administer
Created a Script | NoRead | Container/build container
```

Configuring Agents and Nodes Security

For distributed builds using multiple agents/nodes, secure communication between the Jenkins master and its agents is essential. This includes:

- Enforcing the use of SSH agents for secure connections.
- Using node monitors to detect and react to suspicious activities.
- Ensuring agents are run with the least privilege necessary.

Example of configuring an SSH agent securely:

```
# Add a new node via SSH
Manage Jenkins -> Manage Nodes -> New Node

# Enter details:
Node Name: Agent-1
Remote Root Directory: /home/jenkins
Labels: linux
Launch method: Launch agents via SSH
Host: agent1.example.com

# Ensure agents only possess necessary permissions for their tasks.
Overall permissions: Disconnect, Connect, Configure
Job permissions: Configure, Read, Build
```

CSRF Protection

Cross-Site Request Forgery (CSRF) is a type of attack that can be mitigated by enabling CSRF protection in Jenkins. This sets a security token that must be included in any request modifying data. To enable CSRF protection:

- Navigate to *Manage Jenkins*.
- Click on *Configure Global Security*.
- Under the *CSRF Protection* section, check the *Enable CSRF Protection* box.
- Select *Default Crumb Issuer*.

Miscellaneous Security Settings

Additional security settings are crucial for strengthening Jenkins security posture:

- **Agent-to-Master Access Control**: Restrict what Jenkins agents can do, minimizing risk if an agent gets compromised.
- **CLI Over Remoting**: Consider disabling it if not in use to reduce attack surface.
- **Markup Formatter**: Set to *Safe HTML* to sanitize user inputs and prevent script injection.

Securely configure agent-to-master access:

```
# Enable Agent-to-Master Access Control
Manage Jenkins -> Configure Global Security -> Agent to master security subsystem

# Restrict agent permissions
Per-project security:
  - Disable administrative operations for agents
  - Limit script executions
  - Restrict file access to necessary directories
```

Implementing these configurations establishes a secure baseline for Jenkins operations, significantly mitigating potential security risks while ensuring that only authorized users access the system with appropriately controlled permissions.

2.9 Setting Up User Accounts and Roles

In **Jenkins**, managing user accounts and defining roles is pivotal to maintaining a secure and organized build environment. This section provides detailed instructions on setting up user accounts and roles to ensure that access to Jenkins and its various functionalities is appropriately controlled.

Jenkins supports multiple security mechanisms out-of-the-box and offers a robust user management structure. To begin, it is essential to navigate to the 'Manage Jenkins' page and select 'Configure Global Security'.

- **Security Realm**: This determines the authentication mechanism. You can employ Jenkins' own user database, integrate with LDAP, or use other security realms such as Active Directory for authentication.
- **Authorization**: Define who has access to what within Jenkins. Here, you specify the strategy Jenkins uses to authorize users.

Using Jenkins' Own User Database

When opting to use Jenkins' own user database, you can manage users directly within Jenkins.

- **Enabling Jenkins' Own User Database:**
  Navigate to Manage Jenkins > Configure Global Security. In the Security Realm section, select Jenkins' own user database. Ensure that Allow users to sign up is enabled if you wish to permit self-registration of users.
- **Creating a New User:**
  To create a new user, navigate to Manage Jenkins > Manage Users, then click Create User. Fill in the required fields, such as username, password, full name, and email address.

```
<jenkins>
  <users>
    <user>
      <id>username</id>
      <passwordHash>#jbcrypt:hashedpassword</passwordHash>
      <fullName>John Doe</fullName>
      <emailAddress>john.doe@example.com</emailAddress>
    </user>
  </users>
</jenkins>
```

- **Managing Existing Users:**
  Existing users can be managed from the same Manage Users menu where you can edit or delete users as required.

Configuring Authorization Strategies

Given the importance of defining what users can and cannot do, Jenkins provides several authorization strategies:

- **Logged-in users can do anything**: Suitable for smaller teams where everyone needs full access.
- **Matrix-based security**: Offers fine-grained control over permissions, allowing administrators to specify which users and groups have access to specific actions.
- **Project-based Matrix Authorization**: Similar to matrix-based security but extends control to specific projects.
- **Role-based Authorization Strategy**: Allows definition of roles with specific permissions and assigning those roles to users.

Implementing Matrix-based Security

To configure matrix-based security:

- **Enabling Matrix-based Security:**
  Navigate to Manage Jenkins > Configure Global Security. In the Authorization section, select Matrix-based security.
- **Configuring Permissions:**
  Add users or groups and assign permissions by checking the corresponding checkboxes.

```
adminGroup
  Overall: Administer, Read
  Job: Configure, Read, Build, Discover
  Run: Delete, Replay, Update
developersGroup
  Overall: Read
  Job: Read, Discover, Build, Cancel
```

- **Saving the Configuration:**
  Click Save after configuring the necessary permissions.

Utilizing Role-based Authorization Strategy

The Role-based Authorization Strategy plugin provides a sophisticated mechanism for defining roles and assigning them to users. First, you need to install this plugin if it is not already available.

- **Installing Role-based Authorization Plugin:**
  Navigate to Manage Jenkins > Manage Plugins > Available, search for Role-based Authorization Strategy, and install it.

- **Setting Up Roles:**
  After installation, navigate to Manage Jenkins > Manage and Assign Roles. Here, you can define global roles and project roles.

  - **Global roles**: Apply across all Jenkins jobs.
  - **Project roles**: Specific to individual Jenkins jobs.

- **Assigning Roles to Users:**
  Assign the defined roles to users through Manage Jenkins > Manage and Assign Roles > Assign Roles.

Example Configuration:

```
<jenkins>
  <security>
    <roles>
      <role>
        <name>admin</name>
        <permissions>
          <permission>Overall/Administer</permission>
          <permission>Job/Configure</permission>
        </permissions>
      </role>
      <role>
        <name>developer</name>
        <permissions>
          <permission>Job/Read</permission>
          <permission>Job/Build</permission>
        </permissions>
      </role>
    </roles>
    <assignments>
      <user>
        <id>alice</id>
        <roles>
          <role>developer</role>
        </roles>
      </user>
      <user>
        <id>bob</id>
        <roles>
          <role>admin</role>
        </roles>
      </user>
    </assignments>
  </security>
</jenkins>
```

By meticulously configuring user accounts and roles, administrators can facilitate a secure, organized, and efficient Jenkins environment, ensuring users have the necessary permissions to perform their tasks without compromising the system's integrity.

2.10 Installing and Managing Plugins

Jenkins' functionality is significantly extended through the use of plugins. Plugins allow Jenkins to integrate with a wide range of tools, automate complex workflows, and provide additional features not included in the core Jenkins package. Installing and managing these plugins is crucial for tailoring Jenkins to fit various project requirements and organizational workflows.

Jenkins plugins can be installed using the Jenkins web interface or by manually adding *.hpi* files into the Jenkins home directory. This section delves into both methods, along with guidance on managing installed plugins.

Installing Plugins via the Jenkins Web Interface

The Jenkins web interface provides a straightforward method for installing plugins. Here's a step-by-step guide:

- Navigate to the Jenkins dashboard.
- Click on Manage Jenkins in the left-hand menu.
- Select Manage Plugins.

The Manage Plugins page contains several tabs:

- **Updates**: Displays plugins for which updates are available.
- **Available**: Displays plugins that are available for installation.
- **Installed**: Lists all currently installed plugins.
- **Advanced**: Allows for manual plugin installation and configuration.

To install a plugin:

- Click on the Available tab.
- Use the search box to find the desired plugin.

- Check the box next to the plugin name.
- Click the Install without restart button at the bottom of the page. Alternatively, use Download now and install after restart to have the plugin installed after a Jenkins restart.

```
Click on Manage Jenkins -> Manage Plugins -> Available. Search for 'Git Plugin'.
    Select 'Git Plugin' and click 'Install without restart'
```

Installing Plugins Manually

Manual installation is required for some plugins that are not available in the Jenkins Update Center, or when operating within environments with restricted internet access.

Steps for manual plugin installation:

- Download the *.hpi* or *.jpi* file of the desired plugin from the Jenkins Plugins repository or other trusted sources.
- Navigate to Manage Jenkins -> Manage Plugins -> Advanced tab.
- Under the Upload Plugin section, click the Choose File button.
- Select the downloaded *.hpi* or *.jpi* file.
- Click the Upload button.

Alternatively, the plugin file can be directly copied to the $JENKINS_HOME/plugins directory followed by a Jenkins restart to complete the installation.

```
$ wget https://updates.jenkins-ci.org/latest/git.hpi
$ cp git.hpi $JENKINS_HOME/plugins/
$ sudo systemctl restart jenkins
```

Managing Installed Plugins

Efficiently managing installed plugins ensures Jenkins remains scalable and free of unnecessary components, reducing potential security risks.

Updating Plugins:

Regularly updating plugins is crucial to benefit from new features, improvements, and security patches.

- Navigate to Manage Jenkins -> Manage Plugins -> Updates tab.

- Select the plugins to update.
- Click Download now and install after restart.

Disabling Plugins:

Plugins can be temporarily disabled if not required without uninstalling them:

- Navigate to Manage Jenkins -> Manage Plugins -> Installed tab.
- Locate the plugin to disable.
- Click the Disable button next to the plugin.

Uninstalling Plugins:

To remove unnecessary plugins:

- Navigate to Manage Jenkins -> Manage Plugins -> Installed tab.
- Locate the plugin to uninstall.
- Click the Uninstall button.
- Confirm the uninstallation.

Checking Plugin Dependencies:

Before uninstalling a plugin, it's prudent to check if other installed plugins depend on it. Attempting to uninstall a plugin involved in dependencies typically prompts a warning.

```
Warning: Uninstalling this plugin could also uninstall plugins that depend on it. Proceed?
```

Critical plugins form the backbone of many Jenkins pipelines. Understanding their impact and usage is essential before making any changes.

Configuring Plugin Updates:

Automated plugin updates can be configured via the Manage Jenkins -> Manage Plugins -> Advanced tab. It's possible to manage the plugin update schedules and opt for periodic automatic updates, mitigating manual overhead and ensuring the platform's security and efficiency.

Proper plugin management ensures that Jenkins remains robust and aligns with evolving project demands. By following best practices for installation, updating, disabling, and uninstalling, one can maintain an optimal Jenkins environment.

2.11 Configuring External Tools and Integrations

Jenkins provides robust support for integrating with a variety of external tools and services to extend its capabilities and streamline the CI/CD pipeline. This section details how to configure external tools and integrations, ensuring that Jenkins operates cohesively with your development ecosystem.

To begin configuring external tools in Jenkins, navigate to Manage Jenkins → Global Tool Configuration. Here, you can add and configure various tools Jenkins will use. Common tools include JDK installations, Git, and Maven.

Java Development Kit (JDK)

Jenkins requires the Java Development Kit (JDK) to run properly and compile Java-based projects. You can add JDK installations as follows:

- Navigate to Manage Jenkins → Global Tool Configuration.
- Scroll down to the JDK section and click Add JDK.
- Uncheck Install automatically if you prefer to manually specify the JDK installation path.
- Provide a name for this JDK installation (e.g., JDK11).
- Specify the installation directory.

tool

```
Jenkins.instance.getDescriptorByType(
  hudson.model.JDK$DescriptorImpl.class
).installations = [new hudson.model.JDK(
    'JDK11', '/path/to/jdk11'
)]
```

tool

Git

Git is commonly used for version control in Jenkins projects. Configuring Git involves:

- Navigating to Manage Jenkins → Global Tool Configuration.
- Finding the Git section.

- Clicking Git installations....
- Providing a name and the path to the Git executable (e.g., /usr/bin/git).

To verify Git's configuration:

```
if (!git --version ) {
    println 'Git is not installed or not in the PATH'
}
else {
    println 'Git version: ' + git --version
}
```

Apache Maven

Maven is integral for building and managing Java projects. To configure Maven in Jenkins:

- Go to Manage Jenkins → Global Tool Configuration.
- Scroll to Maven installations and click Add Maven.
- Assign a name (e.g., Maven 3.6.3).
- Specify the Maven home directory, or select the option for Jenkins to install it automatically.

```
def mavenHome = '/path/to/apache-maven-3.6.3'
System.setProperty('maven.home', mavenHome)
```

Integrate Maven in a Jenkins job by configuring the build step:

- Add a Build step in the job configuration.
- Choose Invoke top-level Maven targets.
- Specify the desired goals, for example: clean install.
- Select the configured Maven installation under Maven Version.

tool

```
mvn clean install
```

tool

Docker

Jenkins can be configured to use Docker for containerized builds. Ensure Docker is installed and running on the Jenkins server. Then:

- Install the Docker plugin in Jenkins by navigating to Manage Jenkins → Manage Plugins → Available, and search for Docker.
- After installation, configure Docker by going to Global Tool Configuration and adding a Docker installation under the Cloud section.

To utilize Docker in a Jenkins job:

- In the job configuration, add a Build step.
- Select Execute Shell and enter the Docker commands, such as:

```
docker build -t myapp .
docker run myapp
```

Integration with SCMs and Notification Services

Configuring integrations with Source Control Management (SCM) systems like GitHub and Bitbucket, and notification services like Slack, involves plugins.

For GitHub:

- Install the GitHub Integration plugin.
- Navigate to Manage Jenkins → Configure System.
- Add GitHub servers under the GitHub section.
- Provide the API URL and credentials.

For Slack notifications:

- Install the Slack Notification plugin.
- Go to Manage Jenkins → Configure System.
- Find the Slack section, and enter the Workspace, Credentials, and the default channel or user.

Adding a Slack notification to a job:

- In the job configuration, under Post-build Actions, add the Slack Notifications option.
- Specify the desired notification triggers (e.g., Success, Failure).

```
slackSend channel: 'build-notifications',
         message: 'Build #${BUILD_NUMBER} - ${BUILD_RESULT}'
```

These configurations ensure Jenkins interacts proficiently with external tools and services, enhancing the CI/CD workflow.

2.12 Backup and Restore Strategies

Ensuring the reliability and availability of your Jenkins server is paramount, and effective backup and restore strategies form the backbone of this reliability. Jenkins, as a continuous integration and continuous delivery (CI/CD) server, manages numerous configurations, jobs, and plugins which are crucial to the automated build and deployment pipeline. This section will delve into the various methodologies and best practices for backing up and restoring your Jenkins environment.

The Jenkins home directory (JENKINS_HOME) is the primary repository for all configuration data, job data, and plugins. It is essential that any backup strategy encompasses this directory in its entirety to ensure a complete snapshot of the Jenkins environment.

Manual Backup Strategy

The most straightforward method for backing up Jenkins involves manually copying the JENKINS_HOME directory to a secure location. This process can be executed during regular maintenance windows to minimize disruption.

```
$ cp -r $JENKINS_HOME /path/to/backup/location
```

For enhanced security and reliability, it is recommended to compress the backup directory into a tarball, enabling easier handling and reduced storage requirements.

```
$ tar -czvf jenkins_backup.tar.gz -C /path/to/backup/location .
```

Automated Backup Strategy

While manual backups provide a high degree of control, they may not be feasible in highly dynamic environments. Automated backup solutions can address this need by scheduling backups at regular intervals.

A popular and effective tool for automating Jenkins backups is the ThinBackup plugin. This plugin allows for the creation of automated backup jobs within Jenkins itself.

- Install the ThinBackup plugin via the Jenkins Plugin Manager.
- Configure the plugin through the Jenkins Manage Jenkins > ThinBackup options.
- Schedule regular backups by navigating to Manage Jenkins > ThinBackup > Settings, specifying backup locations, frequencies, and retention policies.
- The backup process will execute in the background without manual intervention.

Restoring Jenkins from Backup

Restoring Jenkins from a backup involves replacing the existing JENKINS_HOME directory with the contents of the backup. This process should be executed with caution, and it is wise to stop the Jenkins service beforehand to prevent data corruption.

```
$ service jenkins stop
```

Subsequently, the backup tarball can be extracted to restore the previous state.

```
$ tar -xzvf jenkins_backup.tar.gz -C /path/to/jenkins_home
```

Upon completion of the extraction, the Jenkins service can be restarted.

```
$ service jenkins start
```

External Integration for Backups

In enterprise settings, integrating Jenkins with external backup systems can provide additional layers of reliability. Utilizing network-attached storage (NAS) systems, cloud storage solutions, or databases like MySQL for Jenkins configurations enhances data durability and accessibility.

- Plugins such as the S3 Plugin allow for backups to be stored in Amazon S3, leveraging the scalability and redundancy of cloud services.
- NAS or SAN can be integrated using network file systems (NFS) or similar protocols to provide consistent and reliable backup destinations.

- Incorporating tools like rsync for incremental backups minimizes bandwidth usage and accelerates the backup process.

Backup Verification and Integrity Checking

No backup strategy is complete without regular verification of the backups taken. It is critical to periodically perform restore tests on a separate, non-production Jenkins server instance to validate the integrity and completeness of the backups.

- Restoring on a staging server to verify job configurations, build history, and plugin settings.
- Utilizing checksum tools like md5sum or sha256sum to ensure file integrity throughout the backup and restore process.

The above methodologies, when diligently applied, can drastically reduce the risk associated with system failures, ensuring that your Jenkins instances remain robust and recoverable under various scenarios.

Chapter 3

Jenkins Pipelines

This chapter introduces Jenkins Pipelines, explaining core concepts and terminology, and differentiating between scripted and declarative pipelines. It guides readers through setting up simple pipelines and using pipeline as code. The chapter covers pipeline syntax, stages, steps, parallel execution, and handling pipeline failures. It also discusses shared libraries, best practices for designing pipelines, and utilizing Blue Ocean for enhanced pipeline visualization.

3.1 Introduction to Jenkins Pipelines

Jenkins Pipelines are a suite of plugins that support implementing and integrating continuous delivery pipelines into Jenkins. A key allure of Jenkins Pipelines is the Pipeline-as-Code approach, allowing versioning pipelines alongside the source code they are built to deploy. This practice enhances collaboration as pipelines are treated as a part of the project, with the same version control practices as the application code itself.

Pipelines in Jenkins are defined using a domain-specific language (DSL) that models the entire build, test, and deploy phases of a Continuous Delivery (CD) pipeline. Jenkins Pipelines can be written in two syntaxes: Declarative and Scripted. This flexibility allows users to choose a syntax that best fits their workflow and team expertise.

A Jenkins Pipeline is configured through a 'Jenkinsfile', written in Groovy. This file defines various stages and steps that make up the build process. The syntax and structure of a 'Jenkinsfile' are crucial as they delineate the sequential tasks and parallel workflows necessary for a robust CI/CD pipeline.

```
node {
  stage('Build') {
    // steps to perform build
  }

  stage('Test') {
    // steps to perform tests
  }

  stage('Deploy') {
    // steps to perform deployment
  }
}
```

In the example above, the pipeline consists of three stages: Build, Test, and Deploy. Stages are used to visualize the progression of the pipeline in Jenkins' UI, providing a clear indication of where the process currently stands. Each stage consists of steps that can range from simple shell commands to complex scripted logic.

One important aspect of Jenkins Pipelines is the distinction between agent and workspace. An 'agent' directive specifies where the pipeline, or a specific stage, should execute. It can be any machine or container capable of running Jenkins-provisioned jobs. Conversely, a 'workspace' is a directory on the agent machine where Jenkins stores files related to a pipeline job.

```
pipeline {
  agent any

  stages {
    stage('Build') {
      steps {
        sh 'mvn clean install'
      }
    }
    stage('Test') {
      steps {
        sh 'mvn test'
      }
    }
    stage('Deploy') {
      steps {
        sh 'scp target/my-app.jar user@server:/deploy/my-app.jar'
      }
    }
  }
}
```

The declarative pipeline syntax, depicted above, emphasizes readability and simplicity. It starts with the 'pipeline' block defining the 'agent', and then a series of 'stages', each containing their respective 'steps'.

In contrast, the scripted syntax offers more flexibility and is based on Groovy, a scripting language for the Java platform. While more powerful, it can be less readable, making it a suitable choice for complex pipelines or for developers with proficiency in Groovy.

```
node {
  stage('Checkout') {
    checkout scm
  }
  stage('Build') {
    sh 'mvn clean install'
  }
  stage('Test') {
    try {
      sh 'mvn test'
    } catch (Exception e) {
      echo 'Tests failed!'
      throw e
    }
  }
  stage('Deploy') {
    if (currentBuild.result == 'SUCCESS') {
      sh 'scp target/my-app.jar user@server:/deploy/my-app.jar'
    }
  }
}
```

Incessantly, the robust infrastructure of Jenkins Pipelines supports advanced features like parallel execution of stages and integrating external libraries. Handling pipeline failures gracefully ensures that issues are caught early and handled efficiently, reducing downtime and maintaining the stability of deployment pipelines.

```
[Pipeline] Start of Pipeline
[Pipeline] node
Running on Jenkins in /var/jenkins/workspace/my-pipeline
[Pipeline] {
[Pipeline] stage
[Pipeline] { (Checkout)
[Pipeline] }
[Pipeline] // stage
[Pipeline] stage
[Pipeline] { (Build)
[Pipeline] }
[Pipeline] // stage
[Pipeline] stage
[Pipeline] { (Test)
[Pipeline] }
[Pipeline] // stage
[Pipeline] stage
[Pipeline] { (Deploy)
[Pipeline] }
[Pipeline] // stage
[Pipeline] }
[Pipeline] // node
[Pipeline] End of Pipeline
```

Jenkins's visualization tools, like Blue Ocean, provide an intuitive interface to monitor pipelines and manage their behavior interactively. This visual insight into pipeline status, failures, and logs is indispensable for maintaining pipeline health and identifying optimization areas. By integrating tightly with version control systems such as Git, Jenkins Pipelines bridge the gap between code commit and deployment, enhancing automation and continuous delivery efficiency.

3.2 Pipeline Concepts and Terminology

Understanding pipelines within Jenkins involves comprehending several key concepts and terminology fundamental to Jenkins pipeline syntax and functionality. This section delineates these vital concepts to provide a robust foundation for utilizing Jenkins Pipelines effectively.

A **Pipeline** is a suite of plugins that enables the implementation and integration of continuous delivery pipelines into Jenkins. It represents the workflow of a project's build lifecycle in a series of stages executed sequentially or in parallel. Jenkins pipelines can be configured using either a declarative or scripted syntax.

Declarative Pipeline is a newer and simpler syntax which offers a more structured approach to defining a Jenkins pipeline. It is defined within a pipeline block and contains stages, each encapsulating a sequence of steps. The declarative pipeline syntax supports specific DSL elements like agent, options, triggers, parameters, and post sections to control various aspects of the pipeline behavior.

```
pipeline {
    agent any
    stages {
        stage('Build') {
            steps {
                echo 'Building..'
            }
        }
        stage('Test') {
            steps {
                echo 'Testing..'
            }
        }
        stage('Deploy') {
            steps {
                echo 'Deploying....'
            }
        }
    }
}
```

A **Scripted Pipeline**, on the other hand, provides greater flexibility and power, at the cost of complexity. Scripted pipelines are constructed as a domain-specific language based on Groovy, offering the full range of features available in Groovy within the pipeline definition.

```
node {
    stage('Build') {
        echo 'Building...'
    }
    stage('Test') {
        echo 'Testing...'
    }
    stage('Deploy') {
        echo 'Deploying...'
    }
}
```

Stages are key sections or steps in a pipeline dedicated to executing a series of instructions encapsulated within themselves. Stages are typically used to encapsulate quantum steps in the delivery process such as Build, Test, and Deploy. Each stage in a declarative pipeline is represented as a nested block within the `stages` directive and encapsulates one or more steps.

Steps are the smallest individual unit of operation in a pipeline. They define a single task such as invoking a script, progressing the build, artifact processing, or executing a shell command. A sequence of steps can be included within a `stage` block.

Agent specifies where the entire pipeline or a segment of the pipeline (stages or specific steps) will run. It is typically defined within the pipeline block in declarative pipelines. It can be defined globally or at the individual stage level, offering control over pipeline execution location.

```
pipeline {
    agent any
    stages {
        stage('Build') {
            agent {
                docker { image 'maven:3.3.3' }
            }
            steps {
                echo 'Building...'
            }
        }
    }
}
```

Post is a block that defines one or more additional steps that are run upon the completion of the pipeline, regardless of the pipeline's success or failure, such as cleanup actions after the build process.

```
pipeline {
    agent any
    stages {
        stage('Example') {
            steps {
                echo 'Hello, World!'
            }
        }
    }
    post {
        always {
            echo 'This will always run'
        }
        success {
            echo 'This will run only if successful'
        }
        failure {
            echo 'This will run only if the build failed'
        }
    }
}
```

Pipelines in Jenkins can branch and merge through the use of **Parallel** directive which facilitates parallel execution of sections within pipelines. This is particularly useful for running independent tasks simultaneously to reduce overall pipeline runtime.

```
pipeline {
    agent any
    stages {
        stage('Parallel Stage') {
            parallel {
                stage('Unit tests') {
                    steps {
                        echo 'Running unit tests'
```

```
                }
            }
            stage('Integration tests') {
                steps {
                    echo 'Running integration tests'
                }
            }
        }
    }
  }
}
```

Integration of **Shared Libraries** allows for reusable, modular, and maintainable code housed separately from the pipeline jobs themselves. Shared libraries provide a mechanism for defining custom pipeline functions, helper methods, and pre-configured pipeline tasks that can be utilized across multiple pipelines.

Delving into the terminology and foundational concepts is essential to enable effective pipeline design and utilization. Recognizing the importance of each component within a pipeline ensures logical structuring and efficient execution, paving the way for more complex and robust pipelines. Communicating these principles clearly and applying them consistently lead to a higher degree of reliability and maintainability in continuous delivery processes.

3.3 Differences Between Scripted and Declarative Pipelines

The Jenkins Pipeline system offers two distinct syntaxes for defining your pipelines: Scripted Pipeline and Declarative Pipeline. Understanding the differences between these two approaches is crucial for leveraging the full potential of Jenkins and choosing the most appropriate syntax for your use case. This section delineates the key distinctions between Scripted and Declarative Pipelines, enabling better decision-making for pipeline implementation.

Scripted Pipeline is based on Groovy, a dynamic language for the Java platform. It follows a more programmatic approach, allowing for greater flexibility and customization. Here is a basic example of a Scripted Pipeline:

```
node {
    stage('Compile') {
        echo 'Compiling...'
        // Compile code
```

```
    }
    stage('Test') {
        echo 'Testing...'
        // Run tests
    }
    stage('Deploy') {
        echo 'Deploying...'
        // Deploy application
    }
}
```

Declarative Pipeline provides a more structured and simplified syntax, making it easier to write and understand. This syntax is designed to cover most of the use cases for pipeline definition with minimal Groovy knowledge. Here is an example of a Declarative Pipeline:

```
pipeline {
    agent any
    stages {
        stage('Compile') {
            steps {
                echo 'Compiling...'
                // Compile code
            }
        }
        stage('Test') {
            steps {
                echo 'Testing...'
                // Run tests
            }
        }
        stage('Deploy') {
            steps {
                echo 'Deploying...'
                // Deploy application
            }
        }
    }
}
```

Key differences between Scripted and Declarative Pipelines include syntax, error validation, parameter handling, and flow control.

- ***Syntax Structure***
  - *Scripted Pipeline*: The syntax is more flexible and resembles traditional scripting languages. The script execution starts from the 'node' block and is highly imperative, providing rich control over the flow.
  - *Declarative Pipeline*: The syntax is prescriptive and enforceable, providing a clear structure with specific blocks such as 'pipeline', 'agent', 'stages', and 'steps'.
- ***Error Validation and Handling***

  - *Scripted Pipeline*: Errors may be less predictable due to the flexible nature of the language. Error handling is often done using traditional try-catch blocks within Groovy.

```
node {
    try {
        stage('Compile') {
            echo 'Compiling...'
            // Possible compilation task
        }
    } catch(Exception e) {
        echo 'Error occurred: ' + e.toString()
    }
}
```

  - *Declarative Pipeline*: Built-in error validation tends to be stricter, as the pipeline structure enforces certain behaviors. Declarative Pipelines support predefined error-handling constructs such as 'post' conditions.

```
pipeline {
    agent any
    stages {
        stage('Compile') {
            steps {
                echo 'Compiling...'
            }
        }
    }
    post {
        failure {
            echo 'Pipeline failed.'
        }
        success {
            echo 'Pipeline succeeded.'
        }
    }
}
```

- ***Parameter Handling and Environment Variables***

  - *Scripted Pipeline*: Parameters and environment variables can be defined and manipulated dynamically throughout the pipeline. For instance:

```
node {
    def buildParam = 'Build-1'
    env.BUILD_STAGE = 'Production'

    stage('Build') {
        echo "Building ${buildParam} in ${env.
            BUILD_STAGE}"
        // Build process
    }
}
```

  - *Declarative Pipeline*: Parameters and environment variables are defined within the 'parameters' and 'environment' blocks at the top level of the pipeline. This provides clarity and maintains consistency in parameter handling.

```
pipeline {
    agent any
    parameters {
        string(name: 'buildParam', defaultValue: 'Build-1',
            description: 'Build Parameter')
    }
    environment {
        BUILD_STAGE = 'Production'
    }
    stages {
        stage('Build') {
            steps {
                echo "Building ${params.buildParam} in ${env.
                    BUILD_STAGE}"
                // Build process
            }
        }
    }
}
```

- ***Flow Control***

  - *Scripted Pipeline*: Offers greater control for complex conditional branching and iterative loops, similar to traditional programming languages. Explicit flow controls can be implemented using standard Groovy constructs.

```
node {
    for (int i = 0; i < 5; i++) {
        stage("Stage ${i}") {
            echo "Running iteration ${i}"
            // Iterative tasks
        }
    }
}
```

  - *Declarative Pipeline*: Flow control is more defined and somewhat constrained, primarily using the 'when' condition for defining stage execution based on specific criteria or parameters.

```
pipeline {
    agent any
    stages {
        stage('Example') {
            when {
                expression { return params.someCondition }
            }
            steps {
                echo "Conditionally executed stage"
                // Conditional tasks
```

```
                }
            }
        }
    }
```

Choosing between Scripted and Declarative Pipelines often depends on the complexity of the requirements and the preferred level of precision and control over the pipeline's behavior. Declarative Pipelines are generally more accessible for those who prefer a clear structure with built-in validations. In contrast, Scripted Pipelines offer more flexibility and may be better suited for highly customized tasks requiring sophisticated logic and flow control.

3.4 Setting Up a Simple Pipeline

Configuring a basic Jenkins Pipeline involves a series of straightforward steps which can be systematically detailed to ensure clarity for users at different proficiency levels. This section outlines the process from the initial setup to the execution of a basic pipeline, focusing on essential commands and configurations.

Step 1: Creating a New Jenkins Job To begin, navigate to your Jenkins dashboard and create a new item by selecting New Item from the menu. You will be prompted to enter a name for your job and to choose the type of project. Select Pipeline and click OK.

Step 2: Configuring the Pipeline Once the new job is created, you will be taken to the job configuration page. Here, you can define the pipeline script. In the Pipeline section, you have the option to enter your script directly in the Pipeline Script textarea or to reference a script from a version control system.

For simplicity, we'll enter the script directly in the textarea. A minimal pipeline script might look like this:

```
pipeline {
    agent any

    stages {
        stage('Build') {
            steps {
                echo 'Building...'
            }
        }

        stage('Test') {
            steps {
```

```
                echo 'Testing...'
            }
        }

        stage('Deploy') {
            steps {
                echo 'Deploying...'
            }
        }
    }
}
```

This script defines three stages: Build, Test, and Deploy. Each stage contains a steps block where the actual steps to be executed are defined. The echo command is used to print a message to the console output for simplicity.

Step 3: Saving and Running the Pipeline After entering the pipeline script, save the configuration by clicking the Save or Apply button. You will be redirected to the job's main page.

To execute the pipeline, click the Build Now button in the left-hand menu. Jenkins will start the pipeline, and you can monitor its progress in real-time by clicking on #1 under the Build History section.

The possible console output will be as follows:

```
[Pipeline] Start of Pipeline
[Pipeline] node
Running on Jenkins in /var/jenkins_home/workspace/<your_job_name>
[Pipeline] {
[Pipeline] stage
[Pipeline] { (Build)
[Pipeline] echo
Building...
[Pipeline] }
[Pipeline] // stage
[Pipeline] stage
[Pipeline] { (Test)
[Pipeline] echo
Testing...
[Pipeline] }
[Pipeline] // stage
[Pipeline] stage
[Pipeline] { (Deploy)
[Pipeline] echo
Deploying...
[Pipeline] }
[Pipeline] // stage
[Pipeline] }
[Pipeline] // node
[Pipeline] End of Pipeline
Finished: SUCCESS
```

Step 4: Analysis and Troubleshooting In the event that the pipeline fails, Jenkins provides detailed logs in the console output. Revisiting and analyzing the logs is essential for diagnosing issues. For instance, a syntax error in the pipeline script will be logged with a descriptive message indicating the nature of the error and the line number where it occurred.

Adjustments can be made directly in the pipeline script on the job configuration page. To apply and test fixes, save the updated script and rebuild the pipeline to observe any changes.

Benefits of Using Pipelines Setting up a pipeline, even a simple one, introduces consistent automation for building, testing, and deploying applications. Pipelines as code are versionable and maintainable, providing a clear audit trail. Moreover, this setup serves as a foundation for more complex workflows, allowing stages to be extended with additional steps, parallel execution, or integration with various plugins and third-party tools supported by Jenkins.

By mastering this process, users can leverage pipelines to standardize CI/CD practices, improving development workflows' efficiency and reliability.

3.5 Pipeline as Code

Pipeline as Code is a fundamental principle in Jenkins pipelines, emphasizing the importance of treating the pipeline configuration as code in a similar way to applications or scripts in your repository. By storing the pipeline definitions as a part of the source code, teams can version and test their continuous integration and continuous delivery (CI/CD) processes alongside their application code. This enhances collaboration, maintains history, and ensures consistency across different environments.

Jenkins pipelines can be defined as code in two main syntaxes: Scripted Pipelines and Declarative Pipelines. The choice between the two depends on the complexity of the project and the team's preference.

Let's begin by understanding how to define a simple pipeline as code using both scripted and declarative syntaxes.

Scripted Pipelines:

Scripted Pipelines use a groovy-based domain-specific language (DSL) that prioritizes flexibility and extensibility. Here's a basic example of a scripted pipeline:

```
node {
    stage('Build') {
        echo 'Building...'
        // Insert build steps here
    }
    stage('Test') {
        echo 'Testing...'
        // Insert testing steps here
    }
    stage('Deploy') {
        echo 'Deploying...'
        // Insert deploy steps here
    }
}
```

In the above example, node is a fundamental step that acquires an executor and a workspace, ensuring that the pipeline runs on an available Jenkins agent. The stage blocks define individual stages in the pipeline, such as Build, Test, and Deploy. Each stage contains specific steps indicated by the echo commands which print messages to the console output. In a real-world scenario, these would be replaced with the actual build, test, and deployment commands.

Declarative Pipelines:

Declarative Pipelines offer a simpler, more structured way of defining pipelines, focusing on readability and ease of use. Here's the equivalent of the above example using declarative syntax:

```
pipeline {
    agent any

    stages {
        stage('Build') {
            steps {
                echo 'Building...'
                // Insert build steps here
            }
        }
        stage('Test') {
            steps {
                echo 'Testing...'
                // Insert testing steps here
            }
        }
        stage('Deploy') {
            steps {
                echo 'Deploying...'
                // Insert deploy steps here
            }
        }
    }
}
```

In this declarative pipeline, the structure is defined within the pipeline block, which specifies that any available agent can be used to run the pipeline (agent any). The stages block wraps multiple stages, each containing steps that execute tasks akin to those in the scripted example.

Using the declarative syntax provides several benefits, such as built-in features for handling environment conditions, post-build actions, and easier error handling, due to its higher level of abstraction.

Version Control Integration:

Integrating the pipeline code with a version control system (VCS) like Git enables tracking changes, rolling back to previous versions, and collaborating seamlessly across different team members. Below is an example configuration of a Jenkinsfile located at the root of a Git repository:

```
pipeline {
    agent any

    stages {
        stage('Checkout') {
            steps {
                git url: 'https://github.com/your-repo.git', branch: 'main'
            }
        }
        stage('Build') {
            steps {
                echo 'Building...'
                // Insert build steps here
            }
        }
        stage('Test') {
            steps {
                echo 'Testing...'
                // Insert testing steps here
            }
        }
        stage('Deploy') {
            steps {
                echo 'Deploying...'
                // Insert deploy steps here
            }
        }
    }
}
```

In this example, the Checkout stage clones the repository from the given URL and branch, ensuring that the pipeline operates on the latest code.

Advanced Pipeline as Code Features:

Declarative Pipeline introduces numerous advanced features, including parallel execution, tools installation, environment variable management, and post-build actions. Below is an advanced declarative pipeline example showcasing these capabilities:

```
pipeline {
```

```
    agent any

    tools {
        maven 'Maven 3.6.3'
    }

    environment {
        JAVA_HOME = '/usr/lib/jvm/java-8-openjdk'
    }

    stages {
        stage('Build') {
            steps {
                sh 'mvn clean package'
            }
        }
        stage('Test') {
            steps {
                parallel (
                    Unit: {
                        sh 'mvn test -Dtest=UnitTest'
                    },
                    Integration: {
                        sh 'mvn verify -Dtest=IntegrationTest'
                    }
                )
            }
        }
        stage('Deploy') {
            steps {
                echo 'Deploying...'
                // Insert deploy steps here
            }
        }
    }

    post {
        always {
            junit 'target/surefire-reports/*.xml'
        }
        success {
            archiveArtifacts artifacts: 'target/*.jar', allowEmptyArchive: true
        }
        failure {
            mail to: 'team@example.com', subject: "Failed Pipeline: ${currentBuild.
                fullDisplayName}", body: "Pipeline ${env.JOB_NAME} failed at ${
                env.BUILD_URL}"
        }
    }
}
```

This pipeline incorporates the tools section to install specific tools (e.g., Maven), sets environment variables, and utilizes the parallel step to run unit and integration tests concurrently. The post section handles actions that should occur regardless of the build status (always), on success (success), and upon failure (failure).

By adopting the Pipeline as Code approach, teams can improve collaboration, maintain a history of CI/CD configurations, and ensure that their automation processes are reproducible and consistent across environments.

3.6 Pipeline Syntax

Understanding the syntax of Jenkins pipelines is crucial for efficiently defining and managing your Continuous Integration (CI) and Continuous Deployment (CD) workflows. The pipeline syntax, which enables the orchestration of complex build processes, varies depending on whether you are using a Scripted Pipeline or a Declarative Pipeline. Here, we'll delve into the specifics of both syntaxes, guiding you through their structures and functionalities.

The Declarative Pipeline syntax, introduced in Jenkins 2.x, aims at simplifying the creation of build pipelines and making it more approachable for users. It enforces a more strict and predefined structure, reducing potential errors and improving readability.

An example of a simple Declarative Pipeline is shown below:

```
pipeline {
    agent any
    stages {
        stage('Build') {
            steps {
                echo 'Building...'
            }
        }
        stage('Test') {
            steps {
                echo 'Testing...'
            }
        }
        stage('Deploy') {
            steps {
                echo 'Deploying...'
            }
        }
    }
}
```

The Declarative Pipeline begins with the pipeline block. This block contains several distinct sections such as agent, stages, and steps. The agent section specifies where the Jenkins pipeline or stage runs. Setting agent any implies that Jenkins can run the pipeline on any available agent.

Within the stages block, individual stage blocks are nested. Each stage signifies a phase in the pipeline and contains a steps block, listing various build steps to be executed in sequence. For instance, the echo statements in each stage demonstrate placeholder commands for Build, Test, and Deploy stages.

Scripted Pipeline syntax, also known as "groovy syntax," offers more control and flexibility and is written in Groovy. An example of a simple Scripted Pipeline is as follows:

```
node {
    stage('Build') {
        echo 'Building...'
    }
    stage('Test') {
        echo 'Testing...'
    }
    stage('Deploy') {
        echo 'Deploying...'
    }
}
```

In the Scripted Pipeline, there is no mandatory pipeline block. Instead, execution starts with the node block, which denotes the Jenkins agent executing the pipeline. Each stage block within the node contains Groovy code articulating the steps in that stage.

Comparing the Declarative and Scripted Pipelines:

1. **Declarative Syntax**:

- Enforces a predefined structure.
- Simplifies pipeline creation.
- Reduces syntax errors with its stringent format.

2. **Scripted Syntax**:

- Provides more flexibility in defining logic.
- Requires familiarity with Groovy programming language.
- Better suited for complex CI/CD processes.

One feature exclusive to Declarative Pipelines is the concept of post blocks, which specify additional steps that run upon the completion of a pipeline or stage:

```
pipeline {
    agent any
    stages {
        stage('Build') {
```

```
            steps {
                echo 'Building...'
            }
        }
    }
    post {
        always {
            echo 'This will always run'
        }
        success {
            echo 'This will run only if the build succeeds'
        }
        failure {
            echo 'This will run only if the build fails'
        }
    }
}
```

The post block runs after the pipeline or specific stage completes and is divided into conditions such as always, success, and failure, which execute based on the build outcome.

Additionally, Declarative Pipelines support precise error handling and recovery with the options, triggers, and parameters directives integrated into the pipeline configuration:

```
pipeline {
    agent any
    options {
        timeout(time: 1, unit: 'HOURS')
    }
    triggers {
        cron('H 4/* 0 0 1-7 *')
    }
    parameters {
        string(name: 'BRANCH_NAME', defaultValue: 'main', description: 'Branch to
            build')
    }
    stages {
        stage('Build') {
            steps {
                echo 'Building...'
            }
        }
    }
}
```

Here, the options directive can set global pipeline options, such as timeout settings. The triggers directive schedules pipeline runs via cron syntax, and the parameters directive allows the definition of pipeline parameters, enabling more dynamic and customizable pipeline executions.

Ultimately, choosing between Declarative and Scripted Pipelines depends on the build complexity, team preference, and need for flexibility versus simplicity. Understanding the nuances of both syntaxes empowers you to architect robust and maintainable Jenkins pipelines tailored to your specific CI/CD requirements.

3.7 Building Blocks of Pipelines

The Jenkins pipeline is composed of several key elements that form the backbone of the automation process. Understanding these fundamental building blocks is crucial for constructing effective and efficient continuous integration and continuous delivery (CI/CD) systems. The primary components are **pipeline**, **node**, **stage**, **step**, and **agent**.

A **pipeline** in Jenkins is a user-defined model of a continuous delivery pipeline, which can be represented as code. This allows for versioning and sharing of the pipeline configuration, enhancing reproducibility and collaboration. Pipelines are written in Groovy-based domain-specific language (DSL) syntax, and they can fall into one of two categories: **scripted** pipelines and **declarative** pipelines. Declarative pipelines provide a more structured and simpler syntax suitable for most use cases, whereas scripted pipelines offer full control and flexibility for complex tasks.

The **node** block is essential for allocating an executor on a Jenkins agent, which runs the instructions coded within the node block. An executor is a computational resource allocated to execute the pipeline's tasks.

```
node {
    // Define tasks to execute inside this block.
}
```

Within the node block, a **stage** block demarcates distinct phases of the pipeline's execution. Stages help in organizing the tasks and visualizing the progression of the pipeline. Each stage can contain multiple steps, allowing for detailed granularity in the execution flow. Stages also enhance clarity when reviewing the pipeline's status, as each stage's status is individually displayed in the Jenkins UI.

```
stage('Build') {
    steps {
        // Build tasks
    }
}
stage('Test') {
    steps {
```

```
        // Test tasks
    }
}
stage('Deploy') {
    steps {
        // Deployment tasks
    }
}
```

A **step** is a single task that defines an action within the pipeline. Steps can range from executing shell commands to invoking specific Jenkins plugins. They form the smallest unit of execution in a pipeline and are the operations that Jenkins agents perform.

```
steps {
    sh 'echo Hello, World!'
    junit 'tests/results.xml'
    archiveArtifacts 'build/*.zip'
}
```

The **agent** directive specifies where the entire pipeline, or a specific stage, is executed. This can be on any available agent, a particular agent, or even within a docker container. Defining agents provide the flexibility to run stages on different environments as required.

```
pipeline {
    agent any
    stages {
        stage('Example Stage') {
            agent {
                // Agent definition
            }
            steps {
                // Steps to execute
            }
        }
    }
}
```

Integrating these building blocks effectively demands an understanding of how different components can be nested and combined. For example, a pipeline can be defined at the top level, with nodes containing stages and stages containing steps. This hierarchy ensures that tasks are executed sequentially within stages and can be parallelized or conditioned based on the requirements.

Complex pipelines may require conditional execution, for which the 'when' directive can be used. The 'when' directive allows stages to be executed only if certain conditions are met, adding an extra layer of customization and control.

```
stage('Deploy to Production') {
    when {
```

```
        branch 'master'
    }
    steps {
        // Deploy steps
    }
}
```

Another crucial aspect of working with pipelines is utilizing environmental variables. These variables can be global or stage-specific and allow for dynamic and reusable pipelines. Environment variables can be predefined by Jenkins, set within the pipeline, or passed from external sources.

```
pipeline {
    environment {
        DEPLOY_ENV = 'production'
    }
    stages {
        stage('Deploy') {
            steps {
                sh 'echo Deploying to ${DEPLOY_ENV}'
            }
        }
    }
}
```

The versatility of Jenkins pipelines is further enhanced by leveraging shared libraries. These libraries enable reusing common code patterns, custom steps, or functions across multiple pipelines. Shared libraries are stored in a source code repository and can be invoked within the pipeline script, promoting modularity and adherence to DRY (Don't Repeat Yourself) principles.

Building robust and maintainable Jenkins pipelines involves not only mastering these fundamental components but also combining them creatively to meet the unique needs of your projects. The interplay between stages, steps, agents, and other constructs forms the blueprint for an automated and reliable CI/CD pipeline.

3.8 Stages and Steps

Within Jenkins Pipelines, the concepts of stages and steps are fundamental. They allow for the organization, modularization, and visualization of a pipeline's workflow, promoting clarity and maintainability. This section delves into the intricacies of stages and steps, elucidating their roles and functionalities.

A **stage** in a Jenkins Pipeline is a high-level component that defines a distinct phase of the CI/CD process. Stages are used to visually segment the pipeline into logical parts, rendering the entire process more comprehensible. Each stage can encompass multiple **steps**, which are more granular actions performed within the stage.

Consider the following illustrative example of a simple declarative pipeline:

```
pipeline {
    agent any
    stages {
        stage('Build') {
            steps {
                echo 'Building...'
                // Insert build step commands here
            }
        }
        stage('Test') {
            steps {
                echo 'Testing...'
                // Insert test step commands here
            }
        }
        stage('Deploy') {
            steps {
                echo 'Deploying...'
                // Insert deploy step commands here
            }
        }
    }
}
```

In this example, the pipeline is divided into three stages: Build, Test, and Deploy. Each stage contains steps that define specific actions. The stages block encapsulates all the stages, ensuring a structured and sequential flow.

Aligning stages with distinct phases of the development lifecycle, such as building, testing, and deployment, is a best practice that enhances readability and manageability. This approach hedges against complexity as pipelines grow in size and complexity.

Steps are individual tasks executed within a stage. They can encompass a wide range of actions, including shell commands, Jenkins-specific operations, and interactions with plugins. The steps syntax varies based on the context and type of pipeline (scripted or declarative).

Below, a more detailed example showcases how shell commands can be executed within steps:

```
pipeline {
    agent any
    stages {
```

```
        stage('Build') {
            steps {
                echo 'Starting Build...'
                sh 'mvn clean install'
                echo 'Build Completed.'
            }
        }
        stage('Test') {
            steps {
                echo 'Running Unit Tests...'
                sh 'mvn test'
                echo 'Unit Tests Completed.'
            }
        }
        stage('Deploy') {
            steps {
                echo 'Deploying Application...'
                sh 'scp target/myapp.war user@server:/deploy-path/'
                echo 'Deployment Completed.'
            }
        }
    }
}
```

In this pipeline, each stage elucidates particular tasks: the Build stage executes the Maven build command, the Test stage runs unit tests, and the Deploy stage transfers the build artifact to a remote server using scp. Integrating echo commands provides additional verbosity, aiding debugging and logging.

Understanding **fail-fast** behavior within stages is pivotal. By default, if any step within a stage fails, subsequent stages are not executed. This behavior is essential for promptly identifying and addressing issues, ensuring subsequent stages do not process erroneous results.

Advanced usage includes stage conditions and parallel execution. Stages can be configured with conditional logic to determine execution based on certain criteria. For example:

```
pipeline {
    agent any
    stages {
        stage('Build') {
            when {
                expression { return params.BUILD == true }
            }
            steps {
                echo 'Building...'
                sh 'mvn clean install'
            }
        }
        stage('Deploy') {
            when {
                branch 'master'
            }
            steps {
                echo 'Deploying...'
```

```
                sh 'scp target/myapp.war user@server:/deploy-path/'
            }
        }
    }
}
```

Here, the Build stage executes conditionally based on the value of a parameter, while the Deploy stage executes only on the master branch. This exemplifies how stages can be dynamically controlled, adapting to complex workflows and requirements.

Parallel execution within stages leverages the parallel directive, enabling concurrent processing. This is advantageous for saving time, especially in extensive test suites or deployments. An example of parallel stages:

```
pipeline {
    agent any
    stages {
        stage('Parallel Tests') {
            parallel {
                stage('Unit Tests') {
                    steps {
                        echo 'Running Unit Tests...'
                        sh 'mvn test'
                    }
                }
                stage('Integration Tests') {
                    steps {
                        echo 'Running Integration Tests...'
                        sh 'mvn verify'
                    }
                }
            }
        }
    }
}
```

In this instance, Unit Tests and Integration Tests run concurrently, thus optimizing the pipeline execution time.

Stages and steps are foundational components of Jenkins Pipelines. They bring structure, clarity, and efficiency to CI/CD workflows, ensuring processes are manageable, scalable, and adaptable. Understanding their effective use is critical to mastering Jenkins Pipelines, enabling sophisticated and robust automation of development and deployment operations.

3.9 Parallel Execution

Parallel execution in Jenkins Pipelines provides a powerful mechanism to run multiple tasks concurrently. This ability greatly enhances the efficiency and speed of testing and deployment processes, especially when managing complex build workflows. By leveraging the parallel directive, various stages or steps of the build can be executed simultaneously, thereby optimizing resource utilization and minimizing pipeline execution time.

To demonstrate parallel execution, consider a scenario where multiple test suites need to be run—unit tests, integration tests, and UI tests. Rather than executing each test suite sequentially, they can be executed in parallel, thus saving significant amounts of time.

In Jenkins Declarative Pipelines, the parallel directive is used within the stages section. The syntax for defining parallel execution is straightforward, organizing concurrent tasks as sub-stages within a main stage. Here is an example of how parallel execution can be implemented:

```
pipeline {
    agent any
    stages {
        stage('Test') {
            parallel {
                stage('Unit Tests') {
                    steps {
                        echo 'Running unit tests'
                        // Commands to execute unit tests
                    }
                }
                stage('Integration Tests') {
                    steps {
                        echo 'Running integration tests'
                        // Commands to execute integration tests
                    }
                }
                stage('UI Tests') {
                    steps {
                        echo 'Running UI tests'
                        // Commands to execute UI tests
                    }
                }
            }
        }
    }
}
```

In this example, the parallel directive within the Test stage initiates three sub-stages: Unit Tests, Integration Tests, and UI Tests. Each substage contains steps to execute the respective test suites, and they all run concurrently.

One critical aspect to consider when using parallel execution is managing the shared resources and ensuring thread safety. It is important to avoid conflicts that could arise from concurrent access to shared files or databases. Solutions include using separate databases for different test environments or employing containerization technologies like Docker to isolate each parallel task.

In addition to running different types of tests, parallel execution can also be leveraged to perform various build tasks such as compiling code for different platforms, scanning for vulnerabilities, and packaging artifacts simultaneously. Here is an example where different build tasks are executed in parallel:

```
pipeline {
    agent any
    stages {
        stage('Build and Test') {
            parallel {
                stage('Compile Code') {
                    steps {
                        echo 'Compiling code'
                        // Commands to compile code
                    }
                }
                stage('Static Code Analysis') {
                    steps {
                        echo 'Running static code analysis'
                        // Commands to perform static code analysis
                    }
                }
                stage('Package Artifacts') {
                    steps {
                        echo 'Packaging artifacts'
                        // Commands to package artifacts
                    }
                }
            }
        }
    }
}
```

Effective use of parallelism can significantly reduce the total pipeline execution time. The pipeline in this example compiles the code, performs static code analysis, and packages the artifacts concurrently, thereby making efficient use of the build agent's resources.

Another advanced feature in Jenkins Pipelines is the failFast option. When set to true, this option ensures that if any task within the parallel block fails, the subsequent parallel tasks are aborted. This can save time and resources in cases where continuing execution of parallel tasks is unnecessary once a failure has occurred. Here is how to use the failFast option:

```
pipeline {
    agent any
    stages {
        stage('Parallel Stage with FailFast') {
            parallel failFast: true, {
                stage('Task 1') {
                    steps {
                        echo 'Executing Task 1'
                        // Commands for Task 1
                    }
                }
                stage('Task 2') {
                    steps {
                        echo 'Executing Task 2'
                        // Commands for Task 2
                    }
                }
                stage('Task 3') {
                    steps {
                        echo 'Executing Task 3'
                        // Commands for Task 3
                    }
                }
            }
        }
    }
}
```

With failFast: true, if any of Task 1, Task 2, or Task 3 fails, the other tasks running in parallel will be stopped, and the pipeline will proceed to the next stage.

Debugging and monitoring parallel execution can sometimes challenge users due to the concurrent nature of tasks. Jenkins' Blue Ocean interface provides an enhanced visualization tool for pipelines, making it easier to understand the flow and status of parallel executions. Each parallel stage is represented clearly, showing in real-time which stages are running, completed, or failed.

Another common practice is to incorporate proper logging and resource monitoring in each parallel step, which aids in identifying bottlenecks or issues when tasks are running concurrently.

Moving beyond simple examples, large-scale projects can include nested parallel stages, combining these with conditional logic to create highly customizable and efficient pipelines. Understanding and implementing parallel execution in Jenkins Pipelines enables developers to maximize build efficiency, reduce feedback times, and maintain high levels of productivity.

3.10 Handling Pipeline Failures

When working with Jenkins Pipelines, addressing failures is a critical aspect that can significantly impact the efficiency and reliability of your software delivery process. Failures can stem from various sources, including code errors, infrastructure issues, or misconfigurations in the pipeline. This section delves into strategies and mechanisms to detect, manage, and recover from pipeline failures, ensuring minimal disruption to your deployment cycles.

Detecting pipeline failures in Jenkins involves scrutinizing build logs, configuring appropriate logging levels, and setting up notifications. Jenkins provides several built-in tools and plugins that help in monitoring pipeline health. For instance, the Build Failure Analyzer plugin analyzes build logs to identify known causes of failures, and the Email Extension Plugin can send notifications when builds fail.

Below is an example that demonstrates how to set up a simple Jenkins pipeline that includes error handling and notifications:

```
pipeline {
    agent any
    stages {
        stage('Build') {
            steps {
                script {
                    try {
                        // Build step that might fail
                        sh 'make build'
                    } catch (Exception e) {
                        // Log error and mark current build result as unstable
                        currentBuild.result = 'UNSTABLE'
                        echo "Build failed: ${e.message}"
                        throw e
                    }
                }
            }
        }
        stage('Test') {
            steps {
                script {
                    try {
                        // Test step that might fail
                        sh 'make test'
                    } catch (Exception e) {
                        // Log error and mark current build result as unstable
                        currentBuild.result = 'UNSTABLE'
                        echo "Tests failed: ${e.message}"
                        throw e
                    }
                }
            }
        }
    }
```

```
    post {
        always {
            script {
                // Send notification regardless of build status
                emailext (
                    to: 'dev-team@example.com',
                    subject: "Build ${currentBuild.fullDisplayName}",
                    body: "Build ${currentBuild.fullDisplayName} resulted in ${
                        currentBuild.result}"
                )
            }
        }
        success {
            echo 'Build succeeded!'
        }
        unstable {
            echo 'Build is unstable.'
        }
        failure {
            echo 'Build failed.'
        }
    }
}
```

The pipeline script above demonstrates several key points regarding failure handling:

1. **Try-Catch Blocks**: Each critical step in the ‘Build‘ and ‘Test‘ stages includes a ‘try-catch‘ block to catch exceptions. When an exception is caught, the pipeline marks the build as ‘UNSTABLE‘, logs the error message, and rethrows the exception to ensure that the failure is properly reported.

2. **Post-Build Actions**: The ‘post‘ section includes actions that execute based on the outcome of the pipeline: - ‘always‘: Executes regardless of the build status. In the example, an email notification is sent containing the build result. - ‘success‘: Executes only if the build succeeds. - ‘unstable‘: Executes if the build is unstable, which can be triggered by caught exceptions. - ‘failure‘: Executes if the build fails, capturing unhandled exceptions or errors that occur outside the ‘try-catch‘ blocks.

Using the ‘try-catch‘ mechanism helps to create pipelines that can handle failures gracefully by logging errors for further inspection and ensuring that the necessary notifications are sent out promptly.

Jenkins also offers the catchError step, which simplifies the error handling process. Below is an example demonstrating its usage:

```
pipeline {
    agent any
    stages {
        stage('Build') {
            steps {
```

```
                catchError(buildResult: 'UNSTABLE', stageResult: 'FAILURE') {
                    sh 'make build'
                }
            }
        }
        stage('Test') {
            steps {
                catchError(buildResult: 'UNSTABLE', stageResult: 'FAILURE') {
                    sh 'make test'
                }
            }
        }
    }
    post {
        always {
            emailext (
                to: 'dev-team@example.com',
                subject: "Build ${currentBuild.fullDisplayName}",
                body: "Build ${currentBuild.fullDisplayName} resulted in ${currentBuild
                    .result}"
            )
        }
        success {
            echo 'Build succeeded!'
        }
        unstable {
            echo 'Build is unstable.'
        }
        failure {
            echo 'Build failed.'
        }
    }
}
```

The catchError step in this example ensures that if the nested shell command ('sh 'make build'' or 'sh 'make test'') fails, the build result is set to 'UNSTABLE' and the stage result is set to 'FAILURE'. This provides a more streamlined way to handle errors as compared to the traditional 'try-catch' blocks.

Another powerful mechanism for handling pipeline failures is the use of 'retry'. This step attempts to rerun the enclosed steps a specified number of times before ultimately failing. This is particularly useful when dealing with transient issues:

```
pipeline {
    agent any
    stages {
        stage('Build') {
            steps {
                retry(3) {
                    sh 'make build'
                }
            }
        }
        stage('Test') {
            steps {
                retry(3) {
```

```
                sh 'make test'
            }
        }
    }
}
post {
    always {
        emailext (
            to: 'dev-team@example.com',
            subject: "Build ${currentBuild.fullDisplayName}",
            body: "Build ${currentBuild.fullDisplayName} resulted in ${currentBuild
                .result}"
        )
    }
    success {
        echo 'Build succeeded!'
    }
    unstable {
        echo 'Build is unstable.'
    }
    failure {
        echo 'Build failed.'
    }
}
}
```

In this approach, if the ‘make build‘ or ‘make test‘ commands fail, Jenkins will retry the steps up to three times before marking the build as failed. This can mitigate issues stemming from temporary network blips or other transient conditions.

Proactively managing pipeline failures using the aforementioned strategies helps maintain reliable and resilient CI/CD workflows. This ensures that issues are caught early, accurately logged, and communicated efficiently to the relevant stakeholders, allowing timely resolutions and sustaining the momentum of your development process.

3.11 Shared Libraries in Pipelines

Shared libraries are a powerful feature in Jenkins that facilitate code reuse across multiple pipelines, promoting the DRY (Don’t Repeat Yourself) principle. These libraries allow teams to encapsulate pipeline logic in reusable scripts, providing a standardized way to implement common functionality. By integrating shared libraries, organizations can achieve maintainable and consistent pipeline configurations.

A shared library in Jenkins is structured as a repository containing Groovy scripts and other resources. These libraries can be hosted on any SCM system supported by Jenkins, such as Git or Subversion. To use a shared library, you must define it in your pipeline's configuration and then import it into your pipeline script.

The directory structure of a shared library is essential for Jenkins to correctly identify and load the library. The standard structure includes three main directories: vars, src, and resources. Each directory serves a specific purpose:

- vars: Contains global variable files. Each file in this directory defines a Groovy script with the same name as the file. These scripts are accessible as global variables in your pipeline.
- src: Contains Groovy classes and packages that can be imported and used in your pipeline scripts.
- resources: Contains non-Groovy files that can be used within shared libraries, such as configuration files, templates, or static assets.

Consider the following example of a shared library structure:

```
shared-library
  vars
    myFunction.groovy
  src
    org
      example
        utilities
          Helper.groovy
  resources
    config
      sample-config.yml
```

In this structure, myFunction.groovy defines a globally accessible function, Helper.groovy contains utility classes, and sample-config.yml is a resource file.

To use a shared library in a Jenkins pipeline, you must configure it in the Jenkins system settings or within the pipeline script itself. For system-wide configuration, navigate to *Manage Jenkins → Configure System*, scroll to the *Global Pipeline Libraries* section, and add your library repository details.

After configuring the shared library, you can load and use it in a declarative pipeline script. Here is an example of how to configure and use a shared library in a pipeline:

```
@Library('shared-library') _
pipeline {
    agent any
    stages {
```

```
            stage('Example') {
                steps {
                    script {
                        // Call a global function from the shared library
                        myFunction('Hello, World')

                        // Use a class from the shared library
                        def helper = new org.example.utilities.Helper()
                        helper.doSomething()
                    }
                }
            }
        }
}
```

In the pipeline script above, the @Library('shared-library') annotation indicates that the pipeline should use the shared-library library. The myFunction global function and the Helper class are used in the Example stage.

Shared libraries also support more advanced features like versioning and loading libraries dynamically. To specify a version of the shared library, you can modify the @Library annotation as follows:

```
@Library('shared-library@v1.0') _
```

Dynamic loading of libraries can be useful in scenarios where different stages of the pipeline require different versions of the shared library. Here is an example of dynamically loading shared libraries:

```
pipeline {
    agent any
    stages {
        stage('Pre-Processing') {
            steps {
                script {
                    library 'shared-library@v1.0'
                    myFunction('Running Pre-Processing')
                }
            }
        }
        stage('Processing') {
            steps {
                script {
                    library 'shared-library@v2.0'
                    myFunction('Running Processing')
                }
            }
        }
    }
}
```

In this script, the Pre-Processing stage uses version v1.0 of the shared library, while the Processing stage uses version v2.0.

Shared libraries enhance modularity, reduce code duplication, and promote best practices in Jenkins pipeline development. By leveraging shared libraries, teams can streamline their CI/CD processes, improve maintainability, and achieve more reliable builds. Properly structuring and utilizing shared libraries plays a crucial role in the efficiency and robustness of Jenkins pipelines.

3.12 Best Practices for Designing Pipelines

Effective pipeline design is essential for maximizing the potential benefits that Jenkins Pipelines offer. When designing pipelines, there are several best practices to consider, which can notably improve maintainability, performance, and reliability. The following guidelines will help refine pipeline architecture.

1. Ensure Modularity and Reusability: Break down the pipeline into modular, reusable components. This approach simplifies maintenance and testing. Utilize shared libraries in Jenkins to encapsulate complex or commonly used functionality. For instance, a reusable library might include a job for checking out code from a repository, executing tests, or deploying artifacts.

```
@Library('my-shared-library') _

pipeline {
    agent any
    stages {
        stage('Checkout') {
            steps {
                checkout scm
            }
        }
        stage('Build') {
            steps {
                mySharedLibraryBuildFunction()
            }
        }
        stage('Test') {
            steps {
                mySharedLibraryTestFunction()
            }
        }
        stage('Deploy') {
            steps {
                mySharedLibraryDeployFunction()
            }
        }
    }
}
```

2. Use Descriptive Naming Conventions: Consistency in naming stages and steps within your pipeline helps in understanding the build process, particularly when troubleshooting issues. Names should accurately reflect the specific actions being carried out.

```
pipeline {
    agent any
    stages {
        stage('Source Checkout') {
            steps {
                checkout scm
            }
        }
        stage('Compile Application') {
            steps {
                sh './build-application.sh'
            }
        }
        stage('Execute Tests') {
            steps {
                junit '**/test-reports/*.xml'
            }
        }
        stage('Package and Deploy') {
            steps {
                sh './deploy.sh'
            }
        }
    }
}
```

3. Leverage Pipeline As Code: Storing pipeline definitions in the source code repository ensures that the pipeline configuration is versioned alongside the application code. This practice promotes transparency and consistency across different environments and teams.

```
pipeline {
    agent any
    stages {
        stage('Setup Environment') {
            steps {
                sh 'scripts/setup.sh'
            }
        }
        stage('Build and Test') {
            parallel {
                stage('Build') {
                    steps {
                        sh 'scripts/build.sh'
                    }
                }
                stage('Test') {
                    steps {
                        sh 'scripts/test.sh'
                    }
                }
            }
        }
        stage('Deploy') {
```

```
            steps {
                sh 'scripts/deploy.sh'
            }
        }
    }
}
```

4. Implement Error and Failure Handling: Using constructs like try-catch or post actions (post section) can make pipelines robust by managing failures gracefully. Define behaviour for various post conditions such as always, success, failure, and unstable.

```
pipeline {
    agent any
    stages {
        stage('Build') {
            steps {
                sh 'make build'
            }
        }
    }
    post {
        always {
            archiveArtifacts artifacts: '**/target/*.jar', allowEmptyArchive: true
        }
        success {
            emailext to: 'team@example.com',
                     subject: "Build Succeeded: ${env.JOB_NAME} #${env.
                         BUILD_NUMBER}",
                     body: "Good news! The build succeeded."
        }
        failure {
            emailext to: 'team@example.com',
                     subject: "Build Failed: ${env.JOB_NAME} #${env.
                         BUILD_NUMBER}",
                     body: "The build failed. Please check the Jenkins logs."
        }
    }
}
```

5. Facilitate Parallel Execution: Leveraging parallel stages improves pipeline efficiency by reducing overall execution time. Careful attention should be paid to resource contention issues that might arise from simultaneous execution of multiple stages.

```
pipeline {
    agent any
    stages {
        stage('Test and Lint') {
            parallel {
                stage('Lint') {
                    steps {
                        sh 'npm run lint'
                    }
                }
                stage('Unit Tests') {
                    steps {
                        junit '**/test-reports/unit/*.xml'
```

```
                }
            }
            stage('Integration Tests') {
                steps {
                    junit '**/test-reports/integration/*.xml'
                }
            }
        }
    }
  }
}
```

6. Keep Pipelines Simple and Maintainable: Avoid overly complicated pipelines. Aim for simplicity by clearly defining stage objectives and keeping scripts within steps concise. Complex logic should be encapsulated within shared library functions or external scripts to maintain readability and ease of updates.

7. Secure Credentials and Sensitive Information: Always use Jenkins' credentials management system to handle sensitive information such as passwords, API tokens, or SSH keys. Environment variables containing secrets should not be exposed or printed in logs.

```
pipeline {
    agent any
    environment {
        DOCKER_HUB_PASSWORD = credentials('docker-hub-password')
    }
    stages {
        stage('Build and Push Docker Image') {
            steps {
                sh 'docker build -t my-app .'
                sh 'echo $DOCKER_HUB_PASSWORD | docker login --username my-
                    username --password-stdin'
                sh 'docker push my-app'
            }
        }
    }
}
```

8. Automate Notifications and Reporting: Integrate automated notifications to alert teams about pipeline status, failures, and key events. Use Jenkins plugins, such as Email Extension or Slack Notification, to keep stakeholders informed automatically.

```
pipeline {
    agent any
    stages {
        stage('Build') {
            steps {
                sh 'make build'
            }
        }
    }
    post {
        always {
```

```
            emailext to: 'dev-team@example.com',
                     subject: "${currentBuild.currentResult}: Job ${env.JOB_NAME} #
                         ${env.BUILD_NUMBER}",
                     body: "See details at ${env.BUILD_URL}"
        }
    }
}
```

These best practices, when consistently applied, contribute to the creation of maintainable, efficient, and resilient Jenkins Pipelines. This ensures smoother CI/CD processes and ultimately supports the delivery of high-quality software.

3.13 Using Blue Ocean for Pipelines

Blue Ocean is a modern interface for Jenkins that provides an improved user experience for managing pipelines. Blue Ocean emphasizes ease of use and visualization, offering an intuitive graphical interface that simplifies pipeline creation, visualization, and troubleshooting.

When utilizing Blue Ocean, the first step is to install the Blue Ocean plugin in Jenkins. This can be achieved via the Jenkins Plugin Manager. Navigate to the Jenkins dashboard, select **Manage Jenkins**, followed by **Manage Plugins**. Search for *Blue Ocean* within the Available tab, select the corresponding checkbox, and initiate the installation process. After installation, restart Jenkins if prompted, to apply changes effectively.

Upon successful installation, Blue Ocean can be launched from the Jenkins dashboard by clicking the **Open Blue Ocean** button. This switches the interface from traditional Jenkins to Blue Ocean. The primary dashboard in Blue Ocean presents a comprehensive and organized view of all Jenkins pipelines.

Creating a new pipeline in Blue Ocean begins by clicking the **New Pipeline** button on the Blue Ocean dashboard. The user must then select the source control repository where the pipeline code is hosted. Blue Ocean supports various version control systems, including GitHub, Bitbucket, and Git. To proceed, the user needs to authenticate and authorize Blue Ocean to access the repository.

The pipeline creation process continues with selecting the relevant repository and, if necessary, specifying the branch to build. Blue Ocean will automatically detect a Jenkinsfile in the repository and utilize it to create the pipeline. If a Jenkinsfile is not detected, Blue Ocean provides a guided experience to create one. This guided experience assists users in configuring stages, steps, and other pipeline components graphically.

Blue Ocean's visualization features play a pivotal role in enhancing the user's understanding of pipeline execution. The pipeline visualization is presented as a series of blocks representing stages. Each block is color-coded based on the status: green for success, red for failure, and yellow for in-progress. This allows users to quickly discern pipeline statuses and identify any issues.

Clicking on a stage block provides detailed logs. This includes console outputs and error messages, aiding in the debugging process. Users can directly navigate through the stages, access logs, and identify failures without switching contexts or dealing with extensive text-based logs. This integrated approach expedites troubleshooting and enhances the maintainability of pipelines.

Parallel execution of stages is another aspect where Blue Ocean excels. Parallel stages are visualized in a grid format, allowing users to readily comprehend the concurrent pipelines' progress. For instance, when running tests across multiple environments or executing different deployment steps simultaneously, Blue Ocean's visualization delivers clarity and insight into each parallel branch's state.

Consider the following example in Blue Ocean, where we have a Jenkinsfile that defines stages for Build, Test, and Deploy. Here is a simplified version of the Jenkinsfile:

```
pipeline {
   agent any

   stages {
      stage('Build') {
         steps {
            echo 'Building...'
            // Add build steps here
         }
      }
      stage('Test') {
         parallel {
            stage('Unit Tests') {
               steps {
                  echo 'Running unit tests...'
                  // Add unit test steps here
               }
            }
            stage('Integration Tests') {
               steps {
                  echo 'Running integration tests...'
                  // Add integration test steps here
               }
            }
```

```
            }
        }
        stage('Deploy') {
            steps {
                echo 'Deploying...'
                // Add deploy steps here
            }
        }
    }
}
```

In this example, Blue Ocean will visualize the *Build*, *Test*, and *Deploy* stages. The *Test* stage will appear as a parallel block comprising *Unit Tests* and *Integration Tests*. In case of any failures, these will be prominently indicated, enabling quick identification and resolution of issues.

Moreover, Blue Ocean facilitates the integration with other plugins and tools. Users can configure notifications, artifact management, and environment variable handling, all within the Blue Ocean interface. For advanced users, further customization is possible by modifying the underlying Jenkinsfile directly, which grants a perfect balance between visual convenience and powerful configurability.

Blue Ocean also integrates seamlessly with Jenkins' core features, such as pipeline triggers and credential management. These integrations are presented in a user-friendly manner, ensuring that users do not need to navigate away from Blue Ocean to configure essential settings.

In essence, utilizing Blue Ocean for managing Jenkins Pipelines dramatically enhances the developer's experience through an improved interface and powerful visualization tools. This results in streamlined pipeline management, better maintainability, and quicker problem resolution.

Chapter 4

Automated Testing with Jenkins

This chapter focuses on implementing automated testing using Jenkins, detailing the setup of unit, integration, and end-to-end tests. It explores configuring test environments, integrating test automation frameworks, and running tests within Jenkins pipelines. The chapter also covers reporting test results, handling test failures, and optimizing testing processes through parallel execution, concluding with best practices for effective automated testing in CI/CD workflows.

4.1 Introduction to Automated Testing

Automated testing is an indispensable aspect of modern software development, fundamentally enhancing the software development lifecycle by ensuring robustness, reliability, and efficiency. In automated testing, software tools are used to execute pre-scripted tests on an application before it is released into production. By automating repetitive but necessary testing in a formalized testing environment, teams can significantly reduce the human effort required, thereby increasing the likelihood of consistency and accuracy in their testing processes. Automated testing can be applied at various stages of development, encompassing unit tests, integration tests, and end-to-end tests. This section will lay the foundation for understanding automated testing and how it integrates with Jenkins.

Automated tests can broadly be classified into three major categories:

- **Unit Testing:** Focuses on verifying the functionality of individual components or functions in isolation.
- **Integration Testing:** Ensures that various modules or services in a system interact correctly.
- **End-to-End Testing:** Simulates real user scenarios and validates the entire application flow, from start to finish.

The role of automated testing in Continuous Integration/Continuous Deployment (CI/CD) is pivotal. In a CI/CD pipeline, every code change is automatically tested at multiple stages before it is deployed to production. Jenkins, a leading automation server, facilitates the integration of automated testing within CI/CD pipelines, enabling developers to detect defects early and improve the overall quality of the software.

Benefits of Automated Testing:

- **Speed:** Automated tests can run significantly faster than human testers, enabling quick feedback cycles.
- **Consistency:** Automated tests perform the same sequence of steps precisely every time they are run, ensuring consistent test execution.
- **Reusability:** Once written, automated tests can be reused across multiple runs, suites, and projects with minimal modification.
- **Scalability:** Automated testing frameworks can handle large volumes of tests, ensuring that applications are thoroughly vetted before production deployment.
- **Comprehensive Testing:** Automated scripts can cover a wide array of scenarios that might be impractical with manual testing, including edge cases and regressions.

Challenges in Automated Testing:

- **Initial Setup Cost:** The initial investment in tools, infrastructure, and time to write tests can be substantial.

- **Maintenance:** Automated tests need to be maintained as the application evolves; otherwise, they may produce false positives or negatives.
- **Complexity:** Writing automated tests can become complex, especially for applications with frequent changes or advanced features.
- **Tool Selection:** Choosing the right tools that integrate well with existing systems and provide necessary functionality can be challenging.

Consider the following simple Python example to demonstrate a basic automated unit test using the popular unittest framework:

```
import unittest

def add(x, y):
    return x + y

class TestMathOperations(unittest.TestCase):
    def test_add(self):
        self.assertEqual(add(1, 2), 3)
        self.assertEqual(add(-1, 1), 0)
        self.assertEqual(add(-1, -1), -2)

if __name__ == '__main__':
    unittest.main()
```

Executing this script yields the following output, assuming all tests pass:

```
...
----------------------------------------------------------------------
Ran 1 test in 0.000s

OK
```

In Jenkins, this can be integrated within a Pipeline script as follows:

```
pipeline {
    agent any
    stages {
        stage('Test') {
            steps {
                sh 'python -m unittest discover -s tests'
            }
        }
    }
}
```

The above pipeline script defines a stage called Test that executes the unit tests located in the tests directory using unittest's discovery mode. This demonstrates how simple unit tests can be automated and integrated into Jenkins pipelines, providing continuous feedback on the codebase's integrity.

Automated testing with Jenkins empowers teams to consistently deliver high-quality software by integrating testing practices seamlessly into the development workflow. Focus on automation allows teams to identify and address issues early and often, facilitating a more reliable and efficient development process.

4.2 Types of Automated Tests

To fully leverage Jenkins in an automated testing environment, it is crucial to understand the different types of automated tests commonly employed in software development. These tests are typically categorized into unit tests, integration tests, and end-to-end (E2E) tests. Each type serves a specific purpose within the testing strategy, contributing to a more robust and reliable software application.

Unit tests are the smallest and most granular form of testing. They focus on individual components or functions of the software, typically at the method level. The primary objective is to verify that each unit of the code performs as expected. Unit tests are usually written by developers and are executed in isolation from other parts of the application. This isolation is often achieved using mocking techniques to simulate the behavior of dependencies.

```
import unittest
from my_module import add

class TestAddFunction(unittest.TestCase):
    def test_add_integers(self):
        self.assertEqual(add(1, 2), 3)

    def test_add_floats(self):
        self.assertAlmostEqual(add(1.1, 2.2), 3.3)

if __name__ == '__main__':
    unittest.main()
```

In the example above, the TestAddFunction class includes two unit tests verifying the behavior of the add function with integers and floating-point numbers. The unittest framework is a commonly used tool for writing unit tests in Python.

Integration tests, in contrast, evaluate the interaction between multiple components or systems. These tests ensure that individual units work together as intended. Integration testing can involve databases, external services, or other modules of the application. The setup is more complex than unit tests since it requires a test environment that mirrors the production setup closely.

```
import unittest
from my_module import create_user, get_user

class IntegrationTestUserModule(unittest.TestCase):
    def test_create_and_get_user(self):
        user_id = create_user('John Doe', 'john@example.com')
        user = get_user(user_id)
        self.assertEqual(user.name, 'John Doe')
        self.assertEqual(user.email, 'john@example.com')

if __name__ == '__main__':
    unittest.main()
```

Here, the integration test creates a new user and subsequently fetches the user details to ensure the create_user and get_user functions work together properly. Such tests might need a real or mock database to run.

End-to-end (E2E) tests are the most comprehensive, simulating real user scenarios to verify the entire application flows from start to finish. E2E tests aim to ensure the system as a whole, including all integrated components, behaves as expected under various user actions. These tests require a complete test environment resembling production closely and are often conducted using specialized tools like Selenium for web applications.

```
from selenium import webdriver
import unittest

class E2ETestLogin(unittest.TestCase):
    def setUp(self):
        self.driver = webdriver.Chrome()
        self.driver.get('http://example.com/login')

    def test_login(self):
        driver = self.driver
        driver.find_element_by_name('username').send_keys('user')
        driver.find_element_by_name('password').send_keys('pass')
        driver.find_element_by_name('submit').click()
        welcome_text = driver.find_element_by_id('welcome').text
        self.assertIn('Welcome', welcome_text)

    def tearDown(self):
        self.driver.quit()

if __name__ == '__main__':
    unittest.main()
```

In this E2E test example, the Selenium WebDriver automates browser interaction to test the login functionality of a web application. It involves navigating to the login page, entering credentials, and verifying the resulting user experience.

Understanding the distinctions and applications of these test types is fundamental for implementing effective automated testing in Jenkins. By categorizing tests into unit, integration, and end-to-end tests, developers and testers can structure their testing strategy to cover different layers of the application, ensuring comprehensive validation at each level.

4.3 Setting Up Unit Tests in Jenkins

Unit testing is a critical component of the software development process, aimed at validating the correctness of individual units of code. In this section, we will detail the process of setting up unit tests within Jenkins, leveraging its capabilities to automate and streamline the testing process.

Before proceeding, ensure that you have a Jenkins instance up and running, and the necessary build tools (such as Maven or Gradle) are installed.

1. Configuring the Jenkins Job for Unit Testing

Begin by configuring a Jenkins job to execute unit tests. Follow these steps:

- Navigate to Jenkins Dashboard.
- Click on New Item, provide a name for your job, and select Freestyle Project.
- In the job configuration page, under the Source Code Management section, select the appropriate repository type (e.g., Git). Provide the repository URL and credentials if necessary.
- Under the Build section, add a Build Step to execute the unit tests. For Maven, select Invoke Top-Level Maven Targets and specify test as the goals.

This setup ensures that every time the job runs, it will pull the latest code from the repository and run the unit tests.

Example Jenkins Job Configuration with Maven

```
pipeline {
    agent any
    stages {
```

```
        stage('Checkout') {
            steps {
                git 'https://github.com/user/repository.git'
            }
        }
        stage('Build and Test') {
            steps {
                sh 'mvn clean test'
            }
        }
    }
    post {
        always {
            junit 'target/surefire-reports/*.xml'
        }
    }
}
```

This pipeline example checks out the code from a Git repository, runs the mvn clean test command to execute the unit tests, and then publishes the test results.

2. Integrating Test Reports

Unit tests generate reports that Jenkins can process to display results in a readable format. To configure Jenkins to display test reports:

- In the job configuration page, in the Post-build Actions section, add Publish JUnit test result report.
- Specify the path to the test result files (e.g., target/surefire-reports/*.xml for Maven or build/test-results/test/*.xml for Gradle).

This configuration allows Jenkins to parse the test results and display them on the job's build page.

3. Handling Test Failures

Jenkins provides mechanisms to handle test failures automatically. You can configure build steps to be conditional based on the test results:

- In the Post-build Actions section, select Add post-build action and choose Conditional steps (single).
- Define a condition based on the test results (e.g., Current build status condition with FAILURE as the build status).
- Add steps to be executed if the condition is met, such as notifying a team via email or slack, or generating a bug ticket.

Example configuration:

```
pipeline {
    agent any
    stages {
        stage('Checkout') {
            steps {
                git 'https://github.com/user/repository.git'
            }
        }
        stage('Build and Test') {
            steps {
                sh 'mvn clean test'
            }
        }
    }
    post {
        success {
            junit 'target/surefire-reports/*.xml'
        }
        failure {
            mail to: 'team@example.com',
                 subject: "Build failed in Jenkins: ${currentBuild.fullDisplayName}",
                 body: "Check Jenkins for more details: ${env.BUILD_URL}"
        }
    }
}
```

4. Example Output

Upon successful execution of the job, Jenkins will display the following output:

```
[INFO] -------------------------------------------------------
[INFO] T E S T S
[INFO] -------------------------------------------------------
[INFO] Running com.example.AppTest
[INFO] Tests run: 1, Failures: 0, Errors: 0, Skipped: 0, Time elapsed: 0.002 sec
[INFO]
[INFO] Results:
[INFO]
[INFO] Tests run: 1, Failures: 0, Errors: 0, Skipped: 0
[INFO]
[INFO] -------------------------------------------------------
[INFO] BUILD SUCCESS
[INFO] -------------------------------------------------------
[INFO] Total time: 2.303 s
[INFO] Finished at: 2023-03-10T12:34:56+00:00
[INFO] Final Memory: 20M/334M
[INFO] -------------------------------------------------------
```

By adhering to these guidelines, you can ensure a robust setup for unit testing within Jenkins. This setup facilitates the execution of tests and provides insights into the code's health through detailed reports and handling of test failures.

4.4 Setting Up Integration Tests in Jenkins

Integration tests are essential to ensure that various components of a software application work together as expected. Unlike unit tests, which test individual pieces of code in isolation, integration tests validate the interactions between different units, modules, or services. This section will provide a comprehensive guide on setting up integration tests within a Jenkins environment, leveraging its capabilities to automate and streamline the process.

First, it is crucial to have a well-defined integration test plan. This plan should identify which components need testing together, the scenarios to cover, and the criteria for success. Once this plan is in place, the next steps involve configuring Jenkins to run these tests automatically.

To begin, make sure the relevant integration test framework is installed and configured in your project. Popular frameworks include JUnit, TestNG, and PyTest for Python-based projects.

```
import org.junit.jupiter.api.Test;
import static org.junit.jupiter.api.Assertions.*;

public class IntegrationTest {

    @Test
    public void testServiceInteraction() {
        ServiceA serviceA = new ServiceA();
        ServiceB serviceB = new ServiceB();

        String result = serviceA.performAction();
        assertEquals("expectedResult", serviceB.processResult(result));
    }
}
```

Once your integration tests are defined, follow these steps to set them up in Jenkins:

1. **Create a Jenkins Project**: Navigate to Jenkins and create a new project by selecting **New Item**, then choose the type of project, such as **Freestyle project** or **Pipeline project**.

2. **Configure Source Code Management (SCM)**: Under the **Source Code Management** section, configure the repository from which Jenkins will pull the source code, e.g., Git. Specify the repository URL and credentials if required.

```
Repository URL: https://github.com/your-repository.git
Credentials: [Add if necessary]
Branch Specifier: */main
```

3. **Define Build Triggers**: You can configure Jenkins to trigger builds

automatically. Common triggers include polling the SCM for changes, triggering after other builds, or scheduling times for builds.

4. **Add Build Steps for Integration Tests**: For a freestyle project, you will need to add build steps to invoke the integration tests. Click **Add build step** and select an appropriate option, such as **Invoke Gradle script**, **Execute shell**, or **Invoke top-level Maven targets**.

```
# Example of a shell script to run Maven integration tests
mvn clean verify -Pintegration-tests
```

5. **Add Post-Build Actions**: To capture and visualize test results, configure post-build actions: - **Publish JUnit test result report**: This action processes the JUnit XML output files.

```
Test report XMLs: target/surefire-reports/*.xml
```

6. **Pipeline Script Configuration**: If you are using a Pipeline project, configure the Jenkinsfile to run integration tests as part of the pipeline. Below is an example Jenkinsfile:

```
pipeline {
    agent any

    stages {
        stage('Checkout') {
            steps {
                git 'https://github.com/your-repository.git'
            }
        }
        stage('Build') {
            steps {
                sh 'mvn clean compile'
            }
        }
        stage('Integration Test') {
            steps {
                sh 'mvn verify -Pintegration-tests'
            }
        }
    }
    post {
        always {
            junit 'target/surefire-reports/*.xml'
        }
    }
}
```

In this Jenkinsfile, the ‘agent any‘ directive schedules the pipeline to run on any available agent. The ‘Checkout‘ stage clones the source code repository. The ‘Build‘ stage compiles the code, and the ‘Integration Test‘ stage executes the integration tests. Finally, the ‘post‘ block always collects the test results and archives them using the ‘junit‘ function.

Configuring the Test Environment: For integration tests, it is often necessary to simulate parts of the environment, such as databases, external APIs, or other services. Jenkins allows you to configure these environments either on-the-fly using containers or VMs, or using persistent environments:

- - **Using Docker**: Define a Dockerfile that sets up the environment, and use Jenkins' Docker Pipeline plugin to run tests inside Docker containers.
- - **Using Kubernetes**: For more complex setups, you can use Kubernetes to manage the lifecycle of your test environment. Jenkins' Kubernetes plugin helps you to automate the deployment and management of Kubernetes pods for your integration tests.

```
pipeline {
    agent {
        docker {
            image 'your-docker-image'
            args '-p 8080:8080'
        }
    }
    stages {
        stage('Checkout') {
            steps {
                git 'https://github.com/your-repository.git'
            }
        }
        stage('Build') {
            steps {
                sh 'mvn clean compile'
            }
        }
        stage('Integration Test') {
            steps {
                sh 'mvn verify -Pintegration-tests'
            }
        }
    }
    post {
        always {
            junit 'target/surefire-reports/*.xml'
        }
    }
}
```

This demonstrates the flexibility of Jenkins in accommodating various environments and needs, making it a powerful tool for continuous integration and delivery.

Throughout the configuration process, make sure to validate each step by running your Jenkins job manually to verify it correctly executes the integration tests. Proper validation includes checking the test results, ensuring that reports are generated, and confirming that any configured triggers work as expected. By automating integration tests within Jenkins, teams can detect issues early and ensure that different parts of their applications function together seamlessly.

4.5 End-to-End Testing

End-to-end (E2E) testing is an essential aspect of automated testing, verifying the complete flow of an application from start to finish. At its core, E2E testing ensures that the entire system functions accurately under real-world scenarios. Unlike unit or integration tests, which focus on individual components or their interactions, E2E tests validate the behavior of the application by simulating user interactions.

The primary objective of E2E testing is to identify system dependencies and ensure that the data integrity is maintained across various systems and their components. This type of testing is particularly crucial in verifying complex workflows and user journeys, providing confidence that the application behaves as expected from the end-user perspective.

- Verify complete system flow.
- Ensure data integrity across components.
- Simulate real-world user interactions.

Setting Up E2E Tests in Jenkins

To effectively set up E2E tests in Jenkins, it is essential to follow a structured approach that incorporates the environment setup, test script integration, execution, and result reporting.

1. Environment Setup

The environment must closely resemble the production setup to deliver meaningful test results. This includes setting up databases, external services, and other dependencies. In Jenkins, this can be achieved through various plugins and environment configuration tools.

For instance, the `Docker` plugin can be utilized to create isolated environments:

```
pipeline {
    agent {
```

```
        docker {
            image 'node:14'
        }
    }
    stages {
        stage('Setup') {
            steps {
                sh 'npm install'
            }
        }
    }
}
```

Here, Docker provides a containerized environment matching the production setup, ensuring the tests are executed under consistent conditions.

2. Test Script Integration

The actual E2E test scripts are typically written using frameworks like Selenium, Cypress, or Puppeteer. These scripts simulate user actions and verify the application's responses. Integrating these scripts into the Jenkins pipeline involves adding steps to fetch the test code and dependencies, followed by executing the scripts.

An example using Cypress might look like:

```
pipeline {
    agent any
    stages {
        stage('Checkout') {
            steps {
                git 'https://github.com/your-repo/your-project.git'
            }
        }
        stage('Install Dependencies') {
            steps {
                sh 'npm install cypress'
            }
        }
        stage('Run E2E Tests') {
            steps {
                sh 'npx cypress run'
            }
        }
    }
}
```

In this pipeline, the Git step fetches the project code, followed by installing Cypress, and then running the tests.

3. Execution and Verification

Upon execution, the test framework interacts with the application, performing the defined user actions and verifying expected outcomes. Successful E2E tests indicate the application is functioning correctly from the user's standpoint.

The execution results should be critically analyzed. Jenkins provides several ways to report these outcomes, such as using the **JUnit** plugin to parse and display test results in a readable format.

```
post {
    always {
        junit 'results/*.xml'
    }
}
```

With this configuration, Jenkins will process the XML results generated by the test framework and present them in an accessible format.

4. Reporting and Failure Handling

Comprehensive reporting is vital for understanding test outcomes. The Jenkins Blue Ocean interface offers an intuitive way to visualize the pipeline and test results, making it easier to identify failures and their causes.

In case of test failures, Jenkins supports several strategies for handling and categorizing them, such as:

- Retrying failed tests.
- Categorizing failures by their impact (critical, minor).
- Sending notifications to relevant stakeholders via email or chat services.

An implementation using the retry strategy can be added to the pipeline like this:

```
stage('Run E2E Tests') {
    steps {
        script {
            retry(3) {
                sh 'npx cypress run'
            }
        }
    }
}
```

The retry mechanism ensures that transient issues do not result in overall pipeline failure, enhancing robustness.

Best Practices for E2E Testing

Following a set of best practices can significantly improve the efficacy and maintainability of E2E tests:

- **Isolation of Test Environments**: Ensuring tests run in an isolated environment prevents interference and maintains consistency.
- **Realistic Test Data**: Utilizing data that closely mirrors production data enhances the relevance of test outcomes.
- **Parallel Execution**: Running tests in parallel reduces execution time and accelerates feedback cycles. This can be configured in Jenkins using the parallel directive.
- **Comprehensive Reporting**: Detailed reports aid in quicker diagnosis of issues. Incorporating tools like Allure for enhanced reporting can be beneficial.
- **Regular Maintenance**: E2E tests should be regularly maintained to accommodate application changes, ensuring their continued relevance.

E2E testing thus forms a critical component of a robust CI/CD pipeline, ensuring that applications not only meet functional criteria but also deliver a seamless user experience. By adhering to structured setups, integrating reliable test frameworks, and following best practices, teams can significantly enhance the quality and reliability of their software applications.

4.6 Configuring Test Environments

Configuring test environments in Jenkins is a crucial aspect of ensuring that automated tests run in conditions that closely mirror production environments. This section delves into the process of setting up and managing different types of test environments within Jenkins, detailing the necessary configurations and best practices.

To begin with, test environments can be categorized primarily into two types: local test environments and remote test environments. Local test environments run tests on the Jenkins server itself or on agents connected to it. In contrast, remote test environments extend the testing process to external servers or cloud-based services. Ensuring the accuracy and reliability of these environments can significantly affect the quality of the test results and, consequently, the overall software quality.

Local Test Environments

Local test environments are often simpler to manage and configure. They are usually created on the Jenkins master server or on any connected Jenkins agents. To set up a local test environment, one needs to install and configure the necessary software dependencies and libraries required by the application under test. This involves:

- Installing required language runtimes (e.g., Java, Python, Node.js).
- Setting up databases (e.g., MySQL, PostgreSQL) if needed by the application.
- Deploying required libraries or packages.
- Configuring environment variables.

The following example uses a pipeline script to create a local test environment setup for a Java application that uses Maven for dependency management:

```
pipeline {
    agent any
    stages {
        stage('Setup Environment') {
            steps {
                // Install Java
                sh 'sudo apt-get install -y openjdk-11-jdk'

                // Install Maven
                sh 'sudo apt-get install -y maven'

                // Clone repository
                git 'https://github.com/your-repo/your-app.git'
            }
        }
        stage('Build and Test') {
            steps {
                // Clean and test using Maven
                sh 'mvn clean test'
            }
        }
    }
}
```

Remote Test Environments

Remote test environments can be either on-premises servers, virtual machines, or cloud instances. They provide the flexibility to simulate more complex scenarios and load conditions. Configuring remote test environments involves:

- Setting up Jenkins to interact with remote servers.
- Installing required tools and runtimes on remote machines.
- Ensuring network configurations and permissions allow Jenkins to deploy and run tests remotely.

To configure Jenkins to run tests in a remote environment, one typically utilizes SSH or an API provided by a cloud service (e.g., AWS EC2, Azure VM). Here's an example pipeline script that sets up a remote test environment using SSH:

```
pipeline {
    agent any
    stages {
        stage('Setup Environment') {
            steps {
                // SSH command to install Java and Maven on remote server
                sshagent(['your-ssh-credentials']) {
                    sh 'ssh user@remote-server "sudo apt-get install -y openjdk-11-jdk
                          maven"'
                }
            }
        }
        stage('Deploy Application') {
            steps {
                // SCP command to copy application files to remote server
                sshagent(['your-ssh-credentials']) {
                    sh 'scp -r your-app user@remote-server:/path/to/deploy/'
                }
            }
        }
        stage('Run Tests') {
            steps {
                // SSH command to run tests on remote server
                sshagent(['your-ssh-credentials']) {
                    sh 'ssh user@remote-server "cd /path/to/deploy/your-app && mvn
                          clean test"'
                }
            }
        }
    }
}
```

For cloud-based remote environments, leveraging specific plugins like the Jenkins Amazon EC2 plugin or the Azure VM Agents plugin simplifies the setup. These plugins allow Jenkins to provision cloud instances, deploy code, and execute tests automatically. Example configuration steps for an AWS EC2 instance:

```
pipeline {
    agent {
        label 'ec2-agent'
    }
    stages {
        stage('Setup Environment') {
            steps {
                // Cloud-init script to setup environment on EC2
                sh '''
                #!/bin/bash
                sudo apt-get update
                sudo apt-get install -y openjdk-11-jdk maven
                '''
                // Clone repository
                git 'https://github.com/your-repo/your-app.git'
            }
        }
        stage('Build and Test') {
            steps {
                // Clean and test using Maven
                sh 'mvn clean test'
            }
        }
    }
}
```

Jenkins ensures scalability and flexibility in testing by allowing configuration of test environments that mirror various deployment scenarios. From basic local test setups to complex, distributed cloud environments, each configuration must be meticulously managed for reliability and consistency in test results.

4.7 Running Tests in Pipelines

Integrating automated tests into Jenkins pipelines is a key aspect of continuous integration and continuous delivery (CI/CD) workflows. This section elucidates how to embed various types of tests within Jenkins pipelines, leveraging the capabilities of Jenkins to ensure effective and efficient testing processes.

To incorporate tests into a Jenkins pipeline, you must define steps in a Jenkinsfile. The Jenkinsfile is a text file that contains the definition of a Jenkins pipeline and typically resides at the root of the repository. It can be written using either Declarative or Scripted Pipeline syntax. For the purposes of this section, we will utilize Declarative Pipeline syntax due to its simplicity and readability.

```
pipeline {
    agent any
    stages {
```

```
        stage('Build') {
            steps {
                echo 'Building...'
                sh 'make build'
            }
        }
        stage('Test') {
            steps {
                echo 'Running Tests...'
                sh 'make test'
            }
        }
        stage('Deploy') {
            steps {
                echo 'Deploying...'
                sh 'make deploy'
            }
        }
    }
}
```

The example Jenkinsfile above outlines a basic pipeline with three stages: Build, Test, and Deploy. The primary focus of this section is the Test stage, wherein we execute the test suite to verify the integrity of the application.

Unit Tests in Pipelines

Unit tests are crucial for verifying that individual components of your application behave as expected. To integrate unit tests within a Jenkins pipeline, you can use the following example. Assume the application uses a testing framework, such as JUnit for a Java project.

Firstly, ensure your build tool (e.g., Maven, Gradle) is configured to run unit tests. Here's how you might define a unit test step in a Jenkinsfile:

```
pipeline {
    agent any
    stages {
        stage('Checkout') {
            steps {
                git 'https://your-repo-url.git'
            }
        }
        stage('Unit Test') {
            steps {
                sh './gradlew test'
            }
            post {
                always {
                    junit '**/build/test-results/test/*.xml'
                }
            }
        }
    }
}
```

In this example, within the Unit Test stage, the ./gradlew test command runs the unit tests. The post section collects the test results using the junit command, making them available in Jenkins' test report.

Integration Tests in Pipelines

Integration tests ensure that different modules of your application work together as expected. These tests typically require a more complex environment than unit tests, as they may involve databases, services, and network configurations.

To integrate integration tests, you might define a Jenkinsfile that sets up the necessary environment. Assume Docker is used to facilitate a consistent environment for testing.

```
pipeline {
    agent any
    stages {
        stage('Build Docker Image') {
            steps {
                sh 'docker build -t myapp:latest .'
            }
        }
        stage('Integration Test') {
            steps {
                sh 'docker run --rm myapp:latest ./gradlew integrationTest'
            }
            post {
                always {
                    junit '**/build/test-results/integrationTest/*.xml'
                }
            }
        }
    }
}
```

In this setup, the Build Docker Image stage creates a Docker image of the application. The Integration Test stage then runs the integration tests inside a Docker container. The junit command processes the test results, similar to the unit tests.

End-to-End Tests in Pipelines

End-to-end (E2E) tests assess the complete flow of an application from start to finish, ensuring all elements operate together seamlessly. Tools like Selenium or Cypress are often used for E2E testing.

The following example demonstrates how to run Cypress E2E tests within a Jenkins pipeline:

```
pipeline {
    agent any
    stages {
        stage('Checkout') {
```

```
            steps {
                git 'https://your-repo-url.git'
            }
        }
        stage('Install Dependencies') {
            steps {
                sh 'npm install'
            }
        }
        stage('End-to-End Test') {
            steps {
                sh 'npm run cypress:run'
            }
            post {
                always {
                    cypress junit,
                    '**/results/cypress/*.xml'
                }
            }
        }
    }
}
```

Here, the Install Dependencies stage installs the required dependencies using npm, followed by the End-to-End Test stage, which runs the Cypress test suite with the command npm run cypress:run. The JUnit XML files generated by Cypress test runs are then captured for reporting purposes.

Running Tests in Parallel

One of the advantages of using Jenkins pipelines is the ability to execute tests in parallel, significantly reducing the overall testing time. To run tests in parallel, you can specify multiple branches within a single stage.

```
pipeline {
    agent any
    stages {
        stage('Parallel Test Execution') {
            parallel {
                stage('Unit Test') {
                    steps {
                        sh './gradlew test'
                    }
                    post {
                        always {
                            junit '**/build/test-results/test/*.xml'
                        }
                    }
                }
                stage('Integration Test') {
                    steps {
                        sh 'docker run --rm myapp:latest ./gradlew integrationTest'
                    }
                    post {
                        always {
                            junit '**/build/test-results/integrationTest/*.xml'
```

```
                    }
                }
            }
            stage('End-to-End Test') {
                steps {
                    sh 'npm run cypress:run'
                }
                post {
                    always {
                        junit '**/results/cypress/*.xml'
                    }
                }
            }
        }
    }
  }
}
```

In the example above, the Parallel Test Execution stage runs Unit Tests, Integration Tests, and End-to-End Tests concurrently, optimizing the testing process. Each parallel stage collects its respective JUnit test results for reporting.

By leveraging Jenkins pipelines to automate the execution of unit, integration, and end-to-end tests, you ensure a robust CI/CD workflow. This integration not only improves code quality but also enables rapid feedback, facilitating continuous improvement and delivery.

4.8 Reporting Test Results

Accurately reporting test results is a fundamental aspect of automated testing in Jenkins. Detailed and clear test reports help teams quickly identify problems, understand test coverage, and ensure that the changes in the codebase do not introduce new issues. This section delves into the mechanisms provided by Jenkins for collecting, displaying, and analyzing test results.

Jenkins supports various test result formats, such as JUnit, NUnit, and others, which can be integrated into the Jenkins job to display results on the job dashboard. We will use the JUnit format as an example, but the principles apply to other formats as well.

Firstly, we need to configure the Jenkins job to record and publish test results. Assume we have a Java project that uses JUnit for unit testing. The relevant section of the Jenkinsfile to capture and display JUnit test results looks like this:

```
pipeline {
```

```
    agent any
    stages {
        stage('Build') {
            steps {
                sh 'mvn clean compile'
            }
        }
        stage('Test') {
            steps {
                sh 'mvn test'
                junit '**/target/surefire-reports/TEST-*.xml'
            }
        }
    }
    post {
        always {
            archiveArtifacts artifacts: '**/target/*.jar', allowEmptyArchive: true
            junit '**/target/surefire-reports/TEST-*.xml'
        }
    }
}
```

In the above Jenkinsfile, the junit '**/target/surefire-reports/TEST-*.xml' directive tells Jenkins to look for test result files in the specified path. This path is relative to the workspace root directory. The junit step can be used in both the main stages and the post section to ensure results are always collected, regardless of the build outcome.

When the pipeline executes the sh 'mvn test' command, the build system (Maven in this case) runs the tests and produces the result files in the target/surefire-reports directory. The junit directive captures these result files and displays the results on the Jenkins job page.

Interpreting Test Results Once the build completes, Jenkins provides a number of ways to view the test results:

- **Test Result Trend:** This is available on the Jenkins job main page, showing a graphical representation of test results over time. It is helpful for spotting trends such as increasing test failures or decreasing test execution times.
- **Test Result:** A detailed breakdown of individual test cases, including which tests passed, failed, or were skipped. This information is accessible via the Jenkins job link, typically found under the "Last Successful Artifacts" section.

To illustrate, below is a typical JUnit test result report in Jenkins, showing the status of various test cases:

```
[Test Summary]
Total Tests: 50
Passed: 48
Failed: 2
Skipped: 0
```

Failing Tests and Notifications Dealing with failing tests effectively requires prompt and clear notifications. Jenkins can be configured to send alerts when specific triggers occur, such as a test failure. Email notifications are one of the most commonly used methods. This can be configured in the `post` section of the Jenkinsfile:

```
pipeline {
    agent any
    stages {
        // (Stages omitted for brevity)
    }
    post {
        always {
            archiveArtifacts artifacts: '**/target/*.jar', allowEmptyArchive: true
            junit '**/target/surefire-reports/TEST-*.xml'
        }
        failure {
            mail to: 'team@example.com',
                subject: "Failed Pipeline: ${currentBuild.fullDisplayName}",
                body: "Something is wrong with ${env.JOB_NAME} ${env.
                    BUILD_NUMBER}\nMore info at: ${env.BUILD_URL}"
        }
    }
}
```

The `failure` block ensures that an email is sent to the designated recipient(s) if the build fails for any reason, including test failures. The variables `env.JOB_NAME`, `env.BUILD_NUMBER`, and `env.BUILD_URL` provide contextual information about the failing job, aiding in quick diagnostics.

Plugins for Extended Reporting Jenkins extends its reporting capabilities through various plugins. Some noteworthy plugins include:

- **Test Results Analyzer Plugin:** This plugin offers an enhanced view of test results with detailed dashboards and trends. It allows filtering, comparison between builds, and various visualizations to make test results more comprehensible.

- **JUnit Attachments Plugin:** This plugin enables attachments to be included with the JUnit results, helpful for adding logs, screenshots, or other artifacts relevant to the test results.

The usage of these plugins can provide deeper insights and more detailed reports, empowering teams to understand and react to test outcomes effectively.

```
pipeline {
    agent any
    stages {
        // (Stages omitted for brevity)
    }
    post {
        always {
            archiveArtifacts artifacts: '**/target/*.jar', allowEmptyArchive: true
            junit '**/target/surefire-reports/TEST-*.xml'
        }
    }
    post {
        always {
            step([$class: 'TestResultAnalyzerPublisher'])
        }
    }
}
```

In the above example, the TestResultAnalyzerPublisher class is called as part of the post-build actions to publish the extended test result analysis.

Effective reporting of test results in Jenkins allows development teams to maintain the health of their codebase, quickly identify and fix bugs, and ensure high quality in continuous integration and delivery pipelines. This section demonstrates the basic and advanced methods to harness Jenkins' capabilities to provide valuable feedback from automated tests.

4.9 Handling Test Failures

When managing automated tests with Jenkins, handling test failures effectively is crucial for maintaining code quality and ensuring a stable continuous integration/continuous delivery (CI/CD) pipeline. This section delves into strategies for managing test failures, analyzing failure reports, and remediating issues to maintain a robust testing process.

Analyzing Test Failure Reports

Upon the execution of automated tests, capturing and analyzing failure reports is the first step. Jenkins pipelines can be configured to generate detailed test reports which include logs, stack traces, and diagnostic information. Utilize the Jenkins JUnit plugin to parse test results and generate comprehensive failure reports. Example pipeline snippet for collecting JUnit test results:

```
pipeline {
    agent any

    stages {
        stage('Test') {
            steps {
                script {
                    // Execute test cases
                    sh 'mvn test'

                    // Archive test results
                    junit 'target/surefire-reports/*.xml'
                }
            }
        }
    }
}
```

The above script ensures that after running the tests using Maven, the resulting XML files containing test results are archived in Jenkins. These archived files facilitate the generation of detailed reports which can be reviewed for identifying root causes of failures.

Integrating Failure Reports for Insights

Jenkins can be integrated with various tools for enhanced reporting capabilities. Tools like Allure, TestNG, and xUnit provide additional visualization and reporting features. Integration example with Allure reports:

```
pipeline {
    agent any

    stages {
        stage('Test') {
            steps {
                script {
                    // Run tests with Allure
                    sh 'mvn clean test'
                    // Generate Allure report
                    allure includeProperties: false, jdk: '', results: [[path: 'target/allure-
                        results']]
                }
            }
        }

        stage('Allure Report') {
            steps {
                script {
                    allure includeProperties: false, jdk: '', results: [[path: 'target/allure-
                        results']]
                }
            }
        }
    }

    post {
        always {
```

```
            // Archive Allure report
            archiveArtifacts artifacts: 'target/allure-results/**'
        }
    }
}
```

The script integrates the Allure testing framework with Jenkins, allowing the generation and archiving of insightful visual reports.

Automatic Test Failure Notification

Configuring Jenkins to send automatic notifications upon test failures can inform the team instantly, expediting the resolution process. Email notifications or integrations with messaging platforms like Slack can be used. Example of email notification configuration:

```
pipeline {
    agent any

    stages {
        stage('Build') {
            steps {
                sh 'mvn clean package'
            }
        }

        stage('Test') {
            steps {
                junit 'target/surefire-reports/*.xml'
            }
        }
    }

    post {
        failure {
            mail to: 'team@example.com',
                subject: "Build ${env.BUILD_NUMBER} Failed",
                body: "The build failed. Check Jenkins for details."
        }
    }
}
```

In the snippet above, an email is sent to the designated recipient if a build fails, aiding in quick communication of test issues.

Retry Mechanisms

Implementing retry mechanisms in pipelines ensures transient issues do not halt the entire testing process. Jenkins provides ways to retry stages if they fail. Example of retrying a test stage:

```
pipeline {
    agent any

    stages {
        stage('Test') {
            steps {
```

```
                retry(3) {
                    sh 'mvn test'
                }
            }
        }
    }
}
```

This configuration retries the test stage up to three times before declaring a failure, thus mitigating temporary issues impacting the test outcomes.

Quarantining Flaky Tests

Identifying and quarantining flaky tests - those that fail intermittently without consistent reasons - is essential. Jenkins allows marking specific tests to be skipped or run in isolation to prevent them from affecting the overall build:

```
pipeline {
    agent any

    stages {
        stage('Test') {
            steps {
                script {
                    try {
                        sh 'mvn -Dtest=!FlakyTest test'
                    } catch (Exception e) {
                        println 'Flaky tests identified and skipped.'
                    }
                }
            }
        }
    }
}
```

Quarantine flaky tests to maintain the integrity of the test suite while working on permanent fixes.

Maintaining Historical Data

Archiving historical test data over multiple runs helps in tracking test failure trends and identifying recurring issues. Using Jenkins' built-in capabilities to keep track:

```
pipeline {
    agent any

    stages {
        // Build and test stages as needed
        stage('Archive') {
            steps {
                archiveArtifacts artifacts: 'target/surefire-reports/*.xml',
                                 allowEmptyArchive: true
            }
```

```
        }
    }

    post {
        always {
            junit 'target/surefire-reports/*.xml'
        }
    }
}
```

Archiving the results ensures that historical data is available for analysis and metrics.

Incorporating these strategies within your Jenkins workflow enables managing and resolving test failures efficiently, maintaining a productive and reliable CI/CD pipeline.

4.10 Parallel Testing in Jenkins

Parallel testing is an essential aspect of Continuous Integration and Continuous Deployment (CI/CD) practices aimed at minimizing test execution time and enhancing efficiency. By executing multiple tests concurrently, Jenkins can significantly decrease the overall time required to complete the testing phase, leading to faster feedback cycles. This section elucidates the rationale, setup, and implementation strategies for parallel testing in Jenkins, ensuring optimized utilization of resources and expediting the validation process.

Parallel testing is predicated on the ability to distribute test execution across multiple nodes or agents within a Jenkins environment. This distribution can be achieved through the configuration of the Jenkins pipeline to utilize parallel steps.

A fundamental Jenkinsfile exemplifying the configuration for parallel testing is provided below:

```
pipeline {
    agent any
    stages {
        stage('Build') {
            steps {
                echo 'Building...'
                // Add build steps here
            }
        }
        stage('Test') {
            parallel {
                stage('Unit Tests') {
                    steps {
                        echo 'Running Unit Tests...'
```

```
                    // Add unit test execution steps here
                }
            }
            stage('Integration Tests') {
                steps {
                    echo 'Running Integration Tests...'
                    // Add integration test execution steps here
                }
            }
            stage('End-to-End Tests') {
                steps {
                    echo 'Running End-to-End Tests...'
                    // Add end-to-end test execution steps here
                }
            }
        }
    }
    stage('Deploy') {
        steps {
            echo 'Deploying...'
            // Add deployment steps here
        }
    }
  }
}
```

In the above pipeline script, the parallel directive within the Test stage allows for the concurrent execution of Unit Tests, Integration Tests, and End-to-End Tests. Each block within the parallel directive represents an independent activity that Jenkins orchestrates simultaneously.

Configuring Jenkins Nodes for Parallel Testing

To efficiently execute tests in parallel, Jenkins must be configured with multiple nodes (or agents). Each node represents a computational resource capable of executing a part of the Jenkins pipeline.

To configure a node in Jenkins: 1. Navigate to Manage Jenkins > Manage Nodes and Clouds. 2. Add a new node and configure its attributes, ensuring that it has the necessary executors, labels, and availability settings. 3. Ensure that the environment on each node contains the required tools and dependencies needed for executing the tests.

```
Node configuration successfully updated.
```

Allocating Specific Nodes or Labels

Allocating specific nodes or using labels helps direct the parallel steps to the appropriate resources. This is achieved using the agent directive within each parallel branch.

```
pipeline {
    agent any
    stages {
        stage('Build') {
```

```
            steps {
                echo 'Building...'
                // Add build steps here
            }
        }
        stage('Test') {
            parallel {
                stage('Unit Tests') {
                    agent { label 'unit-test-node' }
                    steps {
                        echo 'Running Unit Tests on unit-test-node...'
                        // Add unit test execution steps here
                    }
                }
                stage('Integration Tests') {
                    agent { label 'integration-test-node' }
                    steps {
                        echo 'Running Integration Tests on integration-test-node...'
                        // Add integration test execution steps here
                    }
                }
                stage('End-to-End Tests') {
                    agent { label 'e2e-test-node' }
                    steps {
                        echo 'Running End-to-End Tests on e2e-test-node...'
                        // Add end-to-end test execution steps here
                    }
                }
            }
        }
        stage('Deploy') {
            steps {
                echo 'Deploying...'
                // Add deployment steps here
            }
        }
    }
}
```

In this script, specific nodes are allocated for different test stages by using the label attribute within the agent directive. This allocation ensures tests are executed on the nodes with the requisite environment and capabilities.

Optimizing Resource Utilization

Parallel testing should not sacrifice stability for speed. To ensure optimal resource utilization, it is prudent to: - Monitor the resource consumption of each node. - Adjust the number of executors based on the node's hardware capabilities. - Use the throttle feature to limit the number of concurrent jobs executed on a node, preventing overload.

```
options {
    throttle(['Unit Tests', 'Integration Tests', 'End-to-End Tests'])
}
```

Including the throttle option regulates the concurrency, ensuring that excessive parallelism does not degrade performance.

Handling Test Dependencies

Tests often have dependencies that could affect their concurrent execution. Ensuring independence between parallel steps is crucial. Dependencies can be addressed by: - Isolating test environments for each parallel branch. - Using containerization (e.g., Docker) to encapsulate dependencies. - Employing environment variables to distinguish between parallel executions.

```
pipeline {
    agent any
    environment {
        E2E_ENV = 'staging'
    }
    stages {
        stage('Build') {
            steps {
                echo 'Building...'
                // Add build steps here
            }
        }
        stage('Test') {
            parallel {
                stage('Unit Tests') {
                    environment {
                        TEST_ENV = 'unit'
                    }
                    steps {
                        echo "Running Unit Tests in ${TEST_ENV} environment..."
                        // Add unit test execution steps here
                    }
                }
                stage('Integration Tests') {
                    environment {
                        TEST_ENV = 'integration'
                    }
                    steps {
                        echo "Running Integration Tests in ${TEST_ENV} environment...
                            "
                        // Add integration test execution steps here
                    }
                }
                stage('End-to-End Tests') {
                    steps {
                        echo "Running End-to-End Tests in ${E2E_ENV} environment..."

                        // Add end-to-end test execution steps here
                    }
                }
            }
        }
        stage('Deploy') {
            steps {
                echo 'Deploying...'
                // Add deployment steps here
            }
        }
    }
```

```
}
```

By specifying environments within each stage, tests are executed independently, mitigating the risks of conflicts.

Managing Failures in Parallel Execution

It is critical to handle failures gracefully within a parallel context. Each parallel branch can utilize the post directive to define actions on successful or failed executions.

```
pipeline {
    agent any
    stages {
        stage('Build') {
            steps {
                echo 'Building...'
                // Add build steps here
            }
        }
        stage('Test') {
            parallel {
                stage('Unit Tests') {
                    steps {
                        echo 'Running Unit Tests...'
                        // Add unit test execution steps here
                    }
                    post {
                        failure {
                            echo 'Unit Tests failed.'
                            // Add failure handling steps here
                        }
                    }
                }
                stage('Integration Tests') {
                    steps {
                        echo 'Running Integration Tests...'
                        // Add integration test execution steps here
                    }
                    post {
                        failure {
                            echo 'Integration Tests failed.'
                            // Add failure handling steps here
                        }
                    }
                }
                stage('End-to-End Tests') {
                    steps {
                        echo 'Running End-to-End Tests...'
                        // Add end-to-end test execution steps here
                    }
                    post {
                        failure {
                            echo 'End-to-End Tests failed.'
                            // Add failure handling steps here
                        }
                    }
                }
            }
        }
```

```
        stage('Deploy') {
            steps {
                echo 'Deploying...'
                // Add deployment steps here
            }
        }
    }
}
```

Each post block captures the outcome of its respective stage, ensuring that appropriate steps are taken if a failure occurs.

Parallel testing in Jenkins, when properly configured and executed, significantly enhances the CI/CD pipeline efficiency. By optimizing resource usage, managing dependencies, and gracefully handling failures, the approach ensures robust and swift test processes conducive to accelerated software delivery.

4.11 Test Automation Frameworks Integration

To leverage the full potential of Jenkins in automated testing, it is essential to understand the integration of various test automation frameworks. Jenkins supports a wide range of frameworks for unit, integration, and end-to-end testing, facilitating a streamlined and efficient testing process. This section focuses on integrating some of the most commonly used test automation frameworks with Jenkins.

JUnit for Java: JUnit is a popular testing framework for Java, widely used for unit testing. Integrating JUnit with Jenkins involves several steps, starting with the installation of necessary plugins and configuration of Jenkins to recognize JUnit test reports.

First, ensure that the *JUnit Plugin* is installed. This plugin allows Jenkins to parse the test results generated in the JUnit XML format. To install the plugin, navigate to *Manage Jenkins* → *Manage Plugins*, and select the *Available* tab. Search for and install the *JUnit Plugin*.

Once the plugin is installed, configure your Jenkins job to execute JUnit tests and publish test results. Below is a sample *Jenkinsfile* for a Maven project:

```
pipeline {
    agent any

    stages {
        stage('Build') {
```

```
            steps {
                sh 'mvn clean compile'
            }
        }
        stage('Test') {
            steps {
                sh 'mvn test'
            }
        }
        stage('Report') {
            steps {
                junit 'target/surefire-reports/*.xml'
            }
        }
    }
}
```

In this pipeline, mvn test runs the JUnit tests, and junit 'target/surefire-reports/*.xml' instructs Jenkins to process and display the test results in the Jenkins Dashboard.

PyTest for Python: PyTest is a robust testing framework for Python, supporting simple unit tests and complex functional testing. Integrating PyTest with Jenkins involves generating JUnit-compatible XML reports that Jenkins can read.

First, ensure that PyTest is installed in your Python environment. Then, use the *pytest* command with the *–junitxml* option to generate reports in a format Jenkins understands. Below is a sample *Jenkinsfile* for a Python project:

```
pipeline {
    agent any

    stages {
        stage('Install Dependencies') {
            steps {
                sh 'pip install pytest'
            }
        }
        stage('Test') {
            steps {
                sh 'pytest --junitxml=reports/results.xml'
            }
        }
        stage('Report') {
            steps {
                junit 'reports/results.xml'
            }
        }
    }
}
```

In this script, PyTest generates an XML report that is specified by the –junitxml=reports/results.xml flag. Jenkins then uses the junit 'reports/results.xml' command to process the results.

Selenium for End-to-End Testing: Selenium is a widely-used framework for automating web browser interactions, often utilized for end-to-end testing. Integrate Selenium tests with Jenkins by generating JUnit or TestNG reports that Jenkins can process.

Below is a sample *Jenkinsfile* for a Selenium testing project using Maven and TestNG:

```
pipeline {
    agent any

    stages {
        stage('Build') {
            steps {
                sh 'mvn clean compile'
            }
        }
        stage('Test') {
            steps {
                sh 'mvn test'
            }
        }
        stage('Report') {
            steps {
                junit 'target/surefire-reports/*.xml'
            }
        }
    }
}
```

Ensure the Selenium tests are configured to use TestNG and the TestNG plugin is installed in Jenkins. Configuring the Maven pom.xml file to produce JUnit-compatible reports is essential.

Jest for JavaScript Applications: Jest is a popular testing framework for JavaScript, commonly used with Node.js applications. To integrate Jest with Jenkins, use the *jest-junit* reporter to generate test results in a format Jenkins can parse.

First, install *jest* and *jest-junit* in your Node.js project:

```
npm install --save-dev jest jest-junit
```

Next, configure Jest to use the jest-junit reporter by adding the following configuration to your package.json file:

```
"jest": {
    "reporters": [
        "default",
        ["jest-junit", {
            "outputDirectory": "reports",
            "outputName": "results.xml"
        }]
```

```
    ]
}
```

Below is a sample *Jenkinsfile* for a JavaScript project using Jest:

```
pipeline {
    agent any

    stages {
        stage('Install Dependencies') {
            steps {
                sh 'npm install'
            }
        }
        stage('Test') {
            steps {
                sh 'npm test'
            }
        }
        stage('Report') {
            steps {
                junit 'reports/results.xml'
            }
        }
    }
}
```

Here, Jest tests are run using the `npm test` command, producing results in the `reports/results.xml` file. Jenkins then processes this file for the test report.

This section has provided detailed steps for integrating widely-used test automation frameworks with Jenkins, demonstrating how to configure Jenkins to execute tests and report results effectively. Leveraging these integrations ensures a robust and efficient automated testing process within Jenkins.

4.12 Best Practices for Automated Testing

Automated testing plays a critical role in the continuous integration and continuous delivery (CI/CD) pipeline, helping to ensure software quality and reliability. Implementing best practices is essential to maximize the effectiveness of automated tests. This section discusses several key practices that can be adopted to enhance the testing process.

1. Prioritize Maintainability

Maintainability is crucial for automated tests as it impacts the ease of updates and the ability to extend the test suite over time. To ensure maintainability, tests should be organized in a clear and logical structure, following naming conventions and appropriate directory/file hierarchies. Tests should avoid hard-coding values; instead, use configuration files or parameters that can be easily modified.

2. Write Clear and Concise Tests

Automated tests should be clear and concise to facilitate understanding and debugging. Each test should focus on verifying a single piece of functionality, following the principle of "one assertion per test". This approach simplifies identifying the cause of a failure. Additionally, comments and documentation within the test code can provide context and explanation for the tests' purpose and logic.

3. Implement Comprehensive Test Coverage

While achieving 100% test coverage is often unrealistic, aiming for high coverage ensures that most parts of the application are tested. This includes both positive and negative test cases, boundary value analysis, and edge cases. Various types of tests, such as unit, integration, and end-to-end, should be blended to provide thorough coverage across the application stack.

4. Optimize Test Execution Time

Test suites should be optimized for execution time to ensure the CI/CD pipeline remains efficient. Comprehensive test coverage does not necessarily mean lengthy test executions. Techniques such as test parallelization, selective testing (e.g., running only affected tests based on recent changes), and optimizing test setups can significantly reduce execution times.

5. Ensure Tests are Idempotent

Tests should be idempotent, meaning they produce the same result regardless of how many times they are run. This requires tests to properly set up and tear down any state they modify. Mocking dependencies and isolating test environments can help achieve idempotency. Consistent test results lead to more reliable detection of actual issues versus intermittent failures.

6. Use Reliable Test Data

Reliable and representative test data are essential for meaningful tests. Data should be deterministic and reset to a known state before each test run. In cases where real data is used, ensure it is anonymized to avoid privacy concerns and regulatory compliance issues. Generating test data that closely mimics production data enhances the validity of test outcomes.

7. Incorporate Continuous Feedback

Continuous feedback from testing is vital for early detection of issues. Jenkins pipelines should be configured to provide immediate notifications for test failures through emails, messaging systems, or dashboard alerts. This prompt feedback allows developers to address issues quickly, minimizing the impact on the overall development process.

8. Review and Refactor Tests Regularly

Regular review and refactoring of test suites help eliminate obsolete or redundant tests and improve test efficiency. Code reviews for tests should be as rigorous as those for production code. Furthermore, refactoring tests to adopt new testing tools or frameworks can improve the maintainability and execution performance of the test suite.

9. Leverage Test Automation Frameworks

Utilizing well-established test automation frameworks can simplify the creation and maintenance of tests. Frameworks provide reusable components, standardized methods for assertions, and built-in reporting capabilities. Integrating these frameworks within Jenkins pipelines allows for streamlined test execution and result collection.

10. Maintain an Isolated Test Environment

Tests should run in isolated environments that mirror the production environment's configuration as closely as possible. This isolation prevents side effects from other tests or environments, ensuring a consistent baseline for test runs. Tools like Docker and Kubernetes can facilitate the provisioning of isolated and disposable test environments.

11. Monitor and Report Test Metrics

Monitoring and reporting test metrics provide insights into the health and effectiveness of the test suite. Metrics such as test coverage, execution time, pass/fail rates, and flakiness should be regularly reviewed. Visual dashboards in Jenkins can help track these metrics over time and identify trends or areas needing improvement.

12. Encourage a Testing Culture

Fostering a culture that values testing within the development team is vital for long-term success. Encouraging practices like Test-Driven Development (TDD) or Behavior-Driven Development (BDD), incentivizing quality code, and providing training on testing tools and frameworks can elevate the overall quality of the software and the proficiency of the team.

By adhering to these best practices, teams can create robust and efficient automated testing processes that enhance software reliability and support smooth CI/CD operations.

Chapter 5

Continuous Integration (CI) with Jenkins

This chapter provides an in-depth look at implementing Continuous Integration (CI) with Jenkins. It covers the setup and integration of source code management systems, automated build processes, and managing dependencies. The chapter details steps for building and testing code changes, configuring notifications and reports, and addressing build failures. It also explores how CI integrates into broader CI/CD pipelines and outlines best practices to optimize the CI process for improved software quality and development efficiency.

5.1 Introduction to Continuous Integration

Continuous Integration (CI) is a software development practice whereby developers integrate code into a shared repository frequently, ideally several times a day. Each integration is then verified by an automated build and automated tests. The primary goal of CI is to identify integration issues as early as possible, thus reducing the time and effort required to debug and fix problems that can arise from merging code changes.

A typical CI process comprises the following key steps:

- Developers write code and commit changes to a source code

repository.

- The CI server monitors this repository for changes.
- Upon detecting a change, the CI server triggers a new build.
- The build process executes a series of steps, including compiling the code, running tests, and generating reports.

In practice, CI involves several crucial components and steps:

Source Code Management (SCM): A repository where the project's source code is stored. Examples include Git, Subversion, and Mercurial. The SCM tool tracks code changes, maintains version history, and facilitates collaboration among developers.

Automated Builds: The process of automatically compiling the source code to create an executable or deployable artifact. This is achieved using build tools such as Maven, Gradle, or Ant in the Java ecosystem, make for C/C++, or npm for Node.js applications.

Automated Testing: Executing a predefined set of tests to validate the functionality, performance, and security of the software. Automated tests range from unit tests, which check individual components, to integration tests that validate the interaction between components.

A simple example of an automated build configuration for a Java project using Maven can be defined in a pom.xml file:

```
<project xmlns="http://maven.apache.org/POM/4.0.0" xmlns:xsi="http://www.w3.
    org/2001/XMLSchema-instance" xsi:schemaLocation="http://maven.apache.org/
    POM/4.0.0 http://maven.apache.org/xsd/maven-4.0.0.xsd">
  <modelVersion>4.0.0</modelVersion>
  <groupId>com.example</groupId>
  <artifactId>example-project</artifactId>
  <version>1.0-SNAPSHOT</version>
  <dependencies>
    <dependency>
      <groupId>junit</groupId>
      <artifactId>junit</artifactId>
      <version>4.12</version>
      <scope>test</scope>
    </dependency>
  </dependencies>
</project>
```

Build Automation Server: A dedicated server, such as Jenkins, which continuously monitors the source code repository. When changes are detected, the server initiates the build and test process, and provides feedback regarding the build status.

Feedback Mechanism: Effective CI relies on timely feedback. Notifications through email, instant messaging, or dashboards inform developers about the build status and test results, enabling prompt action on any issues detected.

A typical Jenkins build configuration involves setting up a project build in the Jenkins UI, linking it to the SCM repository, and defining build triggers. Below is an example Jenkins pipeline script for a simple Java project:

```
pipeline {
    agent any
    stages {
        stage('Checkout') {
            steps {
                git url: 'https://github.com/example/repo.git'
            }
        }
        stage('Build') {
            steps {
                sh 'mvn clean package'
            }
        }
        stage('Test') {
            steps {
                sh 'mvn test'
            }
        }
        stage('Archive') {
            steps {
                archiveArtifacts artifacts: '**/target/*.jar', allowEmptyArchive: true
            }
        }
    }
    post {
        always {
            junit '**/target/surefire-reports/*.xml'
            mail to: 'developer@example.com',
                 subject: "Build \${currentBuild.fullDisplayName}: \${currentBuild.
                        currentResult}",
                 body: "Details: \${env.BUILD_URL}"
        }
    }
}
```

In this pipeline script:

- The Checkout stage pulls the latest code from the specified Git repository.
- The Build stage compiles the project using Maven.
- The Test stage runs the project's tests.
- The Archive stage saves the compiled artifacts.

- The post block includes an email notification mechanism providing feedback about the build status.

CI plays a fundamental role in modern software development:

- By integrating code frequently, developers reduce the scope of each integration, making it faster and easier to locate and fix defects.
- Automated builds ensure that code changes don't break the existing functionality, promoting a stable codebase.
- Rapid feedback from automated testing helps maintain high code quality and ensures that the software remains functional as it evolves.

5.2 The Role of Jenkins in CI

In the landscape of Continuous Integration (CI), Jenkins has established itself as a pivotal tool for streamlining development workflows and enhancing software quality. Its capabilities go far beyond merely automating build processes; Jenkins provides a robust platform that facilitates comprehensive integration, deployment, and project management tasks. This section delves deep into the functionalities and roles that Jenkins plays in a modern CI environment, elucidating its essential features and illustrating its impact on development practices.

At its core, Jenkins functions as an automation server that orchestrates a series of tasks required in the software development lifecycle. By enabling developers to integrate changes into a shared repository frequently, Jenkins helps to detect issues early, provides timely feedback, and ensures that the codebase remains in a deployable state.

One significant role of Jenkins in CI is its ability to manage and integrate with various Source Code Management (SCM) tools. Through plugins, Jenkins supports a wide array of SCM systems such as Git, Subversion, Mercurial, and Perforce. This flexibility allows Jenkins to fetch the latest code changes, which are then subjected to a series of automated processes, including builds, tests, and deployments.

The user can configure Jenkins to pull from the SCM repository at regular intervals or trigger builds based on specific events, such as a push to the repository. This ensures that Jenkins is constantly updated with the latest changes, ready to execute a new pipeline whenever modifications are detected. Integrating Jenkins with SCM is typically accomplished via the "Source Code Management" section in a Jenkins job configuration:

```
pipeline {
    agent any
    stages {
        stage('Checkout') {
            steps {
                git 'https://github.com/user/repository.git'
            }
        }
        // Additional stages follow
    }
}
```

Jenkins' versatility extends to its build automation capabilities. Jenkins can compile and build code written in various programming languages, utilizing a range of build tools like Maven, Gradle, Ant, and others. By defining build steps within Jenkins pipelines, developers gain the advantage of automating complex build processes, ensuring consistency, and drastically reducing the potential for human errors. Here is a typical Jenkinsfile snippet for a Maven build:

```
pipeline {
    agent any
    stages {
        stage('Build') {
            steps {
                script {
                    sh 'mvn clean install'
                }
            }
        }
    }
}
```

Testing is another crucial phase where Jenkins excels. By integrating testing frameworks and tools such as JUnit, Selenium, and others, Jenkins automates the execution of unit tests, integration tests, and end-to-end tests. Automatic triggering of test suites can immediately validate the integrity of the code after each build, providing rapid feedback on the success or failure of the latest changes. This ensures problems are caught early and resolved before they escalate.

```
pipeline {
    agent any
    stages {
        stage('Test') {
            steps {
                script {
                    sh 'mvn test'
```

```
            }
            junit '**/target/surefire-reports/*.xml'
        }
      }
   }
}
```

In addition to source control integration, build automation, and testing, Jenkins is also integral in the deployment process. By leveraging deployment tools and environments, Jenkins can automate the deployment of applications to various stages, such as development, testing, staging, and production environments. For instance, integrating with Docker allows Jenkins to build, test, and deploy containerized applications seamlessly. A typical deployment step may look like the following:

```
pipeline {
   agent any
   stages {
      stage('Deploy') {
         steps {
            script {
               sh 'docker build -t your-app .'
               sh 'docker run -d -p 8080:8080 your-app'
            }
         }
      }
   }
}
```

Jenkins also supports extensive reporting and notification plugins. By generating and publishing reports on the build and test results, Jenkins keeps the team informed about the project's status. Notifications through email, Slack, or other communication tools can be configured to alert developers of build failures, ensuring prompt attention to issues:

```
pipeline {
   agent any
   stages {
      stage('Build') {
         steps {
            script {
               try {
                  sh 'mvn clean install'
               } catch (Exception e) {
                  mail to: 'dev-team@example.com',
                       subject: "Build Failed: ${env.BUILD_TAG}",
                       body: "The build failed. Please check the logs."
                       throw e
               }
            }
         }
      }
   }
}
```

In wrapping up the exploration of Jenkins' role in CI, it is evident that Jenkins serves as a cornerstone of the modern development lifecycle. Integrating seamlessly with other tools and services, Jenkins automates, monitors, and manages the entire CI pipeline, significantly enhancing efficiency, reducing risk, and streamlining the path from code commit to deployment.

5.3 Setting Up CI in Jenkins

Setting up Continuous Integration (CI) in Jenkins involves several steps tailored to ensure a seamless and automatic integration, testing, and quality assurance process. This section will guide you through the necessary configurations and settings required to set up CI successfully.

Jenkins Installation and Initial Setup

To begin, Jenkins needs to be installed and configured on a server. Jenkins installation is straightforward and involves following these steps:

1. **Download the Jenkins WAR file:** Obtain the Jenkins WAR file from the official Jenkins site (jenkins.io).

2. **Run Jenkins:** Execute the following command in the terminal to run Jenkins.

```
java -jar jenkins.war
```

3. **Access Jenkins via Browser:** Open your browser and navigate to http://localhost:8080. Follow the initial setup instructions prompted by Jenkins.

4. **Unlock Jenkins:** Use the initial admin password located in the specified file path on your local machine to unlock Jenkins and proceed with the setup.

5. **Install Suggested Plugins:** Select 'Install suggested plugins' to install essential Jenkins plugins automatically.

6. **Create Admin User:** Create an admin user to manage the Jenkins instance and complete the setup.

Configuring Jenkins for CI

After the basic setup, Jenkins requires additional configuration to suit Continuous Integration tasks.

Global Tool Configuration

Proper configuration of build tools is necessary for Jenkins to execute build jobs effectively:

1. **Navigate to Global Tool Configuration:** Go to Manage Jenkins > Global Tool Configuration.
2. **Configure JDK:** Add JDK installations by providing an accurate name and path or allowing Jenkins to install automatically.
3. **Configure Maven:** For Maven projects, add and configure Maven installations. Configure the installation with a name and path.
4. **Configure Git:** Add the Git executable by specifying the path to ensure Jenkins can access and use Git repositories.

Creating a New Jenkins Job for CI

With tools in place, the next step is to create and configure a new Jenkins job:

1. **Create a New Item:** Select 'New Item' from the Jenkins Dashboard.
2. **Job Name and Type:** Provide a unique name for the job and select the 'Freestyle Project' option. Click 'OK' to create the job.
3. **Configure Source Code Management (SCM):** Under the 'Source Code Management' section, select 'Git' and provide the repository URL. Ensure credentials are set up for repository access.
4. **Define Build Triggers:** Under 'Build Triggers', select 'Poll SCM' and set the polling schedule using cron syntax. For example, 'H/5 * * * *' checks for changes every five minutes.
5. **Specify Build Steps:** Under 'Build', select 'Add build step > Invoke top-level Maven targets' for Maven projects. Provide goals such as 'clean install'.

6. **Post-build Actions:** To add post-build actions, such as archiving artifacts, select 'Archive the artifacts' and specify the file patterns, e.g., '**/*.jar'.

Executing a Build

Once the job is configured, a build can be executed manually or automatically based on the triggers defined. To run a build manually:

1. **Navigate to the Job:** Click on the job name from the Jenkins dashboard.
2. **Start Build:** Click 'Build Now' to trigger a build.
3. **Monitor Build Progress:** Monitor the build progress under 'Build History'. Click on the build number to view details and console output.

```
[INFO] Scanning for projects...
[INFO]
[INFO] ----------------------< com.example:demo >-----------------------
[INFO] Building demo 1.0-SNAPSHOT
[INFO] --------------------------------[ jar ]---------------------------------
[INFO]
[INFO] --- maven-resources-plugin:2.6:resources (default-resources) @ demo ---
[INFO] Using 'UTF-8' encoding to copy filtered resources.
[INFO] skip non existing resourceDirectory /path/to/resource
[INFO]
[INFO] --- maven-compiler-plugin:3.8.1:compile (default-compile) @ demo ---
[INFO] Changes detected - recompiling the module!
[INFO] Compiling 5 source files to /path/to/target/classes
[INFO]
[INFO] --- maven-resources-plugin:2.6:testResources (default-testResources) @ demo ---
[INFO] Using 'UTF-8' encoding to copy filtered resources.
[INFO] skip non existing resourceDirectory /path/to/test/resources
[INFO]
[INFO] --- maven-compiler-plugin:3.8.1:testCompile (default-testCompile) @ demo ---
[INFO] Changes detected - recompiling the module!
[INFO] Compiling 1 source file to /path/to/target/test-classes
[INFO]
[INFO] --- maven-surefire-plugin:2.22.2:test (default-test) @ demo ---
[INFO]
[INFO] -------------------------------------------------------
[INFO]  T E S T S
[INFO] -------------------------------------------------------
[INFO] Running com.example.MyServiceTest
[INFO] Tests run: 1, Failures: 0, Errors: 0, Skipped: 0, Time elapsed: 0.254 s - in com.example.MyServiceTest
[INFO]
[INFO] Results:
[INFO]
[INFO] Tests run: 1, Failures: 0, Errors: 0, Skipped: 0
[INFO]
[INFO]
[INFO] --- maven-jar-plugin:3.2.0:jar (default-jar) @ demo ---
[INFO] Building jar: /path/to/demo-1.0-SNAPSHOT.jar
[INFO]
[INFO] --- maven-install-plugin:2.5.2:install (default-install) @ demo ---
[INFO] Installing /path/to/demo-1.0-SNAPSHOT.jar to /local/repo/com/example/demo/1.0-SNAPSHOT/demo-1.0-SNAPSHOT.jar
[INFO] ------------------------------------------------------------------------
[INFO] BUILD SUCCESS
[INFO] ------------------------------------------------------------------------
[INFO] Total time: 5.678 s
[INFO] Finished at: 2023-10-10T10:32:14Z
[INFO] ------------------------------------------------------------------------
```

The execution log verifies the successful completion of the build, indicating the CI setup is operational. In the following sections, further details on Source Code Management integration and continuous testing will be explored.

5.4 Source Code Management (SCM) Integration

Proper integration of Source Code Management (SCM) systems is a cornerstone of implementing effective Continuous Integration (CI) with Jenkins. SCM systems, such as Git, Subversion (SVN), and Mercurial, provide repositories to store, track, and manage changes to source code over time. These systems facilitate collaboration among development teams and maintain a history of the code base, allowing for the reconstruction of past versions for debugging or auditing purposes.

Jenkins supports a wide array of SCM systems through plugins. The most commonly used SCM with Jenkins is Git, which is ubiquitous in modern software development. Other supported systems include, but are not limited to, Subversion, Mercurial, Perforce, and CVS. This section will focus on the configuration of Git within Jenkins, while the principles can be adapted to other SCM systems with their respective plugins.

Step 1: Installing Git Plugin

First, ensure the Git plugin is installed in Jenkins. Navigate to Manage Jenkins → Manage Plugins → Available tab. Query for the Git Plugin and install it if not already present. The Git plugin provides Jenkins with the ability to clone repositories, retrieve changes, and trigger builds based on repository events.

Step 2: Configuring Global Git Settings

Once the plugin is installed, configure Jenkins to use the system's Git installation. This involves specifying the path to the Git executable and setting up credentials for accessing private repositories.

In the Jenkins dashboard, navigate to Manage Jenkins → Global Tool Configuration. Under the Git section, configure the following settings:

- **Git Installations**: Define the path to the local Git installation.

```
Path to Git executable: /usr/bin/git
```

- **Credentials**: Add valid credentials for accessing private repositories. This can be done through Jenkins' credentials management system.

Step 3: Setting Up SCM in a Jenkins Job

Next, configure the SCM for a specific Jenkins job. Create a new item (job) in Jenkins by clicking on New Item, give it a suitable name, and select Freestyle project. Once created, proceed to configure this job:

- **Source Code Management**: Under this section and select Git. Specify the repository URL and the branch to build.

```
Repository URL: https://github.com/username/repository.git
Branch Specifier (blank for 'any'): master
```

- **Credentials**: Use the credential added previously for accessing the repository.

Jenkins will create a workspace for this job and clone the specified branch into this directory on each build trigger.

Step 4: Advanced Options

Additionally, explore the advanced options for more granular control:

- **Name**: Allocate a name to identify this repository configuration.
- **Refspec**: Specify additional refspecs for more precise branch or tag selection.

```
+refs/heads/*:refs/remotes/origin/*
```

- **Shallow Clone**: Opt for a shallow clone if only recent history is required. This reduces network usage and speeds up clone time.

Step 5: Polling SCM for Changes

Automate builds by setting Jenkins to poll the SCM for changes. This can be done in the Build Triggers section:

- **Poll SCM**: Enable this and define a cron-style schedule for polling.

```
Schedule: H/5 * * * *
```

Jenkins will check for changes in the specified repository every 5 minutes in the example above, triggering a build if changes are detected.

Step 6: Hooks for Immediate Builds

For even more timely builds, configure Git hooks. When a commit is pushed to the repository, a post-commit hook can trigger Jenkins builds immediately. This requires configuring a webhook in the Git repository settings to notify Jenkins of changes.

Jenkins provides an endpoint for accepting webhook notifications:

```
http://your-jenkins-url.com/git/notifyCommit?url=<repository_url>
```

Add this webhook in the settings of the Git repository management platform (e.g., GitHub, GitLab).

Step 7: Checking Jenkins Job Status

It is essential to monitor the status of your Jenkins jobs to identify and resolve issues promptly. The job's status, along with detailed console output, can be accessed from the Jenkins dashboard. To view job outputs:

- Click on the specific job from the Jenkins dashboard.
- Click on a particular build number from the Build History view.
- Navigate to Console Output to see detailed logs.

Sample log from a successful Git checkout:

```
Started by user jenkins-user
Building in workspace /var/jenkins_home/workspace/my-project
using credential abc12345-6789-def0-1234-56789abcdef0
Cloning the remote Git repository
Cloning repository https://github.com/username/repository.git
 > git init /var/jenkins_home/workspace/my-project # timeout=10
Fetching upstream changes from https://github.com/username/repository.git
 > git fetch --tags --progress https://github.com/username/repository.git
 > +refs/heads/*:refs/remotes/origin/*
Checking out Revision 6b1c1b3fb15526e17ba3babd02e3c3f2f5f7758e (origin/master)
 > git checkout -f 6b1c1b3fb15526e17ba3babd02e3c3f2f5f7758e
Commit 6b1c1b3fb15526e17ba3babd02e3c3f2f5f7758e
 > git rev-list --no-walk 6b1c1b3fb15526e17ba3babd02e3c3f2f5f7758e # timeout=10
Finished: SUCCESS
```

Integration of SCM within Jenkins forms the backbone of Continuous Integration, as it allows automated processes to be initiated based on version-controlled changes. Proper configuration ensures a seamless flow from source code commits to automated builds and tests, facilitating rapid feedback and iterative development.

5.5 Building and Testing Code Changes

Once the source code management (SCM) integration is configured and operational, the next crucial step in the Continuous Integration (CI) process with Jenkins involves building and testing code changes. This section details the steps and best practices for configuring Jenkins to handle automated builds and tests efficiently.

The Jenkins job configuration for build and test cycles can be achieved through Freestyle Projects, Pipeline scripts, or Multibranch Pipelines. Each method has its specific advantages, depending on the project's requirements. This section demonstrates the setup using Jenkins Pipeline, which offers better scalability and maintainability.

Jenkinsfile Definition

A Jenkins Pipeline is defined using a Jenkinsfile. This file is typically stored in the root directory of the project's repository. It contains a domain-specific language (DSL) that models the entire CI/CD pipeline as code.

```
pipeline {
    agent any
    stages {
        stage('Build') {
            steps {
                echo 'Building...'
                // Insert build steps here
            }
        }
        stage('Test') {
            steps {
                echo 'Testing...'
                // Insert test steps here
            }
        }
    }
    post {
        success {
            echo 'The build and tests were successful.'
        }
        failure {
            echo 'The build or tests failed.'
        }
    }
}
```

In this example, the pipeline is composed of two stages: Build and Test. Each stage contains steps that are executed sequentially. The post section indicates actions to take based on the pipeline's success or failure.

Stage: Build

The Build stage is responsible for compiling the source code and producing build artifacts. This stage ensures that the code changes are integrated and built correctly. For example, in a Java project, the build step might involve invoking Maven or Gradle:

```
pipeline {
    agent any
    stages {
        stage('Build') {
            steps {
                script {
                    def mvnHome = tool 'M3'
                    sh "${mvnHome}/bin/mvn clean install"
                }
            }
        }
        // Other stages...
    }
    // Post actions...
}
```

The tool method specifies the Maven installation configured in Jenkins. The sh step executes the shell command to clean and install the Maven project.

Stage: Test

The Test stage ensures the integrity of the application by running automated tests. Automated tests can range from unit tests to integration tests and end-to-end tests. Here's an example using JUnit with Maven:

```
pipeline {
    agent any
    stages {
        stage('Build') {
            steps {
                script {
                    def mvnHome = tool 'M3'
                    sh "${mvnHome}/bin/mvn clean install"
                }
            }
        }
        stage('Test') {
            steps {
                script {
                    def mvnHome = tool 'M3'
                    sh "${mvnHome}/bin/mvn test"

                    junit '**/target/surefire-reports/*.xml'
                }
            }
        }
    }
    // Post actions...
}
```

In this stage, after executing the mvn test command, the junit step is used to archive JUnit test results using the wildcard pattern that matches the test report files. This enables Jenkins to present test reports and trends in the Jenkins UI.

Parallel Execution of Tests

To optimize the testing process, Jenkins allows parallel execution of tasks. For large projects with an extensive test suite, running tests in parallel can significantly reduce execution time.

```
pipeline {
    agent any
    stages {
        stage('Build') {
            steps {
                script {
                    def mvnHome = tool 'M3'
                    sh "${mvnHome}/bin/mvn clean install"
                }
            }
        }
        stage('Test') {
            parallel {
                stage('Unit Tests') {
                    steps {
                        script {
                            def mvnHome = tool 'M3'
                            sh "${mvnHome}/bin/mvn test -Dtest=*UnitTest"

                            junit '**/target/surefire-reports/*.xml'
                        }
                    }
                }
                stage('Integration Tests') {
                    steps {
                        script {
                            def mvnHome = tool 'M3'
                            sh "${mvnHome}/bin/mvn test -Dtest=*IntegrationTest"

                            junit '**/target/surefire-reports/*.xml'
                        }
                    }
                }
            }
        }
    }
    // Post actions...
}
```

Here, Unit Tests and Integration Tests are run in parallel, therefore reducing the overall time needed for test execution.

Environment Configuration

In some cases, specific environment configurations are required during the build or test stages. Jenkins provides mechanisms to set environment variables both globally and per stage.

```
pipeline {
    agent any
    environment {
        JAVA_HOME = "/usr/lib/jvm/java-11-openjdk"
        PATH = "${env.JAVA_HOME}/bin:${env.PATH}"
```

```
    }
    stages {
        stage('Build') {
            steps {
                script {
                    def mvnHome = tool 'M3'
                    sh "${mvnHome}/bin/mvn clean install"
                }
            }
        }
        stage('Test') {
            steps {
                script {
                    def mvnHome = tool 'M3'
                    sh "${mvnHome}/bin/mvn test"

                    junit '**/target/surefire-reports/*.xml'
                }
            }
        }
    }
    // Post actions...
}
```

In this setup, the JAVA_HOME and PATH environment variables are set for all stages within the pipeline.

By following these detailed steps and considering best practices, you can configure Jenkins to effectively build and test code changes, ensuring a robust and reliable CI process. This approach not only improves code quality through continuous feedback but also accelerates development by identifying integration issues early in the development cycle.

5.6 Automated Builds with Jenkins

Automated builds are a cornerstone of Continuous Integration (CI) that ensure consistency and reliability in the software development process. Jenkins, being a robust CI tool, provides extensive capabilities to automate the build process. This section delves into the configuration and execution of automated builds using Jenkins, focusing on various aspects including job configuration, build triggers, and build steps.

Automated build jobs in Jenkins can be configured via the Jenkins web interface. We start with creating a new job:

```
New Item -> Enter an item name -> Select 'Freestyle project' -> OK
```

In the newly created job configuration, settings are divided into several sections. The key sections include **General**, **Source Code Management**, **Build Triggers**, and **Build**. Each of these sections plays a vital role in defining how the build process will be conducted.

General Section: This section includes the basic settings of the job. Here, you can provide a brief description of what the job intends to accomplish. An example is shown below:

```
General -> Description -> "This job builds the master branch of the repository."
```

Source Code Management (SCM) Section: In this section, you integrate the job with your source code repository. Jenkins supports several SCM tools like Git, Subversion, and Mercurial. To configure Git, for instance, you have to specify the repository URL and the branch you want to build.

```
Source Code Management -> Git -> Repository URL -> "https://github.com/
    username/repo.git"
Source Code Management -> Git -> Branches to build -> master
```

Authentication and other configurations (such as SSH keys for private repositories) can also be specified in this section, ensuring secure access to the codebase.

Build Triggers Section: Build triggers define conditions under which the build job should start. Common triggers include polling the SCM, webhooks, scheduled builds, and builds triggered by other jobs. For example, to set up polling, which checks for changes in the repository periodically, you may use the following:

```
Build Triggers -> Poll SCM -> "H/5 * * * *"
```

The example above configures Jenkins to poll the SCM every 5 minutes.

Build Section: This is the heart of the automated build process. Here, you define the steps required to compile, test, and package your application. Jenkins supports multiple build steps like invoking shell scripts, executing batch commands, or running build tools such as Maven, Gradle, Ant, and others.

For a Maven project, a build step may look like this:

```
Build -> Add build step -> Invoke top-level Maven targets -> Goals -> "clean install"
```

To execute a shell script, you can add a shell build step:

```
Build -> Add build step -> Execute Shell -> Command -> "echo Building the project
    && mvn clean install"
```

Once the build steps are configured, Jenkins executes them in the order specified. Any output and errors generated during the build process are captured in the job's console output for later inspection.

Post-build Actions: After the build steps are executed, you might want to perform additional actions such as archiving the build artifacts, publishing JUnit test results, sending notifications, or even triggering other jobs. Archiving artifacts might look like:

```
Post-build Actions -> Archive the artifacts -> Files to archive -> "target/*.jar"
```

Incorporating notifications might involve setting up email notifications:

```
Post-build Actions -> E-mail Notification -> Recipients -> "developers@example.com"
```

Given this configuration, Jenkins will send an email to the specified recipients whenever a build completes, detailing the build status and providing links to the build logs and artifacts.

By combining and fine-tuning these elements, Jenkins enables a highly customizable automated build process that integrates seamlessly into the broader CI workflow, ensuring that code changes are continuously validated and that build automation is consistently maintained.

5.7 Managing Dependencies

Effective management of dependencies is crucial in a Continuous Integration (CI) workflow, ensuring that the builds are reliable, reproducible, and consistent across different environments. Jenkins, as a robust CI tool, allows for comprehensive handling of dependencies, integrating seamlessly with various dependency management systems.

Dependencies in software development refer to the external libraries, frameworks, and modules that a project requires to function correctly. Managing these dependencies involves specifying, fetching, and maintaining them across different environments such as development, testing, and production. Jenkins facilitates this through various plugins and tools, integrating with dependency management systems like Maven, Gradle, and npm.

Specifying Dependencies

In any CI setup, the first step toward managing dependencies is to specify them clearly. Each build tool has its way of defining dependencies:

- **Maven**: Dependencies are specified in the pom.xml file.

- **Gradle**: Dependencies are listed in the build.gradle file.
- **npm**: Dependencies are declared in the package.json file.

Here is an example of specifying dependencies in a Maven pom.xml file:

```
<dependencies>
    <dependency>
        <groupId>org.springframework</groupId>
        <artifactId>spring-core</artifactId>
        <version>5.3.9</version>
    </dependency>
    <dependency>
        <groupId>junit</groupId>
        <artifactId>junit</artifactId>
        <version>4.13.2</version>
        <scope>test</scope>
    </dependency>
</dependencies>
```

Fetching Dependencies

Once dependencies are specified, Jenkins handles fetching them during the build process. This process involves downloading the specified external libraries from repositories, such as Maven Central, npm registry, or custom repositories. Jenkins plugins for these build tools streamline this process.

A Jenkins job configured to use Maven, for example, can be set up to execute the following command:

```
mvn clean install
```

This command triggers Maven to clean the previous build outputs and install the project's dependencies, ensuring that all required libraries are available for the build process.

Maintaining Dependencies

Maintaining dependencies involves keeping them up-to-date, ensuring compatibility, and resolving conflicts. Jenkins supports various strategies to automate and simplify this maintenance:

- **Automated Updates**: Jenkins can be configured to periodically check for updates to dependencies and apply them automatically. Plugins like Versions Maven Plugin help in identifying and updating dependencies in Maven projects.
- **Dependency Management Tools**: Tools such as Dependabot can be integrated with Jenkins to automatically detect outdated

dependencies and create pull requests for updates, making it easier to manage dependency versions.

- **Dependency Analysis**: Jenkins can execute tools that analyze dependency graphs and detect conflicts or vulnerabilities. For instance, the OWASP Dependency-Check plugin identifies vulnerable dependencies within projects.

Scripted Jenkins pipelines further enhance the flexibility for managing dependencies, allowing more fine-grained control over these processes.

```
pipeline {
    agent any
    stages {
        stage('Build') {
            steps {
                // Fetch dependencies and build
                sh 'mvn clean install'
            }
        }
    }
    post {
        always {
            // Run dependency checks
            dependencyCheckAdditionalArguments = '--enableExperimental'
            dependencyCheckPublisher pattern: 'dependency-check-report.xml'
        }
    }
}
```

Handling Transitive Dependencies

Another critical aspect of managing dependencies is dealing with transitive dependencies. Transitive dependencies are the dependencies of your direct dependencies, which can lead to complex dependency trees. Tools like Maven and Gradle manage these transitive dependencies internally, resolving and fetching them as needed.

For instance, in Maven, if a project A depends on B, and B depends on C, Maven will automatically include C when resolving A's dependencies. Below is a snippet demonstrating a transitive dependency scenario:

```
<dependency>
    <groupId>com.example</groupId>
    <artifactId>example-utils</artifactId>
    <version>1.0.0</version>
    <exclusions>
        <!-- Exclude a specific transitive dependency -->
        <exclusion>
            <groupId>com.fasterxml.jackson.core</groupId>
            <artifactId>jackson-databind</artifactId>
        </exclusion>
    </exclusions>
```

```
</dependency>
```

In the example, the example-utils dependency includes a transitive dependency on jackson-databind, which is excluded to avoid conflicts with a different version required by the project.

Caching Dependencies

Efficient CI environments leverage caching mechanisms to reduce build times and improve reliability. Jenkins provides several strategies for caching dependencies, preventing repetitive downloads and ensuring faster builds.

- **Local Repository Caching**: Tools like Maven and npm maintain local caches of downloaded dependencies, reducing network overhead for future builds.

- **Remote Caching**: Jenkins can be configured to use remote caches, such as shared network locations or artifact repositories like Nexus or Artifactory.

- **Pipeline Caching**: Using the Jenkins Pipeline build script, cache dependency directories between builds to avoid re-downloading. For instance, with npm dependencies:

```
pipeline {
    agent any
    stages {
        stage('Install Dependencies') {
            steps {
                script {
                    if (fileExists('node_modules')) {
                        echo 'Using cached node_modules'
                    } else {
                        sh 'npm install'
                    }
                }
            }
        }
    }
}
```

By efficiently managing dependencies through tools and strategies outlined here, Jenkins ensures that the CI process remains robust, scalable, and efficient, ultimately contributing to higher software quality and more streamlined development workflows.

5.8 Code Quality Analysis

Code quality analysis is an essential aspect of Continuous Integration (CI), aiming to ensure that the codebase adheres to defined coding standards and is free from common issues such as bugs, security vulnerabilities, and maintainability problems. Jenkins, with its extensive plugin ecosystem, facilitates the integration of various code quality tools that provide actionable insights into the code's health.

Integrating Static Code Analysis Tools

Static Code Analysis (SCA) tools analyze the source code without executing it, identifying potential issues early in the development cycle. Jenkins supports several SCA tools such as Checkstyle, PMD, and SpotBugs through dedicated plugins.

To use Checkstyle with Jenkins:

1. Install the Checkstyle plugin from the Jenkins plugin management interface.
2. Configure your project's build script (such as Maven's pom.xml or Gradle's build.gradle) to include Checkstyle.
3. Define a Checkstyle rules configuration file (checkstyle.xml) to specify the coding standards.
4. In the Jenkins interface, configure the build job to run Checkstyle and publish the analysis results.

Here's an example configuration snippet for Maven's pom.xml to integrate Checkstyle:

```
<project>
    ...
    <build>
        <plugins>
            ...
            <plugin>
                <groupId>org.apache.maven.plugins</groupId>
                <artifactId>maven-checkstyle-plugin</artifactId>
                <version>3.1.2</version>
                <configuration>
                    <configLocation>checkstyle.xml</configLocation>
                </configuration>
                <executions>
                    <execution>
                        <phase>verify</phase>
                        <goals>
                            <goal>check</goal>
                        </goals>
```

```
                </execution>
            </executions>
        </plugin>
    </plugins>
  </build>
</project>
```

Integrating Dynamic Code Analysis Tools

Dynamic Code Analysis (DCA) tools analyze the application at runtime, providing insights into code behavior under various conditions. Tools such as JaCoCo and JUnit for Java projects are commonly used.

To integrate JaCoCo for code coverage analysis:

1. Install the JaCoCo plugin in Jenkins.

2. Configure your project's build script (e.g., Maven or Gradle) to generate JaCoCo reports.

3. Set up the Jenkins job to collect and visualize JaCoCo reports.

Below is a sample configuration snippet for Maven's pom.xml to use JaCoCo:

```
<project>
    ...
    <build>
        <plugins>
            ...
            <plugin>
                <groupId>org.jacoco</groupId>
                <artifactId>jacoco-maven-plugin</artifactId>
                <version>0.8.7</version>
                <executions>
                    <execution>
                        <goals>
                            <goal>prepare-agent</goal>
                        </goals>
                    </execution>
                    <execution>
                        <id>report</id>
                        <phase>verify</phase>
                        <goals>
                            <goal>report</goal>
                        </goals>
                    </execution>
                </executions>
            </plugin>
        </plugins>
    </build>
</project>
```

Configuration in Jenkins Pipeline

For Jenkins Pipeline, integrating code quality tools requires defining specific stages in the Jenkinsfile. Here's an example of configuring Checkstyle and JaCoCo in a declarative pipeline:

```
pipeline {
    agent any
    tools {
        maven 'Maven_3.6.3'
        jdk 'JDK_11'
    }
    stages {
        stage('Checkout') {
            steps {
                checkout scm
            }
        }
        stage('Build') {
            steps {
                sh 'mvn clean install'
            }
        }
        stage('Code Quality - Checkstyle') {
            steps {
                sh 'mvn checkstyle:check'
            }
            post {
                always {
                    checkstyle pattern: '**/target/checkstyle-result.xml'
                }
            }
        }
        stage('Code Coverage - JaCoCo') {
            steps {
                sh 'mvn test'
            }
            post {
                always {
                    jacoco execPattern: 'target/jacoco.exec'
                }
            }
        }
    }
    post {
        always {
            archiveArtifacts artifacts: '**/target/*.jar', fingerprint: true
            junit 'target/surefire-reports/*.xml'
        }
    }
}
```

Interpreting Results and Taking Action

Once the analysis is configured and executed, Jenkins will display the results in the build report. It is crucial to interpret these results to identify areas for improvement:

- **Warnings and Errors**: Look for patterns in the warnings and errors reported. Common issues should lead to updates in the project's coding standards or additional training for the team.

- **Coverage Reports**: Ensure the code coverage meets the defined thresholds. Low coverage may necessitate writing additional tests.

- **Trend Analysis**: Use Jenkins to track trends over time, allowing you to observe the impact of recent changes on code quality.

By systematically incorporating these analysis tools into Jenkins, the development team can preemptively address potential issues, resulting in a more robust and maintainable codebase.

5.9 Configuring Notifications and Reports

Configuring notifications and reports in Jenkins is critical for maintaining awareness of the build status and ensuring that all stakeholders are informed about the software's state. This section delves into the configuration of notifications using various methods and generating reports to consolidate essential build information.

Notifications

Jenkins provides several plugins to manage notifications effectively. Common notification methods include email notifications, Slack messages, and integrations with other communication tools. The primary goal is to ensure that developers and relevant stakeholders receive timely alerts about build successes, failures, and other significant events.

To configure email notifications in Jenkins:

1. Ensure the Email Extension Plugin is installed.

2. Navigate to **Manage Jenkins** → **Configure System**.

3. Scroll to the **Extended E-mail Notification** section and configure the necessary SMTP server details:

```
SMTP server: smtp.example.com
Default user e-mail suffix: @example.com
Sender e-mail address: no-reply@example.com
```

4. In the project configuration, under the **Post-build Actions** section, select **Editable Email Notification**. Configure the recipients, subject, and content of the email. You can use tokens to dynamically insert build information:

```
Recipients: developer@example.com
Subject: Build $JOB_NAME - Build # $BUILD_NUMBER -
    $BUILD_STATUS!
Content: Build %JOB_NAME% %BUILD_NUMBER% completed with status
    %BUILD_STATUS%.
(Check console output at %BUILD_URL% to view the results.)
```

For more advanced email configurations, the Email Extension Plugin allows for detailed templates and trigger settings, ensuring that notifications can be tailored to specific stages or conditions within the CI process.

To configure Slack notifications, the Slack Notification Plugin can be utilized:

1. Install the Slack Notification Plugin.
2. Navigate to **Manage Jenkins** → **Configure System** and locate the **Globally Slack Notifier Settings**.
3. Fill in the required integration token and Slack channel information:

```
Team subdomain: yourteam
Integration token: xoxp-0123456789-0123456789012345
Channel: #build-notifications
```

4. In the project configuration, add a **Slack Notifications** post-build action. Customize the settings as needed to specify when notifications should be sent (e.g., on success, failure, or always).

Reports

Generating and viewing reports in Jenkins provides insights into the build process, test results, code quality, and other metrics that are crucial for maintaining and improving software quality.

Jenkins supports various reporting tools and plugins, such as JUnit, JaCoCo, Cobertura, and Checkstyle. Below, we provide examples of setting up some common report types:

JUnit Test Reports

JUnit is a widely used testing framework for Java. To integrate JUnit test reports:

1. Add a step in your build process to run your JUnit tests, typically via a Maven or Gradle build script. The following is an example Maven command:

```
mvn test
```

2. In the project configuration, under **Post-build Actions**, add a **Publish JUnit test result report** action.

3. Specify the path to the test result XML files, usually **/target/surefire-reports/ .xml for Maven projects.

This configuration will parse the test result files and display results on the Jenkins job's webpage, allowing users to see which tests passed or failed.

Code Coverage Reports with JaCoCo

JaCoCo is a popular code coverage library for Java. To generate and visualize coverage reports:

1. Add JaCoCo to your build process. For Maven, include the JaCoCo plugin in your pom.xml:

```
<build>
    <plugins>
        <plugin>
            <groupId>org.jacoco</groupId>
            <artifactId>jacoco-maven-plugin</artifactId>
            <version>0.8.5</version>
            <executions>
                <execution>
                    <goals>
                        <goal>prepare-agent</goal>
                    </goals>
                </execution>
                <execution>
                    <id>report</id>
                    <phase>test</phase>
                    <goals>
                        <goal>report</goal>
                    </goals>
                </execution>
            </executions>
        </plugin>
    </plugins>
</build>
```

2. After running the build, configure Jenkins to process these reports. Under **Post-build Actions**, add a **Record JaCoCo coverage report** action.

3. Specify the path to the generated JaCoCo reports, typically **/target/site/jacoco/*.xml.

Jenkins will generate visual reports showing coverage percentages and highlighting untested code areas.

Static Code Analysis Reports with Checkstyle

Checkstyle helps maintain coding standards by analyzing code and reporting deviations. To generate Checkstyle reports:

1. Integrate Checkstyle into your build process. For Maven, add Checkstyle plugin configuration in your pom.xml:

```
<build>
    <plugins>
        <plugin>
            <groupId>org.apache.maven.plugins</groupId>
            <artifactId>maven-checkstyle-plugin</artifactId>
            <version>3.1.1</version>
            <executions>
                <execution>
                    <phase>verify</phase>
                    <goals>
                        <goal>check</goal>
                    </goals>
                </execution>
            </executions>
            <configuration>
                <configLocation>checkstyle.xml</configLocation>
                <encoding>UTF-8</encoding>
            </configuration>
        </plugin>
    </plugins>
</build>
```

2. In the project configuration, under **Post-build Actions**, add a **Publish Checkstyle analysis results** action.

3. Specify the path to the Checkstyle result XML files, typically **/target/checkstyle-result.xml.

Jenkins will present the results with detailed information about violations, helping developers to adhere to the project's coding standards.

Integration of notifications and reports in Jenkins plays a crucial role in facilitating rapid feedback loops and maintaining high code quality.

These configurations ensure that the relevant information is promptly conveyed to stakeholders, empowering informed decision-making and fostering a collaborative development environment. With these tools and techniques, Jenkins acts as an effective CI tool that not only automates builds but also enhances visibility and traceability of the project's progress.

5.10 Dealing with Build Failures

In the context of Continuous Integration (CI) with Jenkins, handling build failures efficiently is crucial for maintaining the health and reliability of the software development lifecycle. This section addresses common causes of build failures, methods to diagnose and fix them, and strategies to minimize their occurrence in future builds.

A build failure happens when the automated build process in Jenkins does not complete successfully. This could be due to a variety of reasons, including but not limited to, compilation errors, test failures, missing dependencies, or configuration issues. To effectively address build failures, follow these steps:

- **Identify the Cause**: The first step is to determine the cause of the build failure. Jenkins provides extensive logs and console outputs that can help identify where the process went wrong.
- **Analyze the Logs**: The console output of the Jenkins build is often the most direct source of information. Reviewing these logs will provide insight into the specific errors and warnings that occurred during the build.
- **Fix the Issues**: Depending on the nature of the issue, fix the underlying problem. This could involve correcting a syntax error, updating a testing script, resolving dependency conflicts, or modifying build configurations.
- **Rebuild**: Once the issues have been fixed, trigger a new build in Jenkins to verify whether the issues have been resolved.

For practical understanding, consider the following example where a build failure occurred due to a missing dependency.

```
[INFO] BUILD FAILURE
[INFO] ------------------------------------------------------------------------
```

```
[INFO] Total time: 2.401 s
[INFO] Finished at: 2023-10-10T13:08:23Z
[INFO] ------------------------------------------------------------------------
[ERROR] Failed to execute goal on project MyApp: Could not resolve dependencies for
    project com.example:MyApp:jar:1.0-SNAPSHOT: Could not find artifact com.
    library:Library:jar:1.2.3 in central (https://repo.maven.apache.org/maven2) -> [
    Help 1]
[ERROR]
[ERROR] To see the full stack trace of the errors, re-run Maven with the -e switch.
[ERROR] Re-run Maven using the -X switch to enable full debug logging.
[ERROR]
[ERROR] For more information about the errors and possible solutions, please read the
    following articles:
[ERROR] [Help 1] http://cwiki.apache.org/confluence/display/MAVEN/
    DependencyResolutionException
```

In this output, the error clearly indicates that the build failed because a required dependency was not found. The solution involves adding the missing dependency to the project's dependency management system, for example, by updating the ‘pom.xml‘ file in a Maven project.

```
<dependency>
    <groupId>com.library</groupId>
    <artifactId>Library</artifactId>
    <version>1.2.3</version>
</dependency>
```

After updating the ‘pom.xml‘ file, commit the changes to the source code repository, and then trigger a new build in Jenkins.

Another common scenario is test failures. Unit tests and integration tests are essential aspects of CI that ensure code changes do not introduce new defects. When a test fails, it is crucial to investigate the root cause.

Consider a trivial JUnit test failure example.

```
[INFO] Results:
[INFO]
[INFO] Failures:
[INFO] CalculatorTest.testAddition:23 expected:<4> but was:<5>
[INFO]
[ERROR] Tests run: 1, Failures: 1, Errors: 0, Skipped: 0
```

In this case, the ‘CalculatorTest‘ failed because the addition method did not return the expected result. The relevant code snippet might look like this:

```
public class CalculatorTest {
    @Test
    public void testAddition() {
        Calculator calc = new Calculator();
        int result = calc.add(2, 2);
        assertEquals(4, result);
    }
```

```
}
```

To fix this, the 'Calculator' class needs to be corrected:

```
public class Calculator {
    public int add(int a, int b) {
        return a + b;
    }
}
```

Once the code changes are made, commit and push them to the repository, then rebuild the project in Jenkins to ensure the tests pass.

To minimize the occurrence of build failures, adopt the following best practices:

- **Pre-Commit Hooks**: Use pre-commit hooks to run basic checks and tests before allowing changes to be committed to the repository. This can catch errors early in the development cycle.
- **Incremental Builds**: Configure Jenkins to trigger builds incrementally for smaller units of code changes. This not only reduces the build time but also makes it easier to isolate and fix issues.
- **Continuous Feedback**: Integrate continuous feedback mechanisms where developers are immediately notified whenever a build fails. Immediate awareness can prompt quicker resolution of issues.
- **Automate Dependency Management**: Ensure that dependency management is automated and up-to-date. Tools like Dependabot or Renovate can be integrated with Jenkins to keep dependencies current.

By following these steps and best practices, the occurrence and impact of build failures can be significantly reduced, ensuring a smoother and more reliable continuous integration process with Jenkins.

5.11 CI/CD Pipeline Integration

Continuous Integration (CI) and Continuous Deployment/Delivery (CD) form the backbone of modern software development practices. Integrating CI/CD pipelines in Jenkins streamlines the processes of developing, testing, and deploying applications, which enhances software quality and accelerates feature delivery.

A CI/CD pipeline is a sequence of processes that automates the delivery of software, ensuring that changes to code are automatically tested and deployed to production environments. Jenkins, as a flexible automation server, is perfectly suited to manage these pipelines.

To start building a CI/CD pipeline, it is essential to understand the key stages involved:

- **Source Code Management (SCM)**: This is the version control system where the source code resides. Examples include Git, Subversion, or Mercurial. Jenkins can integrate seamlessly with these systems to pull the latest changes.
- **Build**: This stage involves compiling the source code into executable artifacts. It may also include running scripts to package the application in a deployable format, such as JAR, WAR, or Docker images.
- **Test**: Automated tests are executed to verify the integrity of the build. This can include unit tests, integration tests, and acceptance tests.
- **Deploy**: The application is deployed to a staging or production environment. Deployment can be configured to be automatic once the tests pass or manual to provide controlled releases.
- **Monitor**: Post-deployment monitoring ensures that the application performs as expected in the production environment.

Creating a CI/CD Pipeline in Jenkins

To integrate a CI/CD pipeline in Jenkins, follow these steps:

1. **Install Jenkins**: Ensure that Jenkins is installed and running on a server. Install required plugins such as Git, Pipeline, and Docker if your application uses containerization.

2. **Create a Jenkins Pipeline Project**:

```
Go to Jenkins Dashboard > New Item > Pipeline > OK.
```

3. **Define the Pipeline Script**:

Jenkins pipelines can be defined using a domain-specific language (DSL) known as Jenkinsfile. This file is written in Groovy and resides in the root directory of the source code repository. Below is a sample Jenkinsfile for a basic CI/CD pipeline:

```
pipeline {
    agent any

    stages {
        stage('Checkout') {
            steps {
                git 'https://github.com/your-repo.git'
            }
        }

        stage('Build') {
            steps {
                sh 'mvn clean install'
            }
        }

        stage('Test') {
            steps {
                sh 'mvn test'
            }
            post {
                always {
                    junit '**/target/surefire-reports/*.xml'
                }
            }
        }

        stage('Deploy') {
            steps {
                sh 'scp target/my-app.jar user@server:/deploy/path/'
            }
        }
    }

    post {
        success {
            slackSend (channel: '#ci-cd', message: "Build and Deploy successful for $
                {env.BUILD_NUMBER}")
        }
        failure {
            slackSend (channel: '#ci-cd', message: "Build failed for ${env.
                BUILD_NUMBER}")
        }
    }
}
```

4. **Configure Post-Build Actions**:

Jenkins can send notifications upon build completion. Tools like Slack or email can be used to notify the team. As seen in the example above, the 'post' section in the Jenkinsfile is used to send notifications based on the build status.

5. **Triggering the Pipeline**:

Configure triggers to automate the pipeline. Jenkins supports various triggers such as SCM changes, scheduled builds, and others. For example, adding SCM polling:

Go to Jenkins Dashboard > Your Pipeline > Configure > Build Triggers > Poll SCM > Schedule

Use a cron format to set the polling frequency. For example, 'H/5 * * * *' polls the SCM every 5 minutes.

Alternatively, you can use a webhook to trigger Jenkins on each commit:

- In GitHub: Go to Settings > Webhooks > Add webhook, and set the Payload URL to your Jenkins build URL.

Integrating Additional Tools

Enhance your CI/CD pipeline by integrating additional tools:

- **Code Quality Tools**: Integrate tools such as SonarQube to perform static code analysis. Add a stage in your Jenkinsfile to execute SonarQube analysis.

```
stage('Code Quality') {
    steps {
        sh 'mvn sonar:sonar'
    }
}
```

- **Containerization**: Use Docker to containerize your application. Ensure Docker is installed on Jenkins agents, and add a stage to build and push the Docker image.

```
stage('Build Docker Image') {
    steps {
        sh 'docker build -t your-image-name .'
        sh 'docker push your-image-name'
    }
}
```

- **Deployment Tools**: Use tools like Kubernetes or Ansible for deployments. Add stages in your Jenkinsfile to deploy to these platforms.

```
stage('Deploy to Kubernetes') {
    steps {
        sh 'kubectl apply -f k8s/deployment.yaml'
    }
}
```

Effective CI/CD pipeline integration in Jenkins promotes automation, enhances software quality, and accelerates the deployment process. The seamless orchestration of code building, testing, and deployment reduces manual intervention, ultimately leading to higher efficiency and more robust software solutions.

5.12 Best Practices for Continuous Integration

Ensuring an effective Continuous Integration (CI) process with Jenkins requires adherence to several best practices that enhance reliability, maintainability, and efficiency. This section consolidates these practices, derived from extensive industry experience and academic research.

1. Maintain a Reliable Source Code Repository

The foundation of a successful CI process lies in a robust Source Code Management (SCM) system. All source code, build scripts, and configuration files should be maintained in a version-controlled repository. Tools like Git, Subversion, or Mercurial are commonly used.

2. Automate Builds and Tests

Automating the build and test process is critical. Jenkins allows for the automation of these tasks through pipelines, freeing developers from manual build/test execution. The following script demonstrates a basic Jenkins pipeline setup:

```
pipeline {
    agent any
    stages {
        stage('Build') {
            steps {
                sh 'make build'
            }
        }
        stage('Test') {
            steps {
                sh 'make test'
            }
        }
    }
}
```

3. Build Every Commit

Integrate code frequently, at least daily. Every commit should trigger a build to ensure that integration issues are detected early. This practice is facilitated by configuring webhooks in the SCM system to notify Jenkins of new commits:

```
pipeline {
    agent any
    triggers {
        pollSCM('* * * * *')
    }
```

```
    stages {
        stage('Build and Test') {
            steps {
                sh 'make build'
                sh 'make test'
            }
        }
    }
}
```

4. Maintain a Clean Build Environment

Isolating the build environment prevents inconsistencies due to local system differences. Using Docker containers or virtual machines to replicate a clean, consistent environment ensures that builds are reliable. An example of a Jenkins job configuration using Docker is shown below:

```
pipeline {
    agent {
        docker {
            image 'maven:3.6.3-jdk-8'
        }
    }
    stages {
        stage('Build') {
            steps {
                sh 'mvn clean install'
            }
        }
    }
}
```

5. Fast Feedback Mechanism

Rapid feedback is essential to minimize the time developers spend on debugging. Ensure that build and test cycles are quick and efficient. Parallelizing tests and using lightweight static analysis tools can significantly reduce feedback time:

```
pipeline {
    agent any
    stages {
        stage('Build') {
            steps {
                sh 'make build'
            }
        }
        stage('Parallel Tests') {
            parallel {
                stage('Unit Tests') {
                    steps {
                        sh 'make test-unit'
                    }
                }
                stage('Integration Tests') {
                    steps {
```

```
                    sh 'make test-integration'
                }
            }
        }
    }
}
```

6. Continuous Code Quality Checks

Incorporate static analysis, linting, and other code quality checks into the CI pipeline to ensure code quality. Jenkins has plugins like SonarQube and Checkstyle that integrate seamlessly for this purpose. Setting up a SonarQube analysis in Jenkins:

```
pipeline {
    agent any
    stages {
        stage('Build') {
            steps {
                sh 'mvn clean install'
            }
        }
        stage('Code Quality Analysis') {
            steps {
                withSonarQubeEnv('SonarQube') {
                    sh 'mvn sonar:sonar'
                }
            }
        }
    }
}
```

7. Display and Analyze Metrics

Visualize build and test results. Jenkins provides dashboards and plugins for monitoring metrics. Utilizing plugins like the Blue Ocean plugin, developers can get a comprehensive view of the CI pipeline status.

8. Implement Robust Error Handling

Finally, handling build and test failures systematically is crucial. Configure notifications for failures and ensure logs are easily accessible. Using Jenkins' email-ext plugin, configure email notifications upon failure:

```
pipeline {
    agent any
    stages {
        stage('Build') {
            steps {
                sh 'make build'
            }
        }
        stage('Test') {
            steps {
```

```
                sh 'make test'
            }
        }
    }
    post {
        failure {
            mail to: 'developer@example.com',
                subject: "Build failed in Jenkins: ${env.JOB_NAME}",
                body: "Please check the Jenkins build logs for ${env.BUILD_URL}"
        }
    }
}
```

By adhering to these practices, Jenkins-based CI implementations can be both effective and efficient, ensuring high-quality software delivery.

Chapter 6

Continuous Delivery (CD) with Jenkins

This chapter outlines the principles and implementation of Continuous Delivery (CD) with Jenkins. It covers setting up CD pipelines, deploying applications, and managing different environments. Key topics include release management, automating infrastructure provisioning, rollback and recovery strategies, and measuring the effectiveness of CD processes. The chapter also addresses security within CD pipelines and presents best practices to ensure reliable and efficient software delivery.

6.1 Introduction to Continuous Delivery

Continuous Delivery (CD) represents a software development practice wherein code changes are automatically prepared for release to production. It builds on the foundation of Continuous Integration (CI), which ensures that code changes are continuously integrated into a shared repository. CD extends CI by automating the release process, ensuring that each change to the software is releasable.

The primary goal of Continuous Delivery is to enable a constant flow of changes into production through an automated deployment pipeline, while maintaining stability and reliability. This practice allows teams to deliver software faster and with fewer risks.

The essence of CD lies in the automation and orchestration of all steps in the software delivery process, from code integration, build and test automations, to final deployments. Below, we delve into the critical components and practices that form the basis of Continuous Delivery.

Automation of Build and Testing

The cornerstone of CD is the automated build process. Whenever changes are pushed to the version control system, CI tools like Jenkins are triggered to initiate the build process. This process includes compiling the code, running automated tests, and generating artifacts such as executables or deployment packages. Automating builds ensures that each integration and code merge is validated immediately, preventing integration issues from propagating.

Automated testing is equally crucial in CD pipelines. Tests are categorized into different levels, including unit tests, integration tests, and acceptance tests. Unit tests validate individual components, integration tests ensure that components work together as intended, and acceptance tests verify the overall system functionality against specified requirements. By automating these tests and embedding them into the deployment pipeline, it is possible to detect defects early in the cycle, ensuring the health of the codebase.

Deployment Pipeline

A deployment pipeline is an automated manifestation of the process through which software is delivered. It incorporates all steps required to get a developer's changes into production, including commit, build, test, staging, and deployment.

In the context of Jenkins, a pipeline is configured using either the Jenkins Pipeline DSL (Domain Specific Language) or through the Blue Ocean interface. A simple Jenkins pipeline script might look like this:

```
pipeline {
    agent any
    stages {
        stage('Build') {
            steps {
                sh 'mvn clean package'
            }
        }
        stage('Test') {
            steps {
                sh 'mvn test'
            }
        }
        stage('Deploy') {
            steps {
                sh 'mvn deploy'
```

```
            }
        }
    }
}
```

This example represents a linear sequence of stages that execute the build, test, and deployment steps. In practice, pipelines can be more complex, incorporating parallel stages, conditional actions, and manual approvals.

Version Control and Configuration Management

Central to Continuous Delivery is the use of a robust version control system (VCS) such as Git. Every commit to the repository should be deployable. Branching strategies are often employed to manage feature development, releases, and hotfixes. Feature branches allow developers to work on new functionality without affecting the main branch, while the main branch (often referred to as 'main' or 'master') remains in a deployable state.

Configuration management involves maintaining the consistency and traceability of the software configuration. Tools like Ansible, Puppet, or Chef are used to automate the provisioning and configuration of environments, ensuring that deployments are predictable and repeatable. By keeping configuration data in version control, it is possible to manage different environments consistently and rollback to previous states if necessary.

Monitoring and Feedback

To ensure the effectiveness of CD processes, continuous monitoring and feedback are crucial. Implementing tools for monitoring application performance, logging errors, and tracking system metrics allows teams to proactively address issues and maintain high levels of quality in production.

Moreover, integrating feedback mechanisms into the pipeline helps in real-time detection and resolution of issues. For instance, if a deployment causes a performance regression, the monitoring tools can alert the team, enabling immediate investigation and remediation.

Deployment Strategies

Continuous Delivery supports various deployment strategies, each suited to different contexts and risk profiles. Some of the commonly used strategies include:

- **Blue-Green Deployment**: Involves having two identical production environments, Blue and Green. Traffic is routed to the Blue environment while new changes are deployed to the Green environment. Once the deployment is validated, traffic is switched to Green, and Blue is retained as a backup.

- **Canary Releases**: A small subset of users is directed to the new version of the application to ensure it works as expected before rolling it out to the entire user base.
- **Rolling Updates**: Gradually updates instances of the application to the new version, ensuring that the system remains available.

By understanding and implementing these strategies appropriately, teams can achieve zero-downtime deployments and reduce the impact of changes.

Understanding the fundamental principles and components of Continuous Delivery equips teams with the necessary tools and practices to accelerate their software delivery processes, improve quality, and ensure that their software is always in a releasable state.

6.2 The Role of Jenkins in CD

Jenkins, as an open-source automation server, plays a pivotal role in Continuous Delivery (CD) by facilitating the automation of various stages in the software delivery lifecycle. This section examines the integral functions Jenkins performs in a CD pipeline, focusing on its capabilities that streamline the delivery of software from code commit to deployment in production environments. Jenkins enables teams to adopt CD practices effectively by providing a robust, extensible platform that supports a wide variety of tools and technologies.

At the core of Jenkins' role in CD is its ability to automate repetitive tasks, reducing the manual overhead involved in building, testing, and deploying applications. By defining a series of stages and steps that make up a delivery pipeline, Jenkins can reliably execute these tasks upon triggering events such as code commits, scheduled builds, or manual interventions.

Pipeline as Code

One of the fundamental features Jenkins offers for Continuous Delivery is the concept of "Pipeline as Code." This is typically implemented using Jenkins Pipeline, a suite of plugins that support implementing and integrating continuous delivery pipelines into Jenkins. Pipelines are defined using a Domain-Specific Language (DSL) based on Groovy, which allows developers to write code that describes the entire build process.

An example of a simple Jenkinsfile for a CD pipeline might look like this:

```
pipeline {
    agent any
    stages {
        stage('Build') {
            steps {
                sh 'mvn clean install'
            }
        }
        stage('Test') {
            steps {
                sh 'mvn test'
            }
        }
        stage('Deploy') {
            steps {
                sh 'mvn deploy'
            }
        }
    }
    post {
        always {
            archiveArtifacts artifacts: '**/target/*.jar', allowEmptyArchive: true
        }
        success {
            mail to: 'team@example.com',
                 subject: "Build Successful",
                 body: "The build was successful."
        }
        failure {
            mail to: 'team@example.com',
                 subject: "Build Failed",
                 body: "The build failed."
        }
    }
}
```

This Jenkinsfile defines a pipeline that consists of three stages: *Build*, *Test*, and *Deploy*. Each stage uses Maven commands to perform its respective tasks. The *post* section specifies actions that should occur regardless of the build result (e.g., archiving artifacts) and conditional notifications based on the build outcome.

Integration with Version Control

Jenkins integrates seamlessly with various version control systems (VCS) such as Git, Subversion, Mercurial, and others. This integration is crucial for CD as it allows Jenkins to automatically trigger pipeline executions based on changes detected in the source code repositories.

This is typically configured using webhooks or polling mechanisms.

To set up a Jenkins job to trigger on Git commits, you can configure the Git plugin in the Jenkins job configuration, specifying the repository URL and branch to monitor. For example:

```
pipeline {
    agent any
    triggers {
        scm('H/5 * * * *') // Polls the repository every 5 minutes
    }
    stages {
        stage('Build') {
            steps {
                git url: 'https://github.com/example/repo.git', branch: 'main'
                sh 'mvn clean install'
            }
        }
    }
}
```

In this example, the pipeline is configured to poll the specified Git repository every 5 minutes, and trigger the pipeline if any changes are detected. This ensures that the pipeline is always executing against the latest code in the repository.

Automated Testing

Testing is a critical component of any CD pipeline, and Jenkins provides extensive support for integrating automated tests. Jenkins can run unit tests, integration tests, and other automated tests, collecting results and generating reports. Plugins are available for common testing frameworks such as JUnit, TestNG, Selenium, and many others.

For instance, to integrate JUnit test results into a Jenkins pipeline:

```
pipeline {
    agent any
    stages {
        stage('Build') {
            steps {
                sh 'mvn clean install'
            }
        }
        stage('Test') {
            steps {
                sh 'mvn test'
                junit '**/target/surefire-reports/*.xml'
            }
        }
    }
}
```

Here, after executing the Maven command 'mvn test', the 'junit' step gathers the test results from the specified location and publishes them within Jenkins. This allows developers to easily view test outcomes directly within the Jenkins interface, facilitating rapid identification and resolution of issues.

Environment Management

Managing different environments (e.g., development, staging, production) is essential in CD pipelines. Jenkins supports environment-specific configurations and deployments, enabling seamless transitions across environments. This is often achieved using configuration files, environment variables, and parameterized builds.

For example, a pipeline that deploys to different environments might look like this:

```
pipeline {
    agent any
    parameters {
        choice(name: 'ENV', choices: ['dev', 'staging', 'prod'], description: 'Select
              environment')
    }
    stages {
        stage('Build') {
            steps {
                sh 'mvn clean install'
            }
        }
        stage('Deploy') {
            steps {
                script {
                    if (params.ENV == 'dev') {
                        sh 'mvn deploy -Pdev'
                    } else if (params.ENV == 'staging') {
                        sh 'mvn deploy -Pstaging'
                    } else if (params.ENV == 'prod') {
                        sh 'mvn deploy -Pprod'
                    }
                }
            }
        }
    }
}
```

In this pipeline, the 'parameters' block defines a choice parameter, providing options for different environments. The deployment stage then uses a conditional statement to execute the appropriate deployment command based on the selected environment.

Extensibility with Plugins

Jenkins' extensibility is one of its strongest assets, achieved through a rich ecosystem of plugins. These plugins extend Jenkins' core functionality, adding support for various tools, technologies, and integrations. Examples include Docker plugins for containerized builds, Kubernetes plugins for orchestrating builds within K8s clusters, and many others.

To illustrate, consider using the Docker plugin to run builds inside a Docker container:

```
pipeline {
    agent {
        docker {
            image 'maven:3.6.3-jdk-8'
            args '-v /root/.m2:/root/.m2'
        }
    }
    stages {
        stage('Build') {
            steps {
                sh 'mvn clean install'
            }
        }
    }
}
```

In this example, the 'agent' block specifies a Docker container to run the build steps. The 'image' parameter defines the Docker image to use, and 'args' provide additional arguments; in this case, mounting a volume for Maven's local repository to cache dependencies between builds.

By leveraging these features and integrations, Jenkins serves as a comprehensive tool for implementing CD practices. Its ability to automate, orchestrate, and monitor the entire software delivery process makes it indispensable for teams aiming to achieve continuous and efficient software delivery.

6.3 Setting Up CD in Jenkins

To facilitate the implementation of Continuous Delivery (CD) with Jenkins, certain foundational steps and configurations must be addressed meticulously. This section will delineate the process to establish a robust CD pipeline in Jenkins through methodical configuration, optimal use of available plugins, and proper integration with version control and other essential services.

Install the Necessary Jenkins Plugins

Jenkins' extensibility via plugins is a core strength. For a CD pipeline, the following plugins are indispensable:

- **Pipeline**: Enables defining pipeline jobs using a domain-specific language for defining workflows.

- **Git**: Integrates Jenkins with Git-based source control systems.
- **GitHub**: Enhances interaction with GitHub repositories, useful for webhooks and repository scanning.
- **AnsiColor**: Ensures colored console output for clearer readability of logs.
- **Publish Over SSH**: Facilitates transferring build artifacts and executing remote commands over SSH.
- **Email Extension**: Allows for configuring advanced email notifications.
- **Blue Ocean**: Provides a modern interface for editing, running, and visualizing pipeline flows.

These plugins can be installed via the Jenkins Plugin Manager, which is accessible through *Manage Jenkins* → *Manage Plugins*.

Configure Global Security Settings

Securing the Jenkins instance is imperative for maintaining integrity and preventing unauthorized access. Navigate to *Manage Jenkins* → *Configure Global Security* and configure:

- **Authentication**: Set up Jenkins to authenticate against LDAP, Active Directory, or the Jenkins own user database.
- **Authorization**: Enable matrix-based security and assign roles to restrict access control at granular levels.
- **CSRF Protection**: Enable to thwart Cross-Site Request Forgery attacks.
- **Agent-to-master Security**: Configure to enforce security for connections between agents and the master instance.

Set Up a Git Repository for the Pipeline Code

Central to CD is the version control system. The pipeline configuration, typically defined in a *Jenkinsfile*, should reside in the root directory of the project's repository. Below is a simple *Jenkinsfile* example:

```
pipeline {
    agent any
    stages {
        stage('Checkout') {
            steps {
                git 'https://github.com/your-repository.git'
            }
        }
        stage('Build') {
            steps {
                sh './gradlew build'
            }
        }
        stage('Test') {
            steps {
                sh './gradlew test'
            }
        }
        stage('Deploy') {
            steps {
                sshPublisher(publishers: [sshPublisherDesc(
                    configName: 'remote-server',
                    transfers: [sshTransfer(
                        sourceFiles: 'build/libs/*.jar',
                        removePrefix: 'build/libs',
                        remoteDirectory: '/var/www/app'
                    )],
                    usePromotionTimestamp: false,
                    useWorkspaceInPromotion: false,
                    verbose: true
                )])
            }
        }
    }
    post {
        success {
            emailext(
                subject: "SUCCESS: Build ${currentBuild.fullDisplayName}",
                body: "Great news! The build completed successfully.",
                to: "team@example.com"
            )
        }
        failure {
            emailext(
                subject: "FAILURE: Build ${currentBuild.fullDisplayName}",
                body: "There's been a failure in the build.",
                to: "team@example.com"
            )
        }
    }
}
```

Integrate Jenkins with External Services

Integrations enhance CD efficacy. For example, webhook integration with GitHub to trigger Jenkins jobs on code commits. Configure the webhook through the GitHub repository settings by setting the payload URL to *http://your-jenkins-instance/github-webhook/* and selecting *Just the push event*.

Setting Up Pipeline Jobs

Pipeline jobs use the *Pipeline* job type. In Jenkins UI:

1. Navigate to *New Item*.

2. Enter an item name, select *Pipeline*, and click *OK*.

3. Under *Pipeline*, select *Pipeline script from SCM*.

4. Configure SCM as *Git* and provide repository URL and credentials.

5. Apply configurations related to script path (*Jenkinsfile*) and branch to build.

Environment Configuration for Nodes (Agents)

Nodes in Jenkins are separate machines configured to handle jobs, optimizing load distribution:

1. Navigate to *Manage Jenkins* → *Manage Nodes and Clouds*.

2. Select *New Node*, name it, and specify a node type (e.g., *Permanent Agent*).

3. Configure the node's *Remote root directory*, *Labels* (for node-specific job allocation), and launch method (e.g., via SSH).

A properly configured node ensures enhanced resource scalability and job execution efficiency.

Testing the CD Pipeline

Upon setup completion, initiate a build to validate the pipeline. Monitor the stages and steps via the Jenkins Blue Ocean interface or the classic view. For instance, executing the *Jenkinsfile* above should yield:

```
[Pipeline] Start of Pipeline
[Pipeline] node
Running on Jenkins in /var/lib/jenkins/workspace/sample-pipeline
[Pipeline] {
[Pipeline] stage
[Pipeline] { (Checkout)
[Pipeline] git
 > git rev-parse --is-inside-work-tree # timeout=10
 ...
[Pipeline] }
[Pipeline] // stage
[Pipeline] stage
[Pipeline] { (Build)
[Pipeline] sh
 ...
[Pipeline] }
[Pipeline] // stage
[Pipeline] stage
[Pipeline] { (Test)
[Pipeline] sh
 ...
[Pipeline] }
[Pipeline] // stage
[Pipeline] stage
[Pipeline] { (Deploy)
[Pipeline] sshPublisher
 ...
[Pipeline] }
[Pipeline] // stage
[Pipeline] }
[Pipeline] // node
[Pipeline] End of Pipeline
Finished: SUCCESS
```

Configure notifications and adjust any failures in script stages to fine-tune the CD process. This structured approach ensures a resilient and systematic setup of Continuous Delivery pipelines in Jenkins, fostering effective and seamless software delivery.

6.4 Deploying Applications with Jenkins

Deploying applications with Jenkins involves configuring deployment pipelines that automate the process of moving applications from a development environment through staging and ultimately to production. Jenkins excels at automating these tasks, ensuring that the deployment is consistent, repeatable, and reliable. This section examines the various stages and best practices for successful deployment using Jenkins.

To deploy applications with Jenkins, a pipeline must be created that handles various deployment tasks, such as building containers, provisioning infrastructure, and executing deployment scripts. A typical Jenkins deployment pipeline includes stages for code checkout, building artifacts, running tests, deploying, and verifying the deployment.

We begin by defining a Jenkins pipeline using the ‘Jenkinsfile‘. The ‘Declarative Pipeline‘ syntax is recommended for its readability and simplicity. Here is an example ‘Jenkinsfile‘ for deploying a Java application:

```
pipeline {
    agent any
    environment {
        APP_NAME = 'my-java-app'
        APP_VERSION = '1.0.0'
        DOCKER_REGISTRY = 'my-docker-registry'
    }
    stages {
        stage('Checkout') {
            steps {
                checkout scm
            }
        }
        stage('Build') {
            steps {
                sh 'mvn clean package -DskipTests'
            }
        }
        stage('Test') {
            steps {
                sh 'mvn test'
            }
        }
        stage('Docker Build') {
            steps {
                script {
                    dockerImage = docker.build("${DOCKER_REGISTRY}/${
                        APP_NAME}:${APP_VERSION}")
                }
            }
        }
        stage('Docker Push') {
            steps {
                script {
                    docker.withRegistry("https://${DOCKER_REGISTRY}", 'docker-
                        credentials') {
                        dockerImage.push()
                    }
                }
            }
        }
        stage('Deploy to Staging') {
            steps {
                sh 'kubectl apply -f k8s/staging'
            }
        }
        stage('Deploy to Production') {
            when {
                branch 'master'
            }
            steps {
                sh 'kubectl apply -f k8s/production'
            }
        }
    }
```

```
    post {
        success {
            echo 'Deployment completed successfully!'
        }
        failure {
            mail to: 'dev-team@example.com',
                 subject: "Failed Pipeline: ${currentBuild.fullDisplayName}",
                 body: "Something is wrong with ${env.BUILD_URL}"
        }
    }
}
```

In this pipeline script, the deployment process is broken down into several stages: 'Checkout', 'Build', 'Test', 'Docker Build', 'Docker Push', 'Deploy to Staging', and 'Deploy to Production'.

1. **Checkout** stage: This stage retrieves the source code from the Version Control System (VCS). The 'checkout scm' step fetches the code based on the Jenkins job configuration.

2. **Build** stage: The 'sh 'mvn clean package -DskipTests'' command cleans and compiles the Java application, packaging it into a JAR or WAR file, while skipping the tests for speed.

3. **Test** stage: The tests are executed using 'sh 'mvn test''. This ensures that the application passes all unit tests before moving to the next stage.

4. **Docker Build** stage: This stage creates a Docker image using the Dockerfile specified in the repository. The 'docker.build' command builds the Docker image and tags it with the specified version.

5. **Docker Push** stage: The Docker image is pushed to a Docker registry. The 'docker.withRegistry' function provides the credentials required to authenticate with the registry.

6. **Deploy to Staging** stage: The application is deployed to a staging environment using Kubernetes. The 'sh 'kubectl apply -f k8s/staging'' command applies the Kubernetes configuration files to deploy the application to the staging cluster.

7. **Deploy to Production** stage: This stage is conditional and only runs when the branch is 'master', as specified by the 'when branch 'master' ' condition. It deploys the application to the production environment using the 'sh 'kubectl apply -f k8s/production'' command.

The 'post' block handles notifications. On a successful build, Jenkins will output a success message. On failure, an email notification is sent to the development team with details about the failed pipeline stage.

Monitoring and verifying deployments are essential to ensure that the application operates correctly once deployed. Blue-green deployments or canary releases can be implemented to minimize downtime and reduce risks. Jenkins supports these deployment strategies through plugins and additional scripting in the 'Jenkinsfile'.

Integrating with configuration management tools like Ansible allows for even more sophisticated deployment processes. Ansible playbooks can be called from Jenkins pipelines to configure servers and deploy applications. For example:

```
pipeline {
    agent any
    stages {
        stage('Checkout') {
            steps {
                checkout scm
            }
        }
        stage('Build') {
            steps {
                sh 'mvn clean package'
            }
        }
        stage('Ansible Deploy') {
            steps {
                ansiblePlaybook playbook: 'playbooks/deploy.yaml', inventory: 'inventory
                    .ini'
            }
        }
    }
}
```

In this modified example, the 'Ansible Deploy' stage uses the Jenkins Ansible plugin to execute the 'deploy.yaml' playbook. This playbook might include tasks for copying artifact files, configuring servers, and restarting services.

Based on the deployment approach and tech stack, Jenkins provides the flexibility to integrate with various deployment automation tools. By strategically setting up these pipelines, teams can achieve efficient Continuous Delivery processes, ensuring that applications are frequently and reliably delivered to production with minimal manual intervention.

6.5 Environment Management

Effective environment management is crucial for ensuring seamless Continuous Delivery (CD) with Jenkins. This involves managing multiple environments such as development, testing, staging, and production, each serving a specific purpose in the software delivery pipeline. Proper management entails automated environment setup, configuration consistency, and ensures that each environment reflects the conditions of the production environment as closely as possible.

A typical CD setup with Jenkins involves multiple pipelines corresponding to different stages of software delivery. Each pipeline might have distinct requirements for the underlying environment. Let us delve into the methods and best practices for managing these environments in a Jenkins-centric CD workflow.

1. Environment Configuration Management

Configuration management ensures that environments are consistent and replicable across various stages of the pipeline. One common tool for this purpose is Ansible. Ansible can manage configurations across environments by defining playbooks which specify the desired state of the infrastructure and application settings. Here is a simple Ansible playbook:

```
- name: Configure Application Server
  hosts: app_servers
  become: yes
  tasks:
    - name: Install necessary packages
      apt:
        name:
          - nginx
          - python3
        state: present

    - name: Deploy application code
      copy:
        src: /srv/myapp/
        dest: /var/www/myapp/
        owner: www-data
        group: www-data
```

Executing this playbook with the command below ensures that all target hosts are configured identically:

```
ansible-playbook -i inventory.ini app_server.yml
```

2. Environment Provisioning with Infrastructure as Code (IaC)

Automation of environment provisioning can be achieved using Infrastructure as Code (IaC) tools such as Terraform, AWS CloudFormation, or Azure Resource Manager. These tools enable the definition and management of the infrastructure using declarative configuration files.

For example, a Terraform configuration to provision an AWS EC2 instance might look like this:

```
provider "aws" {
  region = "us-west-2"
}

resource "aws_instance" "app_server" {
  ami = "ami-0c55b159cbfafe1f0"
  instance_type = "t2.micro"

  tags = {
    Name = "AppServer"
  }
}
```

By executing the command:

```
terraform apply
```

Terraform creates the required infrastructure according to the specified configuration.

3. Isolating Environments Using Containers

Containers, managed with Docker, provide a lightweight and portable way of ensuring consistent environments across the pipeline. Docker images encapsulate the application code, runtime, libraries, and configurations required for the application to run, thus facilitating environment consistency.

A Dockerfile example for a simple web application might be:

```
FROM python:3.8-slim

WORKDIR /app

COPY requirements.txt requirements.txt
RUN pip install -r requirements.txt

COPY . .

CMD ["python", "app.py"]
```

To build and run the Docker container:

```
docker build -t myapp .
docker run -d -p 5000:5000 myapp
```

4. Managing Secrets and Environment Variables

Sensitive information such as passwords, API keys, and configuration parameters should not be hardcoded in the application source code or configuration files. Tools like HashiCorp Vault, AWS Secrets Manager, or Azure Key Vault securely manage secrets and environment variables.

In Jenkins, environment variables can be securely managed using the Jenkins Credentials plugin. Within a pipeline script, credentials can be referenced as follows:

```
pipeline {
    agent any

    environment {
        DB_PASSWORD = credentials('db-password')
    }

    stages {
        stage('Build') {
            steps {
                sh 'echo Building the application...'
                withEnv(['DB_PASS=' + env.DB_PASSWORD]) {
                    sh './run-database-setup.sh'
                }
            }
        }
    }
}
```

5. Promoting Code Across Environments

Promoting code across different environments (e.g., from development to staging, and then to production) should be carried out methodically. This involves ensuring that all necessary tests are passed before promoting to the next environment.

A Jenkins pipeline for promotion might look like this:

```
pipeline {
    agent any

    stages {
        stage('Deploy to Dev') {
            steps {
                sh 'ansible-playbook -i inventory_dev.ini deploy.yml'
            }
        }

        stage('Test in Dev') {
            steps {
                sh './run-tests.sh'
            }
        }

        stage('Promote to Staging') {
            when {
                branch 'main'
                environment name: 'RUN_TESTS', value: 'true'
            }
            steps {
                sh 'ansible-playbook -i inventory_staging.ini deploy.yml'
            }
        }

        stage('Test in Staging') {
```

```
            steps {
                sh './run-tests.sh'
            }
        }

        stage('Promote to Production') {
            input {
                message "Deploy to Production?"
                ok "Deploy"
            }
            steps {
                sh 'ansible-playbook -i inventory_prod.ini deploy.yml'
            }
        }
    }
}
```

6. Monitoring and Logging

Effective environment management includes comprehensive monitoring and logging to quickly identify and resolve issues. Tools such as Prometheus for monitoring and ELK (Elasticsearch, Logstash, Kibana) stack for logging can be integrated into Jenkins pipelines to provide real-time insights.

Using these tools and practices, managing environments in a Jenkins-driven CD pipeline ensures a reliable, consistent, and efficient software delivery process.

6.6 Configuring Delivery Pipelines

Configuring delivery pipelines in Jenkins involves creating a series of automated steps that take code changes from version control through to production release. This ensures that each change passes through rigorous testing and review stages, providing confidence in the quality and stability of the software. The goal is to streamline the process of delivering software while maintaining high standards of code quality and operational reliability.

To configure a delivery pipeline in Jenkins, one typically relies on the Pipeline plugin, also known as the "Pipeline-as-Code" feature. This functionality allows you to define your build, test, and deploy stages in a Jenkinsfile, which is a text file checked into your project's source control repository.

A basic Jenkinsfile might look like this:

```
pipeline {
    agent any
```

```
    stages {
        stage('Build') {
            steps {
                echo 'Building...'
                sh 'make'
            }
        }
        stage('Test') {
            steps {
                echo 'Testing...'
                sh 'make test'
            }
        }
        stage('Deploy') {
            steps {
                echo 'Deploying...'
                sh 'make deploy'
            }
        }
    }
}
```

Stages and Steps

Each pipeline consists of multiple stages, with each stage performing specific tasks. In the example above, there are three stages: Build, Test, and Deploy. Each stage contains steps, which are individual tasks to be executed in that stage. The steps directive supports various commands and plugins, and it can include shell commands (as shown), script blocks, or more complex Groovy scripts.

When configuring a pipeline, consider:

1. **Agent Declaration**: The agent any line indicates that the pipeline can run on any available agent. You can specify a particular agent, label, or even a Docker container.

```
agent {
    docker {
        image 'maven:3.8.1'
        label 'my-agent'
        args '-v /tmp:/tmp'
    }
}
```

2. **Stage Configuration**: You define the sequence of stages under the stages block. The pipeline executes the stages in the order they are defined. 3. **Steps within Stages**: Inside each stage, the steps block defines the actions to perform. These can range from simple shell commands to invoking other Jenkins plugins.

Parallel Execution

To speed up the pipeline, you can run stages in parallel. For example:

```
pipeline {
    agent any
    stages {
        stage('Parallel Stage') {
            parallel {
                stage('Unit Tests') {
                    steps {
                        sh 'make unit-tests'
                    }
                }
                stage('Integration Tests') {
                    steps {
                        sh 'make integration-tests'
                    }
                }
            }
        }
    }
}
```

In this configuration, Unit Tests and Integration Tests run simultaneously on available agents, reducing the total build time.

Post Actions

Actions that should take place after the main pipeline stages—such as cleanup tasks, archiving artifacts, sending notifications, or attaching reports—can be defined in the post block.

```
pipeline {
    agent any
    stages {
        stage('Build') {
            steps {
                sh 'make'
            }
        }
    }
    post {
        always {
            echo 'Cleaning up...'
            sh 'make clean'
        }
        success {
            echo 'Build succeeded'
            mail to: 'team@example.com', subject: 'Build Success', body: 'The build was
                    successful.'
        }
        failure {
            echo 'Build failed'
            mail to: 'team@example.com', subject: 'Build Failure', body: 'The build
                    failed.'
        }
    }
}
```

Environment Variables

You can set environment variables within the pipeline to use throughout the Jenkinsfile using the environment directive.

```
pipeline {
    agent any
    environment {
        HOME_DIR = '/home/jenkins'
    }
    stages {
        stage('Build') {
            steps {
                sh 'echo $HOME_DIR'
                sh 'make'
            }
        }
    }
}
```

Input Directive

When you require human intervention during a pipeline run—for example, to approve a deployment step—you can use the input directive.

```
pipeline {
    agent any
    stages {
        stage('Deploy') {
            steps {
                input message: 'Approve deployment?', ok: 'Deploy'
                sh 'make deploy'
            }
        }
    }
}
```

Handling Secrets

Managing secrets such as API keys and passwords securely can be achieved using credentials stored in Jenkins. Access these credentials in the pipeline with the credentials binding.

```
pipeline {
    agent any
    environment {
        SECRET_KEY = credentials('my-secret-key')
    }
    stages {
        stage('Deploy') {
            steps {
                sh 'echo $SECRET_KEY'
                sh 'make deploy'
            }
        }
    }
}
```

Utilizing these features ensures a robust, maintainable pipeline configuration. Employing parallel execution, post actions, and secure handling of sensitive information contributes to the efficiency and security of the CI/CD process. The ability to define pipelines as code in Jenkinsfile provides transparency and version control, making it easier to reproduce and modify the build pipeline according to evolving project requirements.

6.7 Release Management

Release management is a critical aspect of Continuous Delivery (CD) that focuses on overseeing, coordinating, and managing the delivery of software applications through various stages and environments. For effective release management, it is essential to have a structured approach that involves planning, scheduling, and controlling the builds and versions efficiently. Leveraging Jenkins as a core component of this process can streamline the workflow and improve the reliability and traceability of releases.

Version Control Integration

A well-integrated version control system (VCS) is fundamental to managing releases effectively. Jenkins supports various VCS providers such as Git, Subversion, and Mercurial. The integration allows Jenkins to automatically detect changes in the codebase and trigger corresponding jobs. Here's an example of how you can configure a Jenkins pipeline to work with Git:

```
pipeline {
    agent any
    stages {
        stage('Checkout') {
            steps {
                git branch: 'main', url: 'https://github.com/example/repo.git'
            }
        }
        // Additional stages
    }
}
```

This configuration ensures that the pipeline checks out the latest code from the specified Git repository and branch before proceeding to subsequent stages.

Build Artifacts

During the release process, Jenkins builds the source code and generates artifacts, which are the deliverables of the build process such as JAR files, WAR files, or Docker images. These artifacts need to be versioned and stored in a binary repository to ensure traceability. An example pipeline stage for building a Java application and archiving the build artifacts could look like this:

```
stage('Build') {
    steps {
        sh 'mvn clean package'
        archiveArtifacts artifacts: '**/target/*.jar', fingerprint: true
    }
}
```

In this example, Maven is used for building the project, and 'archiveArtifacts' is a Jenkins post-build action that collects specified files and stores them as part of the build results.

Release Tagging

To maintain a clear history of releases, tagging the source code at the time of the release is a common practice. Tags should adhere to a versioning scheme, such as semantic versioning (e.g., v1.0.0, v1.0.1). Jenkins can automate this tagging process to ensure consistency. Below is a snippet for adding a Git tag upon a successful build:

```
stage('Tag Release') {
    steps {
        script {
            def tagName = "v${env.BUILD_NUMBER}"
            sh "git tag -a ${tagName} -m 'Release ${tagName}'"
            sh "git push origin ${tagName}"
        }
    }
}
```

This script creates a tag using the Jenkins build number and pushes it to the remote repository.

Release Notes

Generating and distributing release notes is important for communicating the changes, enhancements, bug fixes, and known issues in each release. Jenkins can be configured to generate release notes by gathering information from commit messages or issue tracking systems such as JIRA. Here is an example of a post-build step that generates release notes:

```
stage('Generate Release Notes') {
    steps {
        script {
            def releaseNotes = sh(script: 'git log --oneline ${previousTag}..${env.
                BUILD_NUMBER}', returnStdout: true)
            writeFile file: 'release-notes.txt', text: releaseNotes
        }
```

```
        archiveArtifacts artifacts: 'release-notes.txt'
    }
}
```

This script captures commit messages between the previous tag and the current build to create a release notes file.

Release Approval and Signoff

For certain environments, especially production, it is essential to have a manual approval process before the release is deployed. Jenkins provides various mechanisms for integrating manual intervention. One such mechanism is the use of the 'input' step in the pipeline:

```
stage('Approval') {
    steps {
        input message: 'Approve release?', ok: 'Deploy'
    }
}
```

Adding this step ensures that a designated reviewer can verify and approve the release before it progresses to the deployment stage.

Deployment to Different Environments

One of the key responsibilities of release management is deploying applications to various environments such as development, staging, and production. Jenkins pipelines can be designed to promote artifacts through these environments while applying environment-specific configurations. For instance:

```
stage('Deploy to Staging') {
    steps {
        deployToEnvironment('staging')
    }
}

stage('Deploy to Production') {
    steps {
        deployToEnvironment('production')
    }
}

def deployToEnvironment(env) {
    // Deployment logic for the specified environment
    sh "ansible-playbook -i inventory/${env} deploy.yml"
}
```

This example illustrates a reusable function 'deployToEnvironment' for deploying to different environments using Ansible.

Post-Release Tasks

After a successful deployment, several post-release activities might be necessary, such as notifying stakeholders, updating documentation, or performing sanity checks. Jenkins can automate these activities as part of the pipeline:

```
stage('Post-Release') {
    steps {
        // Notification example
        mail to: 'team@example.com',
            subject: "Release ${env.BUILD_NUMBER} Successful",
            body: "The release was successfully deployed to production."

        // Documentation update example
        sh 'generate-docs.sh'
        archiveArtifacts artifacts: 'docs/*.html'
    }
}
```

This stage sends an email notification to the team and archives the generated documentation.

Monitoring and Logging

Monitoring and logging are essential to track the health and performance of releases. Jenkins integrates with monitoring tools such as Prometheus, Grafana, and ELK stack to provide insights into the deployment process and post-deployment operations. The following snippet shows how to send deployment metrics to Prometheus:

```
stage('Send Metrics') {
    steps {
        sh 'curl -XPOST http://prometheus:9091/metrics/job/deployment'
    }
}
```

By capturing and analyzing these metrics, teams can identify issues early and maintain the stability of production environments.

Effective release management with Jenkins not only ensures smoother deployments but also enhances collaboration, traceability, and accountability within development teams. Each aspect discussed contributes to a comprehensive release management strategy that aligns with the principles of Continuous Delivery.

6.8 Automating Infrastructure Provisioning

Automating infrastructure provisioning is crucial for achieving reliable and repeatable deployments in a Continuous Delivery (CD) pipeline. Jenkins, with its robust ecosystem of plugins and integrations, is an ideal tool for automating the provisioning of various infrastructure components. This section explores the tools, techniques, and best practices for automating infrastructure provisioning using Jenkins.

One of the primary tools for automating infrastructure provisioning is Infrastructure as Code (IaC). IaC allows developers to manage and provision infrastructure through code instead of manual processes. This approach ensures consistency, reduces errors, and enables version control for infrastructure. Tools such as Terraform, Ansible, and CloudFormation are commonly used in conjunction with Jenkins to automate the provisioning process.

```
provider "aws" {
  region = "us-west-2"
}

resource "aws_instance" "example" {
  ami = "ami-0c55b159cbfafe1f0"
  instance_type = "t2.micro"
  tags = {
    Name = "ExampleInstance"
  }
}
```

In Jenkins, you can manage infrastructure provisioning tasks by integrating with these IaC tools using various plugins. For example, the Terraform Plugin allows you to run Terraform scripts directly from Jenkins jobs, applying infrastructure changes as part of your CD pipeline.

To configure the Terraform Plugin in Jenkins, follow these steps:

- Install the Terraform Plugin from the Jenkins plugin manager.
- Create a new Jenkins job or pipeline and select the appropriate build environment.
- Add a build step to execute Terraform commands. Use the sh or shell build step to run Terraform commands such as terraform init, terraform plan, and terraform apply.

```
pipeline {
  agent any

  stages {
    stage('Checkout') {
      steps {
        git 'https://github.com/example/repo.git'
      }
    }
    stage('Initialize Terraform') {
      steps {
        sh 'terraform init'
      }
```

```
    }
    stage('Plan Infrastructure') {
      steps {
        sh 'terraform plan'
      }
    }
    stage('Apply Infrastructure') {
      steps {
        sh 'terraform apply -auto-approve'
      }
    }
  }
}
```

In addition to Terraform, Ansible is another powerful IaC tool that can be easily integrated with Jenkins. With Ansible, you can automate the provisioning, configuration, and management of infrastructure resources. The Ansible Tower plugin for Jenkins enables users to run Ansible playbooks as part of their Jenkins pipelines.

```
- name: Set up web server
  hosts: webservers
  become: yes
  tasks:
    - name: Install Nginx
      apt:
        name: nginx
        state: present

    - name: Start Nginx web server
      service:
        name: nginx
        state: started
```

To configure the Ansible Tower plugin in Jenkins:

- Install the Ansible Tower plugin from the Jenkins plugin manager.
- Set up the Ansible Tower server details in the Jenkins configuration.
- Create a Jenkins job or pipeline and configure the build steps to run Ansible playbooks. Use the ansibleTowerBuild step to trigger Ansible jobs from Jenkins.

```
pipeline {
  agent any

  stages {
    stage('Checkout') {
      steps {
        git 'https://github.com/example/ansible-repo.git'
      }
    }
    stage('Run Ansible Playbook') {
```

```
        steps {
          ansibleTowerBuild(
            server: 'AnsiTowerServer',
            jobTemplate: 'WebServerSetup'
          )
        }
      }
    }
}
```

Another critical aspect of automating infrastructure provisioning is managing configuration and secrets. Tools like HashiCorp Vault, AWS Secrets Manager, and Azure Key Vault can be integrated into Jenkins pipelines to securely manage sensitive data and configuration specifics.

For example, integrating HashiCorp Vault with Jenkins allows you to securely retrieve secrets during the build process. The following example demonstrates how to retrieve a secret from Vault in a Jenkins pipeline:

```
pipeline {
  agent any

  environment {
    VAULT_ADDR = 'http://vault.example.com'
  }

  stages {
    stage('Retrieve Secret') {
      steps {
        withVault([vaultPrefix: 'secret/data', credentialsId: 'vault-token-id']) {
          script {
            def secret = vault path: 'secret/data/myapp', key: 'db_password'
            echo "Database password: ${secret}"
          }
        }
      }
    }
  }
}
```

By following these principles and integrating appropriate tools, Jenkins can be used to automate the complete lifecycle of infrastructure provisioning, from configuring compute resources to managing network and storage assets. This automation leads to smoother deployment processes, reduces manual intervention, and enhances the reliability and reproducibility of your CD pipeline.

An advanced practice is the dynamic provisioning of infrastructure, where resources are provisioned, used, and then decommissioned as part of the CD workflow. This is particularly useful in environments that need scalability and resource optimization. Techniques such as autoscaling and serverless architecture can be orchestrated using Jenkins pipelines to dynamically manage resource usage based on demand and workloads.

Employing these strategies ensures that your Continuous Delivery pipelines are resilient, efficient, and scalable, providing a robust foundation for modern application delivery.

6.9 Rollback and Recovery Strategies

In the context of Continuous Delivery (CD), the ability to roll back and recover from failed deployments quickly is paramount. This section details the strategies, tools, and configurations necessary to implement effective rollback and recovery mechanisms in Jenkins-based CD pipelines.

To mitigate the risk associated with new deployments, establishing robust rollback and recovery strategies is critical. These mechanisms ensure that if a deployment introduces errors, the system can revert to the last known good state with minimal downtime and disruption.

Rollback Strategies

One of the fundamental strategies in handling deployment failures is the rollback. A rollback is the process of reverting a deployment to a previous state. Several rollback strategies can be employed, depending on the nature of the application and the specifics of the deployment:

- **Versioned Artifacts:** Storing versioned artifacts allows the CD pipeline to deploy previous versions readily. This requires meticulous versioning of all artifacts and dependencies.
- **Blue-Green Deployment:** This technique involves maintaining two identical production environments. One (blue) runs the current version, while the other (green) deploys the new version. Switching traffic between environments allows for immediate rollback by redirecting traffic back to the blue environment.
- **Canary Releases:** This method deploys the new version to a small subset of users first. If issues arise, rolling back involves minimal user impact, as the majority still operate on the stable version.
- **Feature Toggles:** By implementing feature toggles, new features can be enabled or disabled at runtime, allowing quick deactivation

of problematic features without a full-scale rollback.

Implementing Rollback in Jenkins Pipelines

Jenkins pipelines offer a flexible structure to implement rollback mechanisms. Consider the following Jenkinsfile that details a basic example using versioned artifacts:

```
pipeline {
    agent any

    environment {
        ARTIFACT_VERSION = "1.0.0"
    }

    stages {
        stage('Deploy') {
            steps {
                script {
                    try {
                        // Deploy new version
                        deployArtifact(env.ARTIFACT_VERSION)
                    } catch (Exception e) {
                        echo "Deployment failed: ${e}"
                        echo "Rolling back to previous version"
                        // Rollback to the last-known GOOD version
                        rollbackArtifact(getLastKnownGoodVersion())
                    }
                }
            }
        }
    }
}

def deployArtifact(version) {
    // Your deployment logic
    echo "Deploying version ${version}"
}

def rollbackArtifact(version) {
    // Your rollback logic
    echo "Rolling back to version ${version}"
}

def getLastKnownGoodVersion() {
    // Logic to get the last known good version
    return "0.9.9"
}
```

This pipeline script demonstrates deploying a new artifact version and, in the event of a failure, rolling back to the last known good version. The functions deployArtifact, rollbackArtifact, and getLastKnownGoodVersion encapsulate the deployment, rollback, and version retrieval logic, respectively.

Recovery Strategies

Recovery strategies aim to restore services swiftly following an incident. Effective recovery not only encompasses reverting to previous versions but also includes database and infrastructure restoration.

- **Regular Backups:** Regularly backing up databases and configurations ensures recovery from data corruption or loss.
- **Automated Recovery Scripts:** Scripts that automate recovery tasks, such as restoring databases or restarting services.
- **Disaster Recovery (DR) Environments:** Establishing DR environments that replicate the production setup to minimize downtime and data loss.
- **Monitoring and Alerts:** Comprehensive monitoring platforms integrated with alerting help detect issues early, initiating recovery processes timely.

Database Backup and Restore in Jenkins Pipeline

To illustrate a practical recovery strategy, consider the following example Jenkins pipeline that incorporates database backup and restoration.

```
pipeline {
    agent any

    environment {
        DB_BACKUP_DIR = "/backups/"
        DB_NAME = "production_db"
    }

    stages {
        stage('Backup Database') {
            steps {
                script {
                    try {
                        backupDatabase(env.DB_NAME, env.DB_BACKUP_DIR)
                    } catch (Exception e) {
                        echo "Database backup failed: ${e}"
                    }
                }
            }
        }
        stage('Deploy') {
            steps {
                script {
                    try {
                        // Deployment logic
                        deployNewVersion()
                    } catch (Exception e) {
                        echo "Deployment failed: ${e}"
                        echo "Restoring database from latest backup"
                        // Restore the database
                        restoreDatabase(env.DB_NAME, env.DB_BACKUP_DIR)
```

```
                }
            }
        }
    }
  }
}

def backupDatabase(dbName, backupDir) {
    // Logic to backup the database
    echo "Backing up database ${dbName} to ${backupDir}"
    sh "pg_dump ${dbName} > ${backupDir}/${dbName}_$(date +%F).sql"
}

def restoreDatabase(dbName, backupDir) {
    // Logic to restore the database
    echo "Restoring database ${dbName} from ${backupDir}"
    sh "psql ${dbName} < ${backupDir}/${dbName}_$(date +%F).sql"
}

def deployNewVersion() {
    // Your deployment logic
    echo "Deploying new version"
}
```

In this example, the Jenkins pipeline includes stages for both backing up and restoring the database. The backup is performed before deployment, and in case of a deployment failure, the database is restored from the latest backup, minimizing data loss and downtime.

Critical Considerations

When designing rollback and recovery strategies, several critical considerations must be addressed:

- **Consistency and State Management:** Ensure that all components, including databases and services, are synchronized to the correct state post-rollback.
- **Validation and Testing:** Regularly test rollback and recovery procedures to validate their effectiveness and identify potential issues.
- **Documentation and Training:** Maintain comprehensive documentation and conduct training for team members to ensure readiness in the event of a deployment failure.

Effective rollback and recovery strategies are integral to maintaining the stability and reliability of CD pipelines in Jenkins, ensuring that deployment issues are managed efficiently and downtime is minimized.

6.10 Measuring Effectiveness of CD

Measuring the effectiveness of Continuous Delivery (CD) is crucial in understanding how well the pipelines perform and identifying areas for improvement. This process involves evaluating various metrics that provide insights into the efficiency, quality, and reliability of the CD practices implemented in Jenkins. These metrics help ensure that the goals of CD, such as faster release cycles and improved software quality, are being met consistently.

Key Metrics for Evaluating CD Effectiveness

Several key metrics provide valuable information on the performance of CD processes. These metrics can be broadly categorized into deployment frequency, lead time, mean time to recovery (MTTR), change failure rate, and cycle time.

- **Deployment Frequency**: This metric measures how often new releases are deployed to production. A higher deployment frequency indicates a mature CD process and the ability to deliver features and bug fixes more rapidly.
- **Lead Time**: Lead time is the duration between a code commit and the deployment of the code to production. Reducing lead time is critical for increasing responsiveness to customer feedback and market demands.
- **Mean Time to Recovery (MTTR)**: MTTR measures the average time taken to restore service after a production failure. Lower MTTR indicates a robust recovery process and a well-maintained pipeline.
- **Change Failure Rate**: This is the percentage of deployments that result in a failure in production. A lower change failure rate signifies a stable pipeline with effective testing and validation.
- **Cycle Time**: Cycle time encompasses the total time from the start of a work item until its completion. Optimizing cycle time contributes to smoother workflow and faster delivery of work items.

Implementing Metrics Collection in Jenkins

In Jenkins, measuring these metrics can be automated through various plugins and integrations. For example, the Pipeline Stage View plugin offers visualization of pipeline performance, while the Build Metrics plugin provides data on build success rates, stability, and duration.

To collect deployment frequency and lead time data, you can use the following Jenkins pipeline script:

```
pipeline {
    agent any
    stages {
        stage('Build') {
            steps {
                script {
                    def startTime = new Date()
                    currentBuild.displayName = "#${env.BUILD_NUMBER} - Started
                          at ${startTime}"
                }
                echo 'Building..'
            }
        }
        stage('Deploy') {
            steps {
                script {
                    def endTime = new Date()
                    currentBuild.displayName = "#${env.BUILD_NUMBER} -
                          Completed at ${endTime}"
                    def leadTime = endTime.getTime() - startTime.getTime()
                    echo "Lead Time: ${leadTime / 1000} seconds"
                }
            }
        }
    }
    post {
        always {
            echo 'Cleaning up..'
        }
    }
}
```

This script captures the start and end times of the pipeline to calculate the lead time. Similar mechanisms can be used to track deployment frequency and other time-based metrics.

Analyzing MTTR and Change Failure Rate

MTTR and change failure rate require monitoring deployment outcomes and any subsequent recovery actions. Jenkins allows capturing these events through post-build actions and custom notifications. The following example demonstrates how to use a post-step to record failures:

```
pipeline {
    agent any
    stages {
        stage('Build') {
            steps {
                echo 'Building..'
            }
```

```
        }
        stage('Test') {
            steps {
                echo 'Testing..'
            }
        }
        stage('Deploy') {
            steps {
                echo 'Deploying..'
            }
        }
    }
    post {
        failure {
            script {
                def failTime = new Date()
                currentBuild.displayName = "#${env.BUILD_NUMBER} - Failed at ${
                    failTime}"
            }
            echo 'Send notification or take recovery action..'
        }
        success {
            script {
                currentBuild.displayName = "#${env.BUILD_NUMBER} - Deployed
                    successfully"
            }
        }
    }
}
```

Visualizing and Reporting Metrics

Visualizing metric data is essential for easy interpretation and decision-making. Jenkins integrates with various tools such as Grafana and Kibana for advanced data visualization. The Prometheus plugin for Jenkins enables exporting pipeline metrics to Prometheus, which can be visualized using Grafana dashboards.

To configure Prometheus:

- Install the Prometheus plugin in Jenkins.
- Configure the plugin to export metrics.
- Set up a Prometheus server to scrape metrics from Jenkins.
- Use Grafana to connect to Prometheus and create dashboards.

A sample Prometheus configuration might look like this:

```
global:
  scrape_interval: 15s

scrape_configs:
  - job_name: 'jenkins'
    static_configs:
```

```
    - targets: ['<Jenkins-URL>:<Port>/prometheus']
```

Sample Grafana query to display build status over time:

```
sum(rate(jenkins_job_builds[5m])) by (status)
```

Continuous Improvement through Metrics

The collected metrics should be periodically reviewed to identify trends and areas for improvement. Regularly update CD practices based on insights derived from the data. For instance, if the lead time consistently exceeds the target, investigate the stages contributing to delays and opt for optimizations such as parallel executions or caching.

Metrics also play a vital role in validating the effectiveness of new tools, practices, and configurations introduced to the pipeline. Before and after comparisons using these metrics help in making informed decisions and maintaining continuous improvement.

Effective measurement of CD processes using Jenkins ensures alignment with organizational goals, maintaining high standards of software delivery while responding swiftly to changing customer needs.

6.11 Handling Security in CD Pipelines

Ensuring security in Continuous Delivery (CD) pipelines is imperative for maintaining the integrity and confidentiality of software throughout its lifecycle. Jenkins, being a robust and highly extensible automation server, provides various mechanisms and best practices to secure CD pipelines against common vulnerabilities and threats.

Authentication and Authorization

The first line of defense in securing a Jenkins CD pipeline is establishing a robust authentication and authorization process. Jenkins supports several authentication methods, such as LDAP, OAuth, SAML, and built-in user database. For instance, integrating Jenkins with an organization's LDAP system ensures that only authenticated users can access the Jenkins server.

```
<securityRealm class="hudson.security.LDAPSecurityRealm">
  <server>ldap://ldap.example.com:389</server>
  <rootDN>dc=example,dc=com</rootDN>
  <userSearchBase>ou=users</userSearchBase>
  <userSearch>uid={0}</userSearch>
  <groupSearchBase>ou=groups</groupSearchBase>
  <groupSearch>cn={0}</groupSearch>
```

```
</securityRealm>
```

Additionally, establishing fine-grained authorization controls to specify what authenticated users are allowed to perform within Jenkins is critical. Jenkins supports matrix-based security to define these permissions accurately.

```
<authorizationStrategy class="hudson.security.GlobalMatrixAuthorizationStrategy">
  <permission>hudson.model.Hudson.Administer:admin</permission>
  <permission>hudson.model.Item.Build:developer</permission>
  <permission>hudson.model.Item.Configure:maintainer</permission>
</authorizationStrategy>
```

Securing User Credentials

Handling sensitive information, such as API tokens, SSH keys, and credentials, require utmost care. The Jenkins Credentials Plugin allows safe storage and retrieval of such information. Ensure all sensitive credentials are encrypted and never hard-coded within the pipeline scripts.

```
pipeline {
    environment {
        API_TOKEN = credentials('api-token-id')
    }
    stages {
        stage('Deploy') {
            steps {
                sh 'curl -H "Authorization: Bearer ${API_TOKEN}" https://api.
                      example.com/deploy'
            }
        }
    }
}
```

Furthermore, sensitive information should only be exposed to the jobs that genuinely need it. Use appropriate scope settings in the credential definitions to limit their accessibility.

Network Security

Securing communication channels between Jenkins and other services is essential. Ensure that all HTTP traffic to and from Jenkins uses HTTPS. Configure the Jenkins server to use SSL by setting up an SSL certificate.

```
java -jar jenkins.war --httpsPort=8443 --httpsKeyStore=/path/to/keystore --
      httpsKeyStorePassword=changeit
```

Use firewall rules and VPNs to restrict access to the Jenkins server and related infrastructure. Additionally, ensure proper inbound and outbound traffic rules are in place to limit unnecessary network exposure.

Code Security Analysis

Integrate static and dynamic code analysis tools within the Jenkins pipeline to continuously evaluate the security of the code being delivered. Tools like SonarQube, Checkmarx, and OWASP Dependency-Check can be integrated within the pipeline to perform these checks and halt the process if vulnerabilities are found.

```
pipeline {
    stages {
        stage('Code Analysis') {
            steps {
                script {
                    def sonarqubeHome = tool name: 'SonarQube', type: 'hudson.plugins.
                        sonar.SonarRunnerInstallation'
                    withSonarQubeEnv('SonarQube') {
                        sh "${sonarqubeHome}/bin/sonar-scanner"
                    }
                }
            }
        }
    }
}
```

Ensure these tools are kept up to date to capture the latest vulnerability definitions and rules.

Audit and Monitoring

Continuously monitor and audit Jenkins activities to detect any suspicious or unauthorized operations. Configure audit logging for Jenkins to capture important events, such as job trigger events, user logins, and configuration changes.

```
<loggers>
    <logger name="com.cloudbees.plugins.audit" level="INFO"/>
    <logger name="hudson.security" level="FINE"/>
</loggers>
```

Use Jenkins plugins, like the Audit Trail plugin, to enhance the auditing capabilities, ensuring all user actions within Jenkins are logged and reviewable.

Regular Security Scans and Updates

Keep the Jenkins server and all installed plugins up to date to protect against known vulnerabilities. Jenkins routinely releases updates that address security issues and improve stability. Regularly run security scans on the Jenkins instance using tools like the Jenkins Security Advisor.

Enable automatic updates for plugins via the Jenkins interface:

```
Manage Jenkins -> Manage Plugins -> Advanced -> Check Now
```

Automate weekly security scans by configuring jobs that run security scan scripts and notify administrators of any issues found.

In practice, maintaining security within a CD pipeline is an ongoing process that involves consistent vigilance and up-to-date knowledge of potential threats and mitigation strategies.

6.12 Best Practices for Continuous Delivery

In the rapidly evolving landscape of software development, maintaining a robust and efficient Continuous Delivery (CD) pipeline is pivotal. Adhering to industry best practices ensures the reliability, security, and performance of the delivery process. This section discusses several key practices to enhance your CD pipeline with Jenkins, ensuring that software delivery is not only continuous but also consistently high-quality.

1. Automate Everything

Automation is the backbone of Continuous Delivery. All repetitive tasks within the pipeline should be automated, from code integration, testing, deployment, and infrastructure provisioning to monitoring and reporting. Jenkins offers plugins and tools such as Jenkins Pipeline, Jenkinsfile, and various automated testing frameworks (e.g., JUnit, Selenium) that streamline these processes. Below is an example of a Jenkinsfile that automates build, test, and deployment stages:

```
pipeline {
    agent any

    stages {
        stage('Build') {
            steps {
                sh 'make build'
            }
        }
        stage('Test') {
            steps {
                sh 'make test'
            }
        }
        stage('Deploy') {
            steps {
                sh 'make deploy'
            }
        }
    }
}
```

2. Ensure Fast Feedback Loops

The primary aim of Continuous Delivery is to achieve high-frequency releases. Fast feedback loops are critical; they help detect and fix issues promptly. Implementing parallel testing and using lightweight, containerized environments can significantly reduce build and test times. Docker, coupled with Jenkins, can encapsulate applications and their dependencies, providing consistent testing and deployment environments.

```
pipeline {
    agent {
        docker {
            image 'maven:3-alpine'
            reuseNode true
        }
    }

    stages {
        stage('Build') {
            steps {
                sh 'mvn clean package'
            }
        }
    }
}
```

3. Version Control Everything

All code, including application code, infrastructure as code (IaC), and configuration files, should be version controlled. Tools like Git, in conjunction with Jenkins plugins like Git Plugin, ensure traceability and facilitate rollback if necessary. This practice allows teams to understand the exact state of any component across the pipeline at any given time.

```
pipeline {
    agent any
    environment {
        GIT_REPO = 'https://github.com/example/repo.git'
    }

    stages {
        stage('Checkout') {
            steps {
                git branch: 'main', url: env.GIT_REPO
            }
        }
    }
}
```

4. Maintain a Single Source of Truth

Centralize all pipeline definitions and environment configurations. This prevents inconsistencies and ensures that all team members are working with the same setup. Jenkins supports this through shared libraries and centralized configuration management tools like Ansible or Puppet. Define environment configurations at a central location accessible by all stages of the pipeline.

```
pipeline {
    agent any
    stages {
        stage('Initialize') {
            steps {
                script {
                    def config = readYaml file: 'config.yaml'
                    env.APP_ENV = config.environment
                }
            }
        }
    }
}
```

5. Implement Continuous Improvement

Adopt a culture of continuous improvement by regularly reviewing and optimizing the pipeline. Metrics and logging are fundamental to this process; implement monitoring tools and gather data on build times, failure rates, and other KPIs. Jenkins integrates with tools like Prometheus and Grafana for comprehensive monitoring and visualization.

```
pipeline {
    agent any

    stages {
        stage('Monitor') {
            steps {
                sh 'curl http://monitoring-service/report'
            }
        }
    }
}
```

6. Secure the Pipeline

Security must be integrated into every phase of the CD pipeline. Implement security scans and vulnerability assessments as part of the build process, utilizing tools such as OWASP ZAP or SonarQube. Jenkins plugins like Dependency-Check Plugin can automate the process of identifying and mitigating vulnerabilities.

```
pipeline {
    agent any

    stages {
        stage('Security Scan') {
            steps {
                sh 'dependency-check.sh --project project --scan .'
            }
```

```
            }
        }
    }
```

7. Managing Dependencies

Manage dependencies cautiously to avoid disruptions caused by incompatible or unstable libraries. Utilize dependency management tools like Maven, Gradle, or npm, and include dependency checks as part of the build process. This ensures that all dependencies are defined, versioned, and immutable.

```
pipeline {
    agent any

    stages {
        stage('Dependency Check') {
            steps {
                sh 'mvn dependency:tree'
            }
        }
    }
}
```

8. Testing in Production Environments

Ensure deployments are made to environments that closely mirror production. This practice reduces the likelihood of encountering environment-specific issues post-deployment. Using orchestration tools like Kubernetes with Jenkins can automate the deployment and management of these consistent environments.

```
pipeline {
    agent any

    stages {
        stage('Deploy to Staging') {
            steps {
                script {
                    kubernetesDeploy configs: 'k8s/staging.yaml', kubeconfigId: 'kube-
                        config-staging'
                }
            }
        }
    }
}
```

9. Use Trunk-Based Development

Adopt trunk-based development practices to ensure that the main branch is always in a deployable state. This involves frequent merging and interaction with the mainline branch, reducing the complexity and risk associated with large integrations. Jenkins provides features like multibranch pipelines that accommodate this approach.

```
pipeline {
    agent any

    stages {
        stage('Merge to Main') {
            steps {
                checkout([$class: 'GitSCM', branches: [[name: '*/main']],
                    doGenerateSubmoduleConfigurations: false, extensions: [[$class: '
                    CleanCheckout']], submoduleCfg: [], userRemoteConfigs: [[url: '
                    https://github.com/example/repo.git']]])
                sh 'git merge feature-branch'
            }
        }
    }
}
```

10. Documentation and Training

Ensure that documentation is comprehensive and accessible. This includes the configuration of Jenkins jobs, pipeline scripts, and infrastructure setups. Additionally, ongoing training and knowledge sharing within the team are essential for maintaining and improving the pipeline. Tools like Confluence and JIRA can aid in documenting and tracking workflow processes.

The practices outlined here aim to instill a disciplined and efficient approach to Continuous Delivery, leveraging Jenkins as the orchestrating tool. By adhering to these practices, teams can ensure that their pipelines are robust, secure, and capable of delivering high-quality software in a seamless and continuous manner.

Chapter 7

Managing Jenkins

This chapter focuses on the comprehensive management of Jenkins, including configuration, monitoring, and maintenance. It covers managing nodes and executors, plugins, global tool integrations, and credentials. The chapter details scheduling jobs, builds, and setting up backup and restore processes. Additionally, it provides strategies for troubleshooting and diagnostics to ensure a stable and efficient Jenkins environment.

7.1 Introduction to Jenkins Management

Jenkins is an open-source automation server widely used for continuous integration and continuous delivery (CI/CD). Efficient management of Jenkins ensures a stable, scalable, and responsive environment, minimizing downtime and maximizing productivity. Effective Jenkins management encompasses various tasks, including configuration, monitoring, maintenance, and optimization of resources. This section provides a detailed introduction to these core management aspects, setting the foundation for the subsequent chapters.

Configuration: Jenkins configuration involves setting up the server and defining how it interacts with external systems and tools. This process includes configuring system properties, managing plugins, and setting up global tool integrations. Proper configuration ensures that Jenkins operates reliably and efficiently within the desired infrastructure and meets the specific needs of your development workflow.

Monitoring: Continuous monitoring of Jenkins is vital to maintain its performance and health. This involves tracking system metrics, such as CPU and memory usage, as well as Jenkins-specific metrics like queue length and job executor status. Utilizing monitoring tools and plugins helps in proactively identifying potential issues, ensuring timely intervention before they impact the development pipeline.

Maintenance: Regular maintenance is crucial to keep Jenkins running smoothly. This includes tasks such as cleaning up old builds, updating plugins, backing up configurations, and upgrading Jenkins itself. Scheduled maintenance activities help prevent unforeseen breakdowns, ensuring a reliable CI/CD pipeline.

Optimization: Optimization involves fine-tuning Jenkins performance to handle higher workloads and reduce execution times. This includes optimizing the configurations of nodes and executors, managing resource allocation efficiently, and using load balancing techniques. Optimization practices lead to faster build times and more efficient resource usage, enhancing the productivity and throughput of development projects.

Managing Nodes and Executors: Jenkins can distribute tasks across multiple nodes and executors to achieve parallel processing, which improves build performance and reliability. Nodes are machines configured to perform build tasks, while executors are the individual threads that run on nodes to execute jobs. Properly managing nodes and executors ensures efficient resource utilization and balanced workload distribution, which is essential for large-scale Jenkins deployments.

Plugins Management: Plugins extend Jenkins' functionality and allow it to integrate with a wide array of tools and services. Managing plugins involves installing, updating, and configuring them to meet specific project requirements. Ensuring that plugins are up-to-date and compatible with the Jenkins core prevents potential conflicts and performance issues.

System Properties Configuration: Configuring system properties involves setting various parameters that control how Jenkins operates. These properties can be set through the Jenkins UI or by editing configuration files. System properties influence various aspects of Jenkins behavior, such as security settings, build options, and resource limits.

Global Tool Integrations: Jenkins integrates with many development tools, such as source code management systems, build tools, and testing frameworks. Configuring global tools allows Jenkins to use these tools across multiple jobs and projects, ensuring consistency and simplifying configuration efforts.

Build Jobs Management: Managing build jobs involves creating, configuring, and maintaining the jobs that Jenkins will execute. A build job defines a series of steps Jenkins performs, such as checking out code, running tests, and deploying applications. Efficient management ensures builds are executed reliably and efficiently.

Credentials Management: Credentials management ensures secure access to external systems and services. Jenkins supports various types of credentials, which can be stored and used in a controlled and auditable manner. Proper management of credentials ensures secure operations and protects sensitive information.

Scheduling Jobs and Builds: Jenkins allows scheduling jobs and builds to run at specific times or intervals. Scheduling is configured using cron-like syntax or trigger-based mechanisms, facilitating automated and recurring tasks. Scheduling helps in optimizing resource usage and ensures timely execution of critical tasks.

Backup and Restore: Regular backup and restore are necessary to protect Jenkins configurations and job histories. Backup strategies involve periodic snapshots of configuration files and job data, which can be restored in case of system failures. Reliable backup and restore processes ensure business continuity and quick recovery from disasters.

Troubleshooting and Diagnostics: Troubleshooting involves identifying and resolving issues that arise during Jenkins operations. Diagnostics tools and logs play a crucial role in understanding the root causes of problems. Effective troubleshooting ensures minimal disruption and maintains the stability of the Jenkins environment.

Efficient Jenkins management is the backbone of a reliable CI/CD pipeline, enabling seamless automation of development tasks. Each aspect of management, from configuration to troubleshooting, contributes to a robust and scalable Jenkins environment capable of handling complex build processes and large development teams. By mastering these management practices, you ensure that Jenkins remains a valuable asset in your software development lifecycle.

7.2 Jenkins Configuration

Configuring Jenkins is a fundamental step in maintaining an efficient and stable CI/CD pipeline. Proper configuration ensures that Jenkins runs smoothly, efficiently manages resources, and integrates seamlessly with various tools and plugins. This section delves into the detailed aspects of Jenkins configuration, helping you set the groundwork for a robust Jenkins environment.

Configuring the System

To access the Jenkins configuration, navigate to Manage Jenkins and then Configure System. This page contains several options to fine-tune the overall behavior of Jenkins.

- **Jenkins URL:** Specify the root URL for Jenkins. This is crucial for generating correct URLs for accessing Jenkins from notifications and links.
- **System Admin e-mail address:** Set an email address for the system administrator. Jenkins uses this address for sending alerts and notifications.
- **Jenkins Paths:** Define the directory paths for Jenkins. The default directory is JENKINS_HOME, where all configuration data and job information are stored. It's advisable to place this directory on a robust storage medium.

Configuring Global Security

Security is essential for protecting your Jenkins instance. Within the Configure Global Security page, several options are available:

- **Enable Security:** Check this option to activate security within Jenkins.
- **Security Realm:** Configure the method Jenkins will use to authenticate users. Common options include Jenkins' own database, LDAP, and Active Directory.
- **Authorization:** Determine how users are authorized to access various parts of Jenkins. Typically, Matrix-based security offers fine-grained control over user permissions. Below is an example of how to configure matrix-based security:

```
Matrix-based security configuration:
- Select 'Matrix-based security'
- Add user or group permissions
- Assign appropriate read, write, execute permissions to users or groups
```

Configuring Global Tools

Jenkins requires numerous tools for building projects, which should be configured globally for consistency:

- **JDK:** Add the Java Development Kit installations that Jenkins will use to compile code.
- **Git:** Define Git installations. Configure multiple Git versions if necessary.
- **Gradle, Maven, Ant, etc.:** Add paths for other build tools that your projects might use.

Below is an example of adding a JDK installation:

```
Name: JDK 11
JAVA_HOME: /usr/lib/jvm/java-11-openjdk
```

Configuring Build Tools and Environments

Customization of the build environment is critical for the reproducibility of builds. The configuration is usually managed within the job configurations, but there are also global configurations for tools like Maven:

- **Configure Maven:** Manage global Maven configurations to ensure consistency across builds.
- **Docker:** Integrate Docker installations to create consistent build environments.

Example configuration for Maven:

```
Maven Name: Apache Maven 3.6.3
MAVEN_HOME: /opt/apache-maven-3.6.3
```

Configuring Notifications

Jenkins can send notifications to users about build statuses and other important events. Configuring email notifications and other forms of communication is crucial for informing the team.

E-mail Notification:

- **SMTP Server:** Set your SMTP server details for Jenkins to send emails.
- **Default Subject:** Customize the subject line for build notifications.
- **Default Content:** Define the content and format of the email notifications. You can use tokens like ${BUILD_NUMBER}, ${JOB_NAME}.

Sample SMTP configuration:

```
SMTP Server: smtp.example.com
Default User e-mail suffix: @example.com
```

Configuring Plugins

Plugins expand Jenkins functionality but need proper configuration and maintenance:

- **Install Plugins:** Use the Plugin Manager to install new plugins from the Jenkins repository.
- **Configure Plugins:** Each plugin might have additional settings accessible via the Configure System page or dedicated configuration pages.

Here's how to install a new plugin:

```
Navigate to Manage Jenkins -> Manage Plugins -> Available tab
Search for the desired plugin
Click "Install without restart" or "Download now and install after restart"
```

System Messages and Notifications

You can set system messages and manage notifications in the Configure System section to communicate with all Jenkins users effectively.

- **System Message:** Display important messages on the Jenkins dashboard.
- **Quiet Period:** Define the quiet period to delay the starting of builds after a commit to realign multiple commits into one build.
- **SCM Checkout Retry Count:** Set the retry count for failed SCM checkouts to handle transient network or SCM server issues.

Here is a sample configuration for displaying a system message:

```
System Message: "Welcome to Jenkins CI server. Scheduled maintenance on Friday, 5
    PM."
```

Proper configuration is vital for harnessing the full potential of Jenkins. Through meticulous setup of system parameters, security, global tools, build environments, notifications, and plugins, Jenkins becomes a powerful tool, streamlining the software development lifecycle.

7.3 Managing Jenkins Nodes and Executors

Effective management of Jenkins nodes and executors is crucial for optimizing resource utilization and ensuring timely execution of build jobs. Nodes, also referred to as agents or slaves, are machines configured to run build jobs, while executors are concurrent build slots available on each node to execute the jobs. Understanding the setup, configuration, and management of nodes and executors can vastly improve the performance and efficiency of your Jenkins environment.

To begin managing nodes in Jenkins, navigate to the Jenkins dashboard and click on **Manage Jenkins**. From there, select **Manage Nodes and Clouds**. This section provides an overview of the available nodes and their status. The functionality here allows for adding new nodes, configuring existing ones, and managing the allocation of executors.

Adding a new node involves specifying a range of configuration parameters. Here is an example configuration for adding a new node via the Jenkins UI:

- **Name**: A unique identifier for the node.
- **Description**: An optional field for describing the node's purpose.
- **Remote root directory**: The directory on the node where Jenkins stores files related to the jobs.
- **Labels**: Labels are used to tag nodes, making it easy to direct specific jobs to nodes with particular capabilities.
- **Usage**: Determines how Jenkins allocates jobs to the node. Options include *Use this node as much as possible* or *Only schedule jobs with label expressions matching this node*.

- **Launch method**: Defines how Jenkins connects to the node. Methods include launching through SSH, via a command on the master, or manually.
- **Availability**: Configures the node's availability, including options for keeping it online permanently or bringing it online/offline at specified times.

Here is an example configuration script for adding a new node using the Jenkins script console:

```
import hudson.model.*
import hudson.slaves.*

def nodeName = 'new-node'
def description = 'A new Jenkins node'
def remoteFS = '/var/jenkins'
def numExecutors = 2
def mode = Node.Mode.EXCLUSIVE
def label = 'linux'
def launcher = new JNLPLauncher()
def retentionStrategy = new RetentionStrategy.Always()
def nodeProperties = new ArrayList<>();

Slave node = new DumbSlave(
    nodeName,
    description,
    remoteFS,
    numExecutors,
    mode,
    label,
    launcher,
    retentionStrategy,
    nodeProperties
)

Jenkins.instance.addNode(node)
```

This script creates a new node named new-node with specific parameters and adds it to the Jenkins instance. Ensure that the parameters are customized per your requirements before execution.

Once nodes are configured, executors are managed through the individual node settings. Each node can have one or more executors, which dictate how many jobs it can handle concurrently. Adjusting the number of executors is a balance between the node's resources and the job requirements. Overloading executors can lead to resource contention and performance degradation, whereas underutilizing them results in inefficient resource use.

To adjust the number of executors on a node, follow these steps:

- Navigate to **Manage Jenkins** > **Manage Nodes and Clouds**.

- Click on the node you wish to configure.
- Select **Configure** from the left-hand menu.
- Adjust the **Number of executors** field as required.
- Save the configuration.

In environments that require dynamic scaling, Jenkins can integrate with cloud providers to automatically provision and de-provision nodes based on demand. Jenkins supports various cloud integrations, including Amazon EC2, Azure, and Google Cloud. Configuring cloud-based nodes involves steps like setting up credentials, defining templates for node instances, and configuring retention strategies to manage costs effectively.

Monitoring the health and status of nodes and executors is an ongoing task. Jenkins provides status indicators and event logs to help administrators keep tabs on node performance and availability. It is vital to regularly check these indicators to preemptively address any issues before they impact job execution.

For example, the **Nodes** screen will display indicators for:

- **Online/Offline status**: Indicates whether the node is currently available for executing jobs.
- **Executor usage**: Shows the number of executors in use versus the total number available.
- **Node log**: Provides detailed logging information about the node's activity and any errors encountered.

Should a node encounter issues, the log details can be invaluable for diagnosing and resolving the underlying problems. Additionally, administrators can configure alerts to notify them when a node goes offline or experiences errors.

Considering security, it is essential to configure nodes with appropriate permissions and credentials. Nodes should use non-privileged accounts with the minimum necessary permissions to run Jenkins agents, and communication between Jenkins and nodes should be encrypted to prevent unauthorized access and data breaches.

Integrating these practices will help in maintaining a robust, efficient, and secure Jenkins environment. Consistently reviewing and optimizing nodes and executors can lead to a significant improvement in build performance and resource utilization.

7.4 Monitoring Jenkins

Monitoring Jenkins effectively is crucial for maintaining a stable and efficient Continuous Integration/Continuous Deployment (CI/CD) environment. Monitoring encompasses tracking the performance, health, and resource utilization of the Jenkins server and nodes. Effective monitoring helps identify potential issues early and ensures the system runs smoothly. This section delves into various strategies and tools for comprehensive monitoring of Jenkins.

Jenkins Dashboard

The Jenkins dashboard provides a bird's-eye view of the overall system status, including currently running jobs, system load, and node status. Key elements to monitor on the Jenkins dashboard include:

- **Build Queue:** Displays jobs waiting for executor availability.
- **Build Executor Status:** Shows the jobs currently being executed on available nodes.
- **Weather Icons:** Reflect the stability of different projects, indicating recent build successes or failures.

Utilizing the dashboard effectively can give quick insights into the system's health and performance.

System Logs

Jenkins maintains extensive logging capabilities to help administrators monitor activity and pinpoint issues. Key log files include:

- **jenkins.log:** Contains information about the Jenkins master's operations.
- **node-specific logs:** Include logs for each configured node, providing insights into node-specific issues.
- **Job logs:** Record the output from individual jobs.

Logs can be accessed through the Jenkins UI under Manage Jenkins > System Log.

System Monitoring Tools and Plugins

Several plugins and tools help in monitoring Jenkins more effectively by providing additional metrics and visualizations:

- **Monitoring Plugin:** Provides comprehensive monitoring including JVM heap usage, CPU load, garbage collection activities, and thread counts. To install and configure this plugin, navigate to Manage Jenkins > Manage Plugins > Available tab and look for the "Monitoring" plugin.
- **Performance Monitoring Tools:** Tools like Prometheus and Grafana can be integrated with Jenkins to provide advanced analytics and visualization capabilities. Prometheus collects metrics data, which can then be visualized using Grafana dashboards.

Example of Prometheus Integration

To integrate Prometheus with Jenkins, follow these steps:

1. Install the Prometheus Plugin from the Jenkins plugin repository.
2. Configure the plugin by navigating to Manage Jenkins > Configure System.
3. Add the Prometheus endpoint URL to the Prometheus configuration file.

The following is an example of the Prometheus configuration file:

```
scrape_configs:
  - job_name: 'jenkins'
    static_configs:
      - targets: ['<Jenkins-Server-IP>:<Port>']
```

This configuration adds Jenkins as a new job in Prometheus. Metrics collected by Prometheus can now be visualized using Grafana.

Health Checks

Regular health checks of the Jenkins server and its nodes are essential. Automated scripts and plugins can facilitate these checks, ensuring that any signs of trouble are identified promptly.

Example Health Check Script

Here is an example of a Bash script that checks various Jenkins health metrics:

```
#!/bin/bash

JENKINS_URL="http://localhost:8080"

# Check Jenkins status
STATUS=$(curl -s "${JENKINS_URL}/login" | grep -c "Dashboard")
if [[ $STATUS -ne 0 ]]; then
  echo "Jenkins is up and running."
else
  echo "Jenkins is down."
fi

# Check for queue size
QUEUE_SIZE=$(curl -s "${JENKINS_URL}/queue/api/json" | jq '.items | length')
echo "Number of Jobs in Queue: ${QUEUE_SIZE}"

# Check number of executors
EXECUTORS=$(curl -s "${JENKINS_URL}/computer/api/json" | jq '.busyExecutors'
    )
echo "Number of Busy Executors: ${EXECUTORS}"
```

Executing this script regularly can provide a quick overview of the Jenkins server's health.

Third-Party Monitoring Services

Integrating Jenkins with third-party monitoring services like New Relic, Datadog, or Nagios can enhance monitoring capabilities. These services offer advanced alerting mechanisms, diverse monitoring metrics, and comprehensive reporting functionalities.

Example Integration with Datadog

To integrate Datadog with Jenkins, follow these steps:

1. Install the Datadog Agent on the Jenkins server.
2. Configure Datadog to collect Jenkins metrics by editing the Datadog agent configuration file (e.g., datadog.yaml).
3. Enable Jenkins integration in the Datadog platform and configure necessary parameters such as the Jenkins server URL and API token.

The configuration file might look like this:

```
init_config:

instances:
  - name: jenkins
    jenkins_host: http://localhost:8080
```

```
  username: <your-username>
  password: <your-api-token>
```

These setups allow Datadog to start collecting and visualizing Jenkins performance metrics, helping in proactive monitoring and issue resolution.

Handling Alerts

Configure thresholds and alerts to notify administrators about potential issues. Thresholds can be set for CPU usage, memory consumption, build queue length, and job failure rates. Alerts can be configured to be sent via email, Slack, or other communication tools to ensure the team is immediately aware of issues.

```
alert:
  name: Jenkins CPU Usage High
  query: (avg by (job) (rate(node_cpu_seconds_total{mode="idle"}[5m])) < 0.1)
  for: 5m
  labels:
    severity: critical
  annotations:
    summary: "High CPU usage on {{ $labels.job }}"
```

This sample Prometheus alert configuration triggers an alert when CPU usage exceeds 90% for more than 5 minutes, helping administrators to take timely action.

Effective monitoring of Jenkins involves continuous tracking of system metrics, regular health checks, and integrating with advanced monitoring and alerting tools. This ensures potential issues are identified and resolved promptly, maintaining a stable and efficient CI/CD environment.

7.5 Managing Plugins

Jenkins plugins are critical components extending the capabilities of the core Jenkins system. Effective plugin management involves tasks such as installation, update, configuration, and troubleshooting. This section details the process for managing plugins in Jenkins, ensuring they contribute to a robust and efficient build environment.

Plugins in Jenkins can be managed via the web interface by navigating to **Manage Jenkins** → **Manage Plugins**. The Plugin Manager allows for the management of plugins in four main tabs: **Updates**, **Available**, **Installed**, and **Advanced**.

Updates tab shows the list of installed plugins that have new versions available. Regularly updating plugins is essential to benefit from bug fixes, security patches, and new features. To update plugins:

- Navigate to the **Updates** tab in the Plugin Manager.
- Select the desired plugins or use *Select all* for batch updates.
- Click on the **Download now and install after restart** option to fetch and apply updates after a Jenkins restart.

Available tab shows plugins that can be installed that are not currently present in the Jenkins instance. To install a new plugin:

- Navigate to the **Available** tab in the Plugin Manager.
- Search for the specific plugin using the search bar or browse through the list.
- Select the desired plugin(s).
- Click the **Download now and install after restart** button. For immediate installation, you may click **Install without restart**; however, this may cause jobs currently running to fail or behave unpredictably.

Installed tab provides a list of all currently installed plugins, offering configuration options and indicating which can be updated or have additional configuration settings. The visualization includes columns such as the plugin name, version, and actions (such as *Enable*, *Disable*, *Update*, and *Remove*).

Advanced tab provides more granular control over plugin management, such as:

- Uploading plugins manually by specifying a '.hpi' or '.jpi' file.
- Managing proxy settings to allow Jenkins to connect to the internet through a proxy, which is essential for environments with restricted internet access.
- Setting up an alternative update center URL if using a private repository for plugins.

Programmatically Managing Plugins

In certain scenarios, managing plugins programmatically may be required for automation and consistency across different Jenkins instances. Jenkins plugins can be managed using 'jenkins-cli.jar' and Groovy scripts.

Creating a Jenkins CLI command to install a plugin:

```
java -jar jenkins-cli.jar -s http://<jenkins_url> install-plugin <plugin_name>
```

To list installed plugins:

```
java -jar jenkins-cli.jar -s http://<jenkins_url> list-plugins
```

For environments where automation is prioritized, Jenkins Configuration as Code (JCasC) plugin can be utilized. JCasC enables you to manage your Jenkins configuration, including plugins, using a YAML file.

Sample YAML configuration for managing plugins via JCasC:

```
jenkins:
  systemMessage: "Managed by code"
  numExecutors: 5
  securityRealm:
    local:
      allowsSignup: false
      users:
      - id: admin
        password: $crypted_password
  authorizationStrategy:
    loggedInUsersCanDoAnything:
      allowAnonymousRead: false

tool:
  git:
    installations:
      - name: "Default"
        home: "/usr/bin/git"

plugins:
  required:
    - git:3.6.4
    - workflow-aggregator:2.6
    - credentials:2.1.18
    - configuration-as-code:1.24
```

The YAML file specified above configures various sections of Jenkins, including the installation of plugins like 'git', 'workflow-aggregator', 'credentials', and 'configuration-as-code'. This ensures consistent environment setup and quicker recovery times.

Troubleshooting Plugins

Managing plugins also entails resolving any issues arising from conflicts or erroneous behavior. Common issues include version incompatibility causing Jenkins to fail or system performance degradation due to poorly functioning plugins. Diagnostic steps include:

- **View Logs:** Inspect Jenkins logs available at **Manage Jenkins → System Log**. Specific plugin-related errors are typically logged here.
- **Safe Restart:** Execute a safe restart to ensure no job is running: <jenkins_url>/safeRestart
- **Plugin Dependency:** Verify plugin dependencies are met by checking the plugin page on the update center or the Jenkins wiki.
- **Disable/Enable:** Sequentially disable and enable plugins to isolate the problematic one through the **Installed** plugins tab.

Resolving such issues maintains system stability and aligns with best practices for Jenkins maintenance. Effective plugin management significantly enhances Jenkins capabilities and contributes to a stable continuous integration/continuous deployment (CI/CD) pipeline.

7.6 Configuring System Properties

Efficient management of Jenkins requires precise configuration of system properties. These properties allow administrators to fine-tune the Jenkins environment for performance, security, and specific project needs. System properties can be set in various ways: through the Jenkins UI, initialization scripts, or directly via configuration files. This section delves into the processes and implications of configuring these properties, reinforcing the stability and scalability of your Jenkins instance.

Jenkins operates based on a variety of system properties, facilitated primarily by Java properties and specific Jenkins settings tailored to manage builds, plugins, user permissions, and more. Configuration can be done via:

- The jenkins.model.JenkinsLocationConfiguration.xml file.

- The JAVA_ARGS environment variable.
- Direct modification through the Jenkins user interface.

Configuring via XML Files

The jenkins.model.JenkinsLocationConfiguration.xml file is a primary file where core system properties can be set. This file typically resides in the Jenkins home directory. Edits to this file require a server restart to take effect. To illustrate, consider a scenario where you need to configure the Jenkins URL and system-admin email address:

```
<?xml version='1.1' encoding='UTF-8'?>
<jenkins.model.JenkinsLocationConfiguration>
  <adminAddress>admin@yourdomain.com</adminAddress>
  <jenkinsUrl>http://yourjenkinsdomain.com/</jenkinsUrl>
</jenkins.model.JenkinsLocationConfiguration>
```

Modifications made in this file explicitly set the administrative contact and Jenkins URL, enabling proper notification workflows and network accessibility.

Setting Properties Using Environment Variables

Java system properties can be manipulated using the JAVA_ARGS variable. This is particularly useful for settings that influence JVM behavior or Jenkins security settings. For example, to adjust the heap size and set a custom system property, you might alter the Jenkins service configuration script (often located in /etc/default/jenkins, /etc/sysconfig/jenkins, or directly in the Jenkins WAR startup script):

```
JAVA_ARGS="-Xmx2048m -Djenkins.install.runSetupWizard=false"
```

In this instance, the maximum heap size is set to 2048MB, and the setup wizard is disabled for initial startup, streamlining the deployment for script-based installations.

Configuring System Properties via the Jenkins UI

For immediate and less invasive changes, Jenkins offers the system configuration through the UI (Manage Jenkins → Configure System). This interface provides a convenient means to adjust settings, including global environment variables, Git configurations, and more.

For example, to set a global environment variable:

1. Navigate to Manage Jenkins → Configure System.
2. Scroll down to the Global properties section.

3. Check the Environment variables option.

4. Add a new variable, e.g., MY_VAR with value myValue.

Such configurations are stored internally and require no service restart, making them ideal for dynamic environments where frequent adjustments are necessary.

Example: Configuring Build Timeout

Adjusting build timeouts is a critical aspect of maintaining Jenkins performance. Long-running builds can consume significant resources, leading to potential bottlenecks. Configuring the build timeout system property ensures builds are terminated after a specified period, freeing resources for other tasks.

This can be done via the Configure System page:

1. Navigate to Manage Jenkins → Configure System.

2. Locate the Build-timeout plugin settings (assuming the plugin is installed).

3. Set the Maximum build time (e.g., 60 minutes).

Alternatively, if using a configuration file such as config.xml for the job:

```
<project>
    ...
    <buildWrappers>
        <hudson.plugins.build___timeout.BuildTimeoutWrapper>
            <strategy class="hudson.plugins.build_timeout.impl.
                    AbsoluteTimeOutStrategy">
                <timeoutMinutes>60</timeoutMinutes>
            </strategy>
        </hudson.plugins.build___timeout.BuildTimeoutWrapper>
    </buildWrappers>
</project>
```

Security Settings

Certain security aspects, such as enabling CSRF protection or setting custom security realms, can be configured via system properties. For instance, enabling CSRF protection:

```
-Djenkins.security.csrf.GlobalCrumbIssuerConfiguration.disabled=false
```

These properties can be set in the Jenkins startup script or via the JAVA_ARGS variable, as previously illustrated.

Verifying Changes

After configuring system properties, it is essential to verify that the settings have been applied correctly:

1. For XML changes, restart the Jenkins service: service jenkins restart.
2. Check the System Information page (Manage Jenkins → System Information) for updated values.
3. Validate through UI elements where changes are reflected, e.g., the Jenkins URL showing the configured value.

This practice ensures consistency and functionality alignment, preventing configuration drift and potential system inconsistencies.

7.7 Configuring Global Tool Integrations

Configuring global tool integrations in Jenkins is a crucial aspect for enabling various build and deployment tools to function seamlessly within the Jenkins environment. This section details the configuration of widely used tools such as JDK (Java Development Kit), Maven, Git, and Gradle. Setting up these tools correctly ensures that Jenkins can execute builds using the necessary software environments and dependencies.

Java Development Kit (JDK)

Java is a predominant programming language in enterprise applications, and Jenkins itself runs on JVM (Java Virtual Machine). To configure the JDK in Jenkins, follow the steps below:

- Go to *Manage Jenkins* from the main Jenkins dashboard.
- Select *Global Tool Configuration*.
- In the *JDK* section, click *Add JDK*.
- Uncheck the *Install automatically* option if you manually manage JDK installations.
- Provide a name for this JDK installation, for example, JDK_11.

- Specify the JAVA_HOME path where JDK is installed on the node.

```
Example: /usr/lib/jvm/java-11-openjdk
```

These configurations allow Jenkins to use the specified JDK version for projects that require it, ensuring compatibility with the Java applications being built.

Maven

Maven is a powerful build automation tool primarily used for Java projects. To set up Maven in Jenkins:

- Navigate to *Manage Jenkins → Global Tool Configuration*.
- Find the *Maven* section and click *Add Maven*.
- Provide a name for this Maven installation, such as Maven_3.6.3.
- If required, check the box for *Install automatically* to let Jenkins download Maven from the Internet.
- Alternatively, specify the local installation path in the MAVEN_HOME field.

```
Example: /opt/maven/apache-maven-3.6.3
```

This configuration allows Jenkins to invoke Maven for building and managing project dependencies, ensuring the right version of Maven is used.

Git

Git is the most widely used version control system. To configure Git in Jenkins:

- Go to *Manage Jenkins → Global Tool Configuration*.
- Locate the *Git* section and click *Add Git*.
- Provide a meaningful name, e.g., Default_Git.

- Specify the path to the Git executable, ensuring it is accessible from Jenkins agents.

```
Example: /usr/bin/git
```

Correct Git setup is crucial for Jenkins to clone repositories, perform checkouts, and manage source code effectively.

Gradle

Gradle is another popular build automation system that supports multiple languages and platforms. To integrate Gradle with Jenkins:

- Access *Manage Jenkins → Global Tool Configuration*.
- In the *Gradle* section, click *Add Gradle*.
- Enter a name for this Gradle installation, such as Gradle_6.7.
- Decide whether to let Jenkins install Gradle automatically or specify an existing installation path.

```
Example: /opt/gradle/gradle-6.7
```

This enables Jenkins to leverage Gradle for building projects, supporting Jenkins pipelines with advanced build configurations.

Example Jenkinsfile with Tool Integrations

Integrating these tools into Jenkins Pipeline is facilitated using the tools directive in Jenkinsfile. Below is an example illustrating how to configure and use JDK, Maven, and Git within a Pipeline.

```
pipeline {
    agent any

    tools {
        // Define the JDK to use
        jdk 'JDK_11'
        // Define the Maven version to use
        maven 'Maven_3.6.3'
    }

    stages {
        stage('Checkout') {
            steps {
                // Checkout source code from Git repository
                git 'https://github.com/example/repository.git'
            }
```

```
        }

        stage('Build') {
            steps {
                // Run Maven build
                sh 'mvn clean install'
            }
        }

        stage('Deploy') {
            steps {
                echo 'Deploying application...'
                // Add deployment steps here
            }
        }
    }
}
```

When executed, the pipeline uses the configured JDK 11 and Maven 3.6.3 to build the project. Git is used for checking out the source code.

Validation and Testing After setting up the tools, validate the configurations by running test builds to ensure Jenkins correctly recognizes and uses the specified tools. Any misconfiguration will typically result in build failures, prompting corrective action.

Properly configuring global tool integrations bridges Jenkins with essential build tools, optimizing the build process and ensuring predictable, reliable builds.

7.8 Managing Build Jobs

Build jobs are a crucial aspect of Jenkins, serving as the core tasks Jenkins executes. These jobs compile, test, and deploy your software. Managing these jobs efficiently can significantly enhance your build pipelines, improving overall productivity and software quality.

A build job in Jenkins can be configured through the Jenkins interface by navigating to **New Item** on the dashboard. The following configuration options need detailed attention:

1. Project Name: The initial step in creating a build job is to specify a unique name for the project. This name should be descriptive and follow a consistent naming convention used in your organization.

2. Project Type: Jenkins supports various project types:

- **Freestyle Project:** A flexible project type to execute multiple build steps.

- **Pipeline:** Defines the entire build process through a Jenkinsfile with a domain-specific language (DSL).
- **Multibranch Pipeline:** Designed to automatically create a pipeline for each branch in a source control repository.
- **External Job:** Designed for jobs that run outside Jenkins but are monitored by Jenkins.

3. Source Code Management (SCM): Jenkins integrates with various SCM tools such as Git, Subversion, and Mercurial. Configuration settings include repository URL, credentials, and branch to build. Example for Git configuration:

```
git('https://github.com/your-repo.git') {
    branch('main')
}
```

4. Build Triggers: Determines when a build job should run. Options include:

- **Build Periodically:** Uses a cron-like syntax to schedule jobs.
- **Poll SCM:** Monitors the repository for changes and triggers a build when changes are detected.
- **Build after other projects:** Specifies that this job should run after one or more other jobs have completed.
- **GitHub Hook Trigger:** Uses a webhook to trigger builds upon repository changes.

Cron-like syntax example:

```
H/15 * * * *
```

5. Build Environment: Configures the environment within which the build should run. Common configurations include:

- **Use secret text(s) or files:** Injects secret files or text into the build environment for secure access.
- **Delete workspace before build starts:** Ensures a clean workspace by deleting files from the previous build.
- **Restrict where this project can be run:** Specifies which nodes or labels are permissible for this build to execute on.

6. Build Steps: Defines the actual tasks that Jenkins performs during the build. Common steps include:

- **Execute shell:** Runs commands in a shell script. Example:

```
echo "Building the project..."
./gradlew build
```

- **Invoke Ant:** Runs Ant tasks.
- **Invoke Gradle script:** Runs Gradle tasks.
- **Execute Windows batch command:** Runs commands in a Windows command line environment.

7. Post-build Actions: Actions to execute after the build completes, such as:

- **Publish JUnit test result report:** Integrates test results from JUnit.
- **Archive the artifacts:** Archives build artifacts for later use. Example:

```
archiveArtifacts artifacts: '**/build/libs/*.jar', allowEmptyArchive: false
```

- **Email notifications:** Sends notifications based on build status (success, failure, etc.).

Visualization through the Jenkins interface helps in monitoring build job history and status. Color codes and icons (e.g., blue for success, red for failure) illustrate build outcomes for easy identification. Logs for each build can be accessed to diagnose issues.

Configurations can be exported as XML for portability. The 'job-dsl' plugin provides another approach to define jobs programmatically. Job DSL can iterate through templates, automatically creating multiple jobs:

```
pipelineJob('example-pipeline') {
    definition {
        cps {
            script(readFileFromWorkspace('Jenkinsfile'))
            sandbox()
        }
    }
}
```

Managing build jobs in Jenkins not only involves setting them up but also continuously reviewing and optimizing them. Jenkins provides plugins and tools to define complex CI/CD pipelines, ensuring efficient and high-quality builds.

This section has distilled the essential aspects of managing build jobs in Jenkins, emphasizing practical configurations and examples to enhance understanding and application.

7.9 Setting Up and Managing Credentials

Setting up and managing credentials in Jenkins is fundamental to maintaining a secure and effective continuous integration environment. Credentials in Jenkins are used for authenticating external systems and services such as source control repositories, deployment platforms, and external APIs. This section will delve into the processes and best practices for managing credentials within Jenkins.

Jenkins supports various credential types, including but not limited to SSH keys, secret texts, username-password pairs, and certificates. Understanding how to create, store, and securely manage these credentials ensures the protection of sensitive information and smooth operation of build and deployment processes.

Creating and Managing Credentials

To create a new credential, follow these steps:

- Navigate to the Jenkins dashboard.
- Click on *Manage Jenkins* in the sidebar.
- Select *Manage Credentials*.
- Choose the appropriate store and domain where the credential should be stored. Typically, the *Global* domain is used for credentials accessible to all jobs.

After selecting the domain, proceed as follows:

- Click on *Add Credentials*.
- From the *Kind* dropdown, select the type of credential you wish to create. The available types may include:

- **Secret text**: A secret string such as an API token.
- **Username with password**: A pair of username and password.
- **SSH Username with private key**: Used for SSH authentication.
- **Certificate**: A client certificate for authentication.
- Fill in the details for the credential based on the selected type.
- Click on *OK* to save the credential.

Usage of Credentials in Jenkins Jobs

Once credentials are added, they can be referenced in Jenkins jobs and pipelines. For instance, when configuring a job to connect to a Git repository that requires authentication, use the following steps:

- In the job configuration, under the *Source Code Management* section, select *Git*.
- Provide the repository URL.
- Click on the *Add* button next to the *Credentials* field to select the appropriate credential. If the desired credential is not listed, ensure that it exists in the appropriate domain.

Example of Using Credentials in a Pipeline Script

When using a Jenkins pipeline (either declarative or scripted), credentials can be accessed using the credentials or withCredentials helper functions. Here is an example of how to use a username-password credential within a declarative pipeline:

```
pipeline {
    agent any
    environment {
        GIT_CREDENTIALS = credentials('my-git-creds-id')
    }
    stages {
        stage('Clone repository') {
            steps {
                git url: 'git@github.com:user/repo.git',
                    credentialsId: "${GIT_CREDENTIALS}"
            }
        }
    }
}
```

In this pipeline:

- The environment block assigns the credential ID my-git-creds-id to the variable GIT_CREDENTIALS.
- The git step references this variable to authenticate and clone the repository.

Security Considerations

Managing credentials necessitates strict security practices:

- Store credentials in the *Global* domain only if they need to be accessible across all jobs. Otherwise, use specific domains to limit their scope.
- Regularly review and rotate credentials to minimize risks associated with credential leaks.
- Follow the principle of least privilege, ensuring that only necessary permissions are granted to the credentials.
- Monitor audit logs to detect unauthorized access attempts to credentials.

Credentials should be encrypted at rest, which Jenkins does by default using the Jenkins Server's main configuration file. To further enhance security, consider using external secret management tools like HashiCorp Vault, CyberArk, or AWS Secrets Manager, which Jenkins can integrate with.

Example: Integrating Jenkins with HashiCorp Vault

Here's an example to illustrate the process of using a HashiCorp Vault plugin to manage secrets within Jenkins:

```
pipeline {
    agent any
    environment {
        VAULT_ADDR = 'https://vault.example.com:8200'
        VAULT_TOKEN = credentials('vault-token-id')
    }
    stages {
        stage('Authenticate with Vault') {
            steps {
                withCredentials([string(credentialsId: 'vault-token-id', variable: '
                        VAULT_TOKEN')]) {
                    sh 'vault login $VAULT_TOKEN'
                }
            }
        }
        stage('Retrieve secrets from Vault') {
            steps {
```

```
                script {
                    def secret = sh (script: 'vault kv get -field=my-secret secret/myapp',
                                        returnStdout: true).trim()
                    echo "Retrieved secret: ${secret}"
                }
            }
        }
    }
}
```

In this script:

- The withCredentials block securely injects the Vault token into the shell command to authenticate with Vault.
- The secret retrieval is performed using the Vault command line interface.

Understanding and implementing these methodologies ensures the secure and efficient use of credentials in Jenkins, thereby protecting sensitive information and maintaining the integrity of the CI/CD pipeline.

7.10 Scheduling Jobs and Builds

In Jenkins, efficient scheduling of jobs and builds is central to maintaining a smooth and productive continuous integration and continuous delivery (CI/CD) environment. Properly scheduled jobs ensure the optimum utilization of resources, prevent bottlenecks, and align with the overall project timelines. This section delves deeply into the mechanisms Jenkins employs for scheduling, the configuration of triggers, and the utilization of various scheduling strategies to meet diverse requirements.

1. Understanding Job Scheduling in Jenkins

Jenkins utilizes a timing mechanism based on cron syntax to schedule jobs and builds. The cron syntax consists of five fields representing different time units: minute, hour, day of month, month, and day of week. The cron expression follows this format:

```
* * * * *
| | | | |
| | | | +---- Day of Week (0 - 7) (Sunday = 0 or 7)
| | | +------ Month (1 - 12)
| | +-------- Day of Month (1 - 31)
| +---------- Hour (0 - 23)
+------------ Minute (0 - 59)
```

For example, to schedule a job to run at 15 minutes past the hour, every hour, the syntax would be:

```
15 * * * *
```

2. Using Build Triggers

Jenkins provides several types of build triggers that can be configured to start builds automatically. These include:

- **Cron Trigger:** Configures periodic scheduling using cron syntax.
- **SCM Trigger:** Initiates builds when changes are detected in the source code repository.
- **Remote Trigger:** Allows the initiation of builds through remote REST API calls.
- **Build After Other Projects:** Triggers builds upon the completion of specified projects.

The following is an example of a Jenkins pipeline configuration utilizing a cron trigger:

```
pipeline {
    agent any
    triggers {
        cron('H 4/* 0 0 1-5')
    }
    stages {
        stage('Build') {
            steps {
                echo 'Building..'
            }
        }
        stage('Test') {
            steps {
                echo 'Testing..'
            }
        }
        stage('Deploy') {
            steps {
                echo 'Deploying....'
            }
        }
    }
}
```

In the above example, the pipeline is triggered at a randomized hour (indicated by 'H') every 4 hours on weekdays.

3. Polling vs. Push Based Triggers

SCM polling is a method where Jenkins periodically polls the source code repository to detect changes and trigger builds. This method involves predetermined intervals for polling, defined as follows:

```
H/5 * * * *
```

The above expression polls the repository every 5 minutes. However, frequent polling can lead to performance degradation, especially in large repositories. To mitigate this, push-based triggers, such as the Webhook mechanism, are preferred. Webhooks are HTTP callbacks that receive event notifications from the SCM, like when changes are pushed to a repository.

To set up a Webhook in Jenkins, one would configure the SCM (e.g., GitHub) to send HTTP POST requests to Jenkins upon changes. Jenkins then processes these requests to trigger the associated jobs.

4. Utilizing Parameterized Builds

Parameterized builds allow for flexible job executions by incorporating dynamic values into the build process. Parameters are inputs defined in the job configuration, which can be passed manually or through automated scripts.

Common parameter types include:

- **String Parameter:** Accepts textual input.
- **Boolean Parameter:** Represents a true/false value.
- **Choice Parameter:** Provides a predefined list of options.

Example of parameterized build script in Jenkinsfile:

```
pipeline {
    agent any
    parameters {
        string(name: 'VERSION', defaultValue: '1.0.0', description: 'Release version')
        booleanParam(name: 'DEPLOY', defaultValue: true, description: 'Deploy
              application')
    }
    stages {
        stage('Build') {
            steps {
                echo "Building version ${params.VERSION}"
            }
        }
        stage('Deploy') {
            when {
                expression { return params.DEPLOY }
            }
            steps {
                echo 'Deploying application...'
```

```
            }
        }
    }
}
```

In this configuration, the ‘VERSION‘ parameter determines the build version, and the ‘DEPLOY‘ boolean parameter controls whether the application is deployed.

5. Concurrent Builds and Build Queuing

Jenkins handles builds execution via executors. By default, Jenkins allows concurrent builds if multiple executors are configured. However, there are scenarios where concurrency control is necessary to avoid resource contention.

You can enforce build concurrency constraints using the ‘Build Blocker‘ plugin, which blocks builds if specified jobs are currently running, or through the ‘Lockable Resources‘ plugin to manage shared resources.

Configuration example for ‘Lockable Resources‘ in Jenkinsfile:

```
pipeline {
    agent any
    options {
        lock(resource: 'sharedResource') {
            echo 'Running with locked resource'
        }
    }
}
```

Restricting concurrent builds ensures critical sections of the build process run exclusively, preventing race conditions and other conflicts.

6. Advanced Scheduling Strategies

For complex CI/CD workflows, advanced scheduling strategies may be necessary. Conditional builds can be implemented based on environment-specific conditions or external parameters.

By combining Jenkins’ job chaining capability (build after projects) and advanced pipeline scripting, multi-stage deployments with conditional triggers can be orchestrated. Declarative and scripted pipelines support intricate conditions and branching logic.

Example of conditional build logic in Jenkinsfile:

```
pipeline {
    agent any
    environment {
        TARGET_ENV = 'production'
    }
    stages {
```

```
        stage('Test Environment') {
            when {
                environment name: 'TARGET_ENV', value: 'production'
            }
            steps {
                echo 'Testing for Production Environment'
            }
        }
        stage('Build Environment') {
            when {
                anyOf {
                    environment name: 'TARGET_ENV', value: 'staging'
                    environment name: 'TARGET_ENV', value: 'production'
                }
            }
            steps {
                echo 'Building for Staging/Production Environment'
            }
        }
    }
}
```

Incorporating conditional logic ensures that stages execute only under predefined circumstances, optimizing the pipeline and matching the deployment needs.

Efficient job scheduling in Jenkins involves understanding cron expressions, configuring various triggers, balancing polling and pushing strategies, and leveraging parameterized builds for flexibility. Advanced scheduling with concurrent build control and conditional stages enhances Jenkins' capability to manage complex workflows, ensuring robust build and deployment processes.

7.11 Backup and Restore

A robust backup and restore strategy is essential for ensuring the continuity and resilience of your Jenkins environment. This section outlines the processes and best practices involved in backing up Jenkins configuration, jobs, and plugins, as well as the steps to restore them in the event of data loss or corruption.

Jenkins maintains its state in a directory referred to as *JENKINS_HOME*. This directory encompasses configuration files, job definitions, build histories, plugin archives, and other crucial data. It is imperative to back up the entirety of *JENKINS_HOME* to safeguard your Jenkins instance.

Regular Backup Procedures

To perform a backup, ensure Jenkins is either minimally active or in a quiescent state to avoid inconsistencies. Utilize either manual or automated methods for this task:

- **Manual Backup**: Stop the Jenkins service to ensure a consistent backup state. Use tar or zip commands to archive the entire *JENKINS_HOME* directory.

```
sudo service jenkins stop
tar -czvf jenkins_backup.tar.gz $JENKINS_HOME
sudo service jenkins start
```

- **Automated Backup**: Employ plugins such as ThinBackup or shell scripts scheduled via cron jobs to automate the process.

```
#!/bin/bash

JENKINS_HOME="/var/lib/jenkins"
BACKUP_DIR="/backup/jenkins"
TIMESTAMP=$(date +"%Y%m%d_%H%M%S")

tar -czvf $BACKUP_DIR/jenkins_backup_$TIMESTAMP.tar.gz
    $JENKINS_HOME

# Ensure backups older than 7 days are deleted
find $BACKUP_DIR -type f -name "jenkins_backup_*.tar.gz" -mtime +7 -
    exec rm {} \;
```

Plugin-Specific Backups

Certain plugins may have their own data storage, located outside of *JENKINS_HOME*. Ensure these directories are also included in the backup strategy. For example, if using the Code Coverage API Plugin, its data might be stored under a different directory defined in the plugin configuration. Always consult the documentation of each plugin for specific backup instructions.

Restoration Procedures

Restoring Jenkins from a backup involves a series of steps to ensure a smooth transition without data loss or corruption:

- **Manual Restore**: Stop the Jenkins service before restoration. Extract the archived backup to the *JENKINS_HOME* directory.

```
sudo service jenkins stop
tar -xzvf jenkins_backup.tar.gz -C $JENKINS_HOME
sudo service jenkins start
```

- **Automated Restore**: Should a catastrophe occur, an automated script can simplify and speed up the restoration process.

```
#!/bin/bash

JENKINS_HOME="/var/lib/jenkins"
BACKUP_ARCHIVE="/backup/jenkins/jenkins_backup_latest.tar.gz"

sudo service jenkins stop
tar -xzvf $BACKUP_ARCHIVE -C $JENKINS_HOME
sudo service jenkins start
```

Verification Post-Restoration

Post-restoration, it is critical to verify the integrity and functionality of the Jenkins environment. This involves:

- Checking the status of the Jenkins service to ensure it is running correctly:

```
sudo service jenkins status
```

- Reviewing log files located in *JENKINS_HOME*/logs for any error messages or warnings.
- Validating that all jobs are present and can be executed without issues. Trigger a few key jobs to confirm their proper operation.
- Ensuring that plugins are active and functioning as expected. This can be verified through the Jenkins Plugin Manager interface.

Regularly scheduled backups and thorough restoration testing are vital components of a dependable Jenkins management strategy. By adhering to these guidelines, administrators can ensure quick recovery from unforeseen events, maintaining a stable and efficient Jenkins environment. Proper documentation and routine audits of the backup and restore processes further enhance system reliability.

7.12 Troubleshooting and Diagnostics

Troubleshooting and diagnostics are crucial components of managing a Jenkins environment. A robust understanding of these elements ensures continuous integration and continuous delivery (CI/CD) pipelines function smoothly. This section provides detailed methodologies and approaches to identify, investigate, and resolve common issues associated with Jenkins deployment and operations.

Effective troubleshooting begins with understanding the common points of failure and familiarizing oneself with various diagnostic tools and logs provided by Jenkins.

Understanding Jenkins Logs

Jenkins maintains several log files crucial for diagnosing issues. Key among these are the "controller log" (also known as "master log"), "node logs," and "build logs." These logs provide a historical record of events and errors that occur during Jenkins operations.

To access the Jenkins controller log, navigate to:

```
Jenkins Dashboard -> Manage Jenkins -> System Log
```

Here, the System Log section displays ongoing activities and historical information vital for debugging and analysis. Additionally, administrative users can configure custom log recorders to capture specific events or activities by clicking the Add New Log Recorder button and specifying the desired loggers.

Node logs can be accessed by navigating to the specific node's page, where Jenkins provides details about the node's status and recent logs. This can be accomplished by:

```
Jenkins Dashboard -> Manage Nodes and Clouds -> Click on Node Name -> Log
```

Build logs are accessible from the build's page. By navigating to a specific build and selecting Console Output, one can view detailed real-time information or logs about the build process.

Identifying Common Issues

Some frequently encountered issues in Jenkins include build failures, executor issues, configuration problems, and plugin errors. Each problem category requires a different approach to diagnostics.

1. Build Failures

Build failures can be caused by a myriad of reasons, including:

- Compilation errors
- Failing unit tests

- Dependency issues
- Script errors in pipeline definitions

Upon encountering a build failure, delve into the build log. Scrutinize the errors logged and trace them back to the root cause. For example, a dependency resolution error might indicate a missing or incorrect dependency in the build configuration (e.g., pom.xml for Maven or build.gradle for Gradle projects).

2. Executor Issues

Issues with Jenkins executors can stem from resource constraints, misconfigurations, or node connectivity problems. When executors fail, assess the following:

- Ensure that the node has adequate CPU, memory, and disk space.
- Verify node connectivity via:

```
Jenkins Dashboard -> Manage Nodes and Clouds -> Click on Node Name ->
    Configure -> Test Connection
```

- Inspect agent logs for disconnection or connectivity issues.

3. Configuration Problems

Configuration-related problems can range from incorrect tool configurations to misconfigured global settings. To diagnose these:

- Validate the global settings under Manage Jenkins -> Configure System.
- Check configurations for tools like JDK, Maven, or Git located under Global Tool Configuration.
- Ensure environment variables and paths are correctly set.

4. Plugin Errors

Plugins enhance Jenkins' capabilities, but they can also introduce instability or incompatibilities. Plugin-related issues can often be diagnosed by:

- Reviewing the Manage Jenkins -> Manage Plugins -> Installed tab to confirm that all plugins are up-to-date.
- Checking compatibility notes and documentation for each plugin, especially after Jenkins core updates.
- Using the Jenkins Plugin Compatibility Tester to evaluate plugin compatibility against different Jenkins versions.

Advanced Diagnostics Tools

Several advanced diagnostic tools can assist in pinpointing and resolving issues effectively.

1. Thread Dumps

A thread dump captures the state of all threads running at a particular moment, valuable for diagnosing performance issues or deadlocks. To generate a thread dump:

```
Jenkins Dashboard -> Manage Jenkins -> Script Console
```

Execute the following Groovy script in the Script Console:

```
Thread.getAllStackTraces().each { thread, stackTrace ->
  println "Thread: ${thread}"
  stackTrace.each { println it }
}
```

2. Heap Dumps

Heap dumps provide a snapshot of the memory heap of the JVM, crucial for diagnosing memory leaks or excessive memory consumption. To generate a heap dump, use the jmap tool:

```
jmap -dump:live,format=b,file=<HeapDumpFilePath> <JenkinsProcessID>
```

Analyze the heap dump using tools like Eclipse Memory Analyzer (MAT).

3. Monitoring Plugins

Plugins such as Metrics, Monitoring, and Performance provide insights into Jenkins performance and operational health. Configure these plugins to monitor important metrics like response times, memory utilization, and build durations.

Automating Diagnostics

Automation can simplify the diagnostics process. Groovy scripts executed via the Script Console can automate routine checks and generate alerts. For example, automating the collection of system metrics:

```
import jenkins.model.Jenkins

def metrics = Jenkins.instance.metricsRegistry
def memoryUsage = metrics.gauges['jvm.memory.heap.usage'].value
println "Heap Memory Usage: ${memoryUsage}"
```

Regular Maintenance and Proactive Monitoring

Regular maintenance tasks, such as updating Jenkins and its plugins, pruning old builds, and ensuring backups, help maintain a healthy Jenkins instance. Proactive monitoring with tools like Prometheus and Grafana provides real-time insights and alerting capabilities to preempt issues.

```
import org.jenkinsci.plugins.metrics.model.LoggingMetricsProvider
import metrics.JenkinsMetricProvider

Metrics.properties.each {
  println "${it.key}=${it.value}"
}
```

Understanding and implementing the above troubleshooting and diagnostics techniques are fundamental for maintaining a robust and efficient Jenkins environment.

Chapter 8

Security in Jenkins

This chapter addresses the critical aspects of securing Jenkins. It includes setting up authentication and authorization, implementing role-based access control, and securing communications with SSL. The chapter discusses securing Jenkins agents, configuring security groups, and managing security settings. It also covers setting up security auditing, handling security incidents, and adhering to compliance and security policies to ensure a robust and secure Jenkins environment.

8.1 Introduction to Jenkins Security

Securing Jenkins is an essential task to ensure the integrity, confidentiality, and availability of your Continuous Integration/Continuous Deployment (CI/CD) environment. Jenkins, being a widely used automation server, can be a target for various security threats if not adequately protected. This section covers core principles and practices necessary to secure Jenkins environment, setting the foundation for more advanced security configurations in subsequent sections.

Jenkins security revolves around multiple key components:

- Authentication
- Authorization
- Secure communication

- Agent security
- Security auditing

Each of these components contributes to an overarching security strategy that keeps the Jenkins environment safeguarded against potential risks.

Authentication ensures that only legitimate users are granted access to Jenkins. Jenkins supports multiple authentication methods, including internal user database, LDAP, and third-party authentication plugins. Through authentication, the system verifies the identity of users attempting to access Jenkins, serving as the first line of defense against unauthorized access.

Authorization involves determining what authenticated users are allowed to do within Jenkins. This is managed through permissions and roles, supporting mechanisms such as Matrix-based security and Project-based Matrix Authorization Strategy. Effective authorization controls prevent users from unintentionally or maliciously performing actions beyond their granted scope, thereby minimizing the risk of operational disruption or data compromise.

Securing communication in Jenkins is critical to protect data in transit between clients and the Jenkins server. SSL (Secure Sockets Layer) or its successor TLS (Transport Layer Security) is employed to encrypt data, ensuring that sensitive information such as credentials and configuration secrets are not exposed to interception during transmission.

Agent security focuses on securing the interaction between the primary Jenkins server and its agents. Agents run on separate machines, executing jobs as directed by the server. Secure agent configuration ensures that compromised agents do not become a vector for attacks on the Jenkins server itself. Ensuring secure channels between agents and the server, along with proper access controls, mitigates this risk.

Security auditing involves logging activities and changes within Jenkins to provide an audit trail. This facilitates the detection of suspicious activities and supports forensic investigations in case of a security incident. Regular audit log reviews are part of maintaining a vigilant security posture.

To configure authentication in Jenkins, one might use the following configuration in the 'config.xml' file located in the Jenkins home directory:

```
<securityRealm class="hudson.security.HudsonPrivateSecurityRealm">
    <disableSignup>true</disableSignup>
```

```
  <enableCaptcha>false</enableCaptcha>
</securityRealm>
```

Here, the built-in security realm is configured, disabling user sign-up ('<disableSignup>true</disableSignup>') to prevent unauthorized user registration.

For securing communication, enabling HTTPS for Jenkins involves configuring the 'jenkins.xml' file. Below is an example of modifying 'jenkins.xml' to include HTTPS:

```
<Jenkins>
  ...
  <systemMessage>...</systemMessage>
  <numExecutors>...</numExecutors>
  <mode>NORMAL</mode>
  <useSecurity>true</useSecurity>
  <authorizationStrategy class="...">...</authorizationStrategy>
  ...
  <httpConnector implementation="org.eclipse.jetty.server.ssl.
        SslSelectChannelConnector">
     <port>8443</port>
     <sslKeyStore>/path/to/keystore.jks</sslKeyStore>
     <sslKeyStorePassword>yourKeystorePassword</sslKeyStorePassword>
     <sslKeyManagerPassword>yourKeyPassword</sslKeyManagerPassword>
  </httpConnector>
</Jenkins>
```

This snippet configures Jenkins to use HTTPS on port 8443, utilizing a specified keystore containing SSL certificates. The use of strong passwords for key and keystore adds an extra layer of security to protect against unauthorized access.

Encryption of sensitive files and artifacts is another important security measure. Jenkins provides plugins such as the Credentials Plugin to store credentials securely. Using the plugin, credentials can be managed within Jenkins without embedding passwords and secrets directly in job configurations.

```
pipelines {
  agent any
  environment {
     MYSECRET = credentials('my-credentials-id')
  }
  stages {
     stage('Build') {
        steps {
           sh 'echo My secret is ${MYSECRET}'
        }
     }
  }
}
```

In this declarative pipeline script, 'MYSECRET' environment variable is set using credentials stored securely in Jenkins. This avoids exposing sensitive information in the pipeline code.

Logging and monitoring activities within Jenkins is achieved using the Audit Trail Plugin. Configuration ensures that all user actions are recorded, providing insights for security auditing.

```
<plugin>
    <auditing>
        <class>jenkins.security.audit.AuditTrailPlugin</class>
        <logFile>/var/log/jenkins/audit.log</logFile>
        <logFormat>%userId %message</logFormat>
    </auditing>
</plugin>
```

This configuration directs audit logs to '/var/log/jenkins/audit.log', capturing user activities in a structured format. Regular review of these logs helps in identifying anomalies and potential security incidents.

The foundational security principles detailed here set the stage for implementing more granular security measures discussed in later sections. Adhering to these principles ensures a robust baseline for securing Jenkins.

8.2 Setting Up Authentication

Authentication is the first line of defense in securing a Jenkins environment. It ensures that only authorized users can access the Jenkins interface and perform actions within the system. This section provides a comprehensive guide on setting up authentication in Jenkins.

Jenkins supports a variety of authentication mechanisms, ranging from basic user-password combinations to integrating with external systems through plugins. One of the most common methods of authentication in Jenkins is the use of Jenkins' own user database, although Jenkins can also integrate with LDAP, Active Directory, and other external identity providers.

1. Configuring Jenkins' Own User Database

To leverage Jenkins' own user database, follow these steps:

1. Navigate to *Manage Jenkins* → *Configure Global Security*.
2. Under the *Security Realm* section, select *Jenkins' own user database*.

3. Make sure the option *Allow users to sign up* is checked if you want users to be able to create their own accounts.

4. Click *Save*.

Jenkins' own user database is now enabled. To create users:

1. Navigate to *Manage Jenkins* → *Manage Users*.

2. Click on *Create User*.

3. Fill in the fields for username, password, full name, and email address.

4. Click *Create User*.

2. Integrating with LDAP

LDAP (Lightweight Directory Access Protocol) is a standard application protocol for accessing and maintaining distributed directory information services over an IP network. To configure LDAP in Jenkins:

1. Navigate to *Manage Jenkins* → *Configure Global Security*.

2. Under *Security Realm*, select *LDAP*.

3. Fill in the required fields such as *Server*, *Root DN*, *User Search Base*, and *User Search Filter*. An example configuration might look like this:

```
Server: ldap://your-ldap-server.com:389
Root DN: dc=example,dc=com
User Search Base: ou=users
User Search Filter: uid={0}
```

1. Click *Save*.

2. Jenkins will now authenticate users against the LDAP directory.

3. Configuring Active Directory

To integrate with Active Directory (AD), a widely used directory service for Windows domain networks:

1. Install the *Active Directory Plugin* if not already present.

2. Navigate to *Manage Jenkins → Configure Global Security*.

3. Under *Security Realm*, select *Active Directory*.

4. Fill in the domain details and credentials. Basic fields include:

```
Domain: your-domain.com
Domain Controller: dc1.your-domain.com
Bind DN: user@your-domain.com
Bind Password: your-password
```

1. Click *Save*.

Jenkins will now validate user credentials against Active Directory.

4. Using Security Plugins

Jenkins offers various plugins to enhance authentication mechanisms. Popular plugins include:

- **OAuth Plugin**: Allows users to authenticate using OAuth providers like GitHub, Google, etc.

- **SAML Plugin**: Enables authentication through SAML (Security Assertion Markup Language). Commonly used for Single Sign-On (SSO) implementations with enterprise identity providers.

Example of OAuth Plugin Configuration (GitHub):

1. Install the *GitHub OAuth Plugin*.

2. Navigate to *Manage Jenkins → Configure Global Security*.

3. Under *Security Realm*, select *GitHub Authentication Plugin*.

4. Configure the *Client ID*, *Client Secret*, and *OAuth Scopes* obtained from GitHub Developer settings.

```
Client ID: your-client-id
Client Secret: your-client-secret
OAuth Scopes: read:org,user:email
```

1. Click *Save*.

Users can now authenticate with their GitHub credentials.

5. Testing Authentication

To verify the authentication setup:

1. Log out of Jenkins.
2. Try logging in with the user credentials created or configured through LDAP, Active Directory, or OAuth.

Successful logins confirm accurate configuration. For failed attempts, review log files under *Manage Jenkins* $\rightarrow$ *System Log* for diagnostic information.

Security Considerations

While configuring authentication, consider these security best practices:

- **Enforce Strong Password Policies**: Mandate complex passwords and regular password changes.
- **Enable Multi-Factor Authentication (MFA)**: Use plugins like the Google Authenticator Plugin to add an extra layer of security.
- **Regularly Update Plugins and Jenkins**: Ensure all plugins and Jenkins itself are up-to-date to mitigate vulnerabilities.
- **Audit Logging**: Maintain and regularly review audit logs to detect any unauthorized access attempts.

Combining robust authentication mechanisms with diligent monitoring establishes a secure base for your Jenkins environment, crucial for preventing unauthorized access and protecting sensitive data.

8.3 Configuring Authorization

In the context of Jenkins security, authorization determines what actions users and agents can perform once authenticated. This configuration ensures that distinct users have adequate and appropriate permissions, preventing unauthorized actions and minimizing the risk of inadvertent system modifications.

Authorization Strategies in Jenkins

Jenkins supports various authorization strategies. The primary methods include:

- **Anyone can do anything**: This option allows any user full control, which is not recommended in any environment requiring security.
- **Legacy mode**: Grants full control to any authenticated user. Public users have read access. This setting poses security risks and is generally discouraged.
- **Logged-in users can do anything**: Restricts full control to authenticated users, enhanced security compared to 'Anyone can do anything.'
- **Matrix-based security**: Provides fine-grained access control by allowing grant-specific permissions at different levels.
- **Project-based matrix authorization**: Extends matrix-based security to individual projects, giving more control over distinct project permissions.
- **Role-based strategy**: Allows the definition and assignment of roles to users or groups for manageable and scalable security configuration.

Setting up Matrix-based Security

Matrix-based security is a flexible and powerful approach to manage user permissions efficiently. Here, permissions are categorized and can be granted individually to users or groups. To set up matrix-based security, follow these steps:

1. Navigate to Manage Jenkins > Configure Global Security. 2. Under Authorization, select Matrix-based security. 3. Configure permissions by adding users or groups and assigning permissions across different functional categories.

```
# Navigate to Manage Jenkins > Configure Global Security
security:
  authorizationStrategy: "matrix-based"
  permissions:
    - job/read:
      users:
        - alice
        - bob
    - job/build:
      groups:
        - developers
```

Implementing Role-Based Strategy

The Role-based strategy facilitates the assignment of pre-defined roles to various users or groups, a scalable option for managing a large number of users. It requires the installation of the 'Role-based Authorization Strategy' plugin.

Steps to implement role-based strategy:

1. Install the Role-based Authorization Strategy plugin:

    1. Navigate to Manage Jenkins > Manage Plugins.
    2. In the Available tab, search for Role-based Authorization Strategy and install it.

2. Configure the authorization strategy:

    1. Navigate to Manage Jenkins > Configure Global Security.
    2. Under Authorization, select Role-based Strategy.

Defining Global Roles

Global roles encompass permissions that affect the entire Jenkins instance. For instance, administering configuration permissions can be granted globally, ensuring critical operations are under controlled access.

To define global roles:

- Navigate to Manage Jenkins > Manage and Assign Roles > Manage Roles.
- Under Global roles, create roles necessary for your setup (e.g., admin, read-only, developer).
- Assign respective permissions to each role.

Creating Project Roles

Project roles restrict permissions to specific projects, ideal for environments where multiple teams work on isolated projects. This ensures that permissions are granted per-project, enhancing security by adhering strictly to the principle of least privilege.

To define project roles:

- Navigate to Manage Jenkins > Manage and Assign Roles > Manage Roles.
- Under Project roles, create project-specific roles (e.g., project-read, project-write).
- Assign project-specific permissions to these roles.

Role Assignment

After defining roles, assign them to users or groups to enforce the authorization configurations:

- Navigate to Manage Jenkins > Manage and Assign Roles > Assign Roles.
- Assign the global and project roles to the respective users or groups.

```
# Navigate to Manage Jenkins > Manage and Assign Roles > Assign Roles
role_assignments:
  globalRoles:
    admin:
      users:
        - admin
  projectRoles:
    project-developer:
      users:
        - alice
        - bob
```

Verifying Authorization Configuration

Once roles and permissions are assigned, verification ensures the implementation aligns with organizational security policies. Test different user accounts to validate that permissions are correctly enforced, ensuring users can only perform actions granted by their assigned roles.

Verification steps:

1. Log in as different users to validate access and actions.
2. Attempt to perform tasks outside the granted permissions to ensure such operations are blocked.

```
$ jenkinsuser@jenkins-server:~$ # Log in as user Alice
$ jenkinsuser@jenkins-server:~$ # Attempt unauthorized action
Error: Access Denied
```

Best Practices

When configuring authorization, adhering to the following best practices ensures a secure and manageable environment:

- Always apply the principle of least privilege—grant only necessary permissions.
- Regularly review and update roles and permissions to reflect organizational changes.
- Document all role and permission configurations for auditing and compliance.
- Utilize group-based assignments for easier management in larger organizations.

Using these strategies and considerations ensures that Jenkins is configured securely and that users have the appropriate permissions for their roles, reducing the risk of unauthorized access and maintaining the integrity of the CI/CD pipeline.

8.4 Role-Based Access Control

Role-Based Access Control (RBAC) is a potent mechanism in Jenkins designed to manage permissions and access systematically. By assigning permissions to roles and then assigning those roles to users or groups, organizations can exercise fine-grained control over who has access to what within Jenkins. This approach not only enhances security but also simplifies the management of permissions across large teams with varying levels of responsibility.

RBAC in Jenkins can be configured using the Role Strategy Plugin, which is robust and flexible, allowing the definition and assignment of roles at different scopes such as global, project, or agent levels. To use this plugin, an understanding of Jenkins' roles and permissions architecture is essential.

First, we need to install the Role Strategy Plugin. Navigate to **Manage Jenkins** → **Manage Plugins**, select the **Available** tab, search for **Role-based Authorization Strategy**, and install it. After installation, configure it under **Manage Jenkins** → **Configure Global Security**. Select **Role-Based Strategy** under the **Authorization** section.

Once the setup is complete, we can start defining roles. The roles are primarily categorized into three types: Global Roles, Project Roles, and Agent Roles. Each of these roles can be controlled with specific permissions suitable for different scopes.

Defining Global Roles

Global Roles control access at the highest level, impacting the entire Jenkins environment.

- Navigate to **Manage Jenkins** → **Manage and Assign Roles** → **Manage Roles**.
- Under **Global roles**, click **Add** to define a new global role.
- Assign your role a name and configure the corresponding permissions from the presented list. Permissions can include overall administration, read access, credentials management, and more.

For example, creating an *admin* role with full access might involve checking all permissions. Below is an example of how a role's permissions might be set in a Jenkinsfile:

```
def adminRole = [
    configure: true,
    read: true,
    write: true,
    create: true,
    delete: true,
    admin: true
]
```

Defining Project Roles

Project Roles apply to specific jobs or projects and are crucial for environments where different teams or users need varying access levels to various projects.

- Under **Manage Jenkins** → **Manage and Assign Roles** → **Manage Roles**, locate the **Project Roles** section.
- Click on **Add Project Role**, enter the role name, and define the associated permissions.
- Use field expressions (regular expressions) to determine which jobs the roles will apply to.

For instance, creating a *developer* role with read and build permissions across all projects might be represented as follows:

```
def developerRole = [
    read: true,
    build: true
]
```

Defining Agent Roles

Agent Roles govern the access rights related to Jenkins agents. These permissions are critical for controlling who can configure or use specific build agents.

- Under the **Agent Roles** section in the same **Manage Roles** page, click **Add Agent Role**.
- Enter the role name and configure the required permissions, such as connect, configure, and build.

An agent role for regular users that allows connection and usage but restricts configuration might look like this:

```
def userAgentRole = [
    connect: true,
    build: true
]
```

Assigning Roles

Once roles are configured, assigning them to specific users or groups is straightforward:

- Go to **Manage Jenkins** → **Manage and Assign Roles** → **Assign Roles**.
- Under **Global Roles**, **Project Roles**, and **Agent Roles**, you can assign roles to users or groups by entering their names and selecting the appropriate roles.

For example, assigning the *admin* role to a user named *jdoe*:

```
roleAssignments.'jdoe' = [ 'admin' ]
```

This assignment ensures that *jdoe* has all permissions specified in the *admin* role across the Jenkins instance.

Practical Considerations

While RBAC provides significant control, it requires meticulous planning to ensure roles are well-defined and assignments are accurate.

Regularly review roles and assignments to adapt to organizational changes. Additionally, incorporating auditing mechanisms, as discussed in a subsequent section, helps monitor access and usage effectively.

The consistent and cautious application of RBAC principles in Jenkins ensures a secure, manageable, and scalable CI/CD environment, safeguarding critical systems and fostering collaborative development practices.

8.5 Securing Jenkins with SSL

Securing communications between Jenkins and its users or agents is paramount to ensure data integrity and confidentiality. Implementing SSL (Secure Sockets Layer) or its successor, TLS (Transport Layer Security), provides a robust mechanism to encrypt data transmitted over the network. This section will detail the steps necessary to secure your Jenkins instance using SSL/TLS.

Step 1: Generating a Self-Signed Certificate

To begin, you need an SSL certificate and a private key. For development and testing purposes, a self-signed certificate will suffice. Below are the commands to generate a self-signed certificate using the openssl tool:

```
openssl req -newkey rsa:2048 -nodes -keyout jenkins.key -x509 -days 365 -out jenkins.crt
```

The command will prompt you to enter several details, such as country, state, organization, and common name (the server's domain name).

Step 2: Creating a Java Keystore

Jenkins runs on Java, which utilizes a keystore to manage certificates. Convert the generated certificate and key into a keystore:

```
openssl pkcs12 -export -in jenkins.crt -inkey jenkins.key -out jenkins.p12 -name jenkins
     -CAfile jenkins.crt -caname root
```

The above command creates a PKCS12 file named jenkins.p12. Next, import this file into a Java keystore:

```
keytool -importkeystore -deststorepass changeit -destkeypass changeit -destkeystore
     jenkins.jks -srckeystore jenkins.p12 -srcstoretype PKCS12 -srcstorepass changeit -
     alias jenkins
```

Replace changeit with your desired password.

Step 3: Configuring Jenkins to Use SSL

The next step is to configure Jenkins to use the generated keystore. Modify the jenkins.xml file, typically located in the Jenkins installation directory on Windows, or the /etc/default/jenkins file on Unix-based systems. Update the 'JENKINS_ARGS' environment variable to include SSL configuration:

```
JENKINS_ARGS="--httpPort=-1 --httpsPort=8443 --httpsKeyStore=/path/to/jenkins
    .jks --httpsKeyStorePassword=changeit"
```

Replace /path/to/jenkins.jks with the actual path to your keystore file and changeit with your keystore password.

Step 4: Restarting Jenkins

After configuring the keystore, restart the Jenkins service to apply the changes. On Unix-based systems, you can use:

```
sudo systemctl restart jenkins
```

On Windows, restart the Jenkins service through the Services management console.

Step 5: Verifying SSL Configuration

Once Jenkins restarts, verify the SSL configuration by navigating to https://<your_jenkins_domain>:8443. Ensure that your browser recognizes the certificate. If using a self-signed certificate, the browser will display a warning, which can be bypassed for testing purposes.

Using Certificates from a Trusted Certificate Authority

For production environments, it is recommended to use a certificate signed by a trusted Certificate Authority (CA). The steps are similar but involve generating a Certificate Signing Request (CSR) and submitting it to the CA. Once you receive the signed certificate, import it into the keystore and configure Jenkins as detailed previously.

Generating a Certificate Signing Request

Generate a CSR using the following openssl command:

```
openssl req -new -newkey rsa:2048 -nodes -keyout jenkins.key -out jenkins.csr
```

Submit the jenkins.csr file to your chosen Certificate Authority. Upon receipt of the signed certificate (usually a .crt file) and the CA's intermediate certificates, create the PKCS12 file and follow the steps to import it into the Java keystore.

Ensuring Secure Communication with Jenkins Agents

If Jenkins agents communicate with the master via JNLP (Java Network Launch Protocol), it is crucial to secure this communication. Configure the Jenkins master URL in the agent configuration to use HTTPS:

```
<JnlpProtocol3>
  <tls>true</tls>
</JnlpProtocol3>
```

Ensure agents trust the master certificate, especially when using self-signed certificates. Place the master certificate in the agent's trust store.

Securing Jenkins with SSL significantly enhances the security posture by preventing eavesdropping and ensuring that data in transit remains confidential and tamper-proof. This practice is vital in safeguarding sensitive information and maintaining the overall integrity of the Jenkins environment.

8.6 Securing Jenkins Agents

Securing Jenkins agents is fundamental to maintaining a robust and secure Jenkins environment. These agents execute build tasks, and their security is paramount because any vulnerability can be exploited to compromise the entire Jenkins infrastructure. Several key strategies and configurations help secure Jenkins agents effectively.

Jenkins agents communicate with the Jenkins master using the JNLP (Java Network Launch Protocol) or through SSH (Secure Shell). Ensuring the security of this communication is crucial as it prevents unauthorized access and potential attacks. Jenkins versions 2.0 and higher have introduced enhanced security features, making it essential to use updated versions.

To begin with, it is crucial to configure agents to use encrypted communication channels. For JNLP agents, configuring them to use the JNLP4 protocol, which supports secure communication through TLS (Transport Layer Security), is recommended. This ensures the integrity and confidentiality of data exchanged between the Jenkins master and the agents.

```
<agentProtocolHandler>
  <enabledProtocols>JNLP4-connect</enabledProtocols>
</agentProtocolHandler>
```

The configuration above ensures that agents only connect using the JNLP4 protocol, enforcing TLS for secure communication.

When using SSH agents, one must ensure that the SSH keys are securely managed and stored. Use strong, unique SSH keys for each agent. Avoid using passwords for SSH connections, as keys provide a much higher level of security. SSH key pairs should be generated using secure algorithms such as RSA with a key length of at least 2048 bits or Ed25519.

Additionally, agents should be configured to restrict access and run with minimum necessary privileges. This could be achieved by setting up dedicated user accounts for Jenkins agents and granting them only the permissions required for their tasks. Ensuring these user accounts are not shared among multiple agents also helps in maintaining better control and auditing.

Network segmentation can also be employed to enhance security. This involves placing Jenkins agents on a separate network segment or virtual LAN (VLAN) and applying firewall rules to restrict traffic only to/from the Jenkins master. This limits the potential attack surface and isolates Jenkins agents from other critical parts of the network.

Here is an example of restricting access via firewall rules on a Linux system using 'iptables':

```
# Allow Jenkins master to connect to agent over port 50000 (JNLP)
sudo iptables -A INPUT -p tcp --dport 50000 -s <JENKINS_MASTER_IP> -j
    ACCEPT
# Allow SSH from Jenkins master to agent
sudo iptables -A INPUT -p tcp --dport 22 -s <JENKINS_MASTER_IP> -j ACCEPT
# Drop all other inbound connections
sudo iptables -A INPUT -p tcp --dport 50000 -j DROP
sudo iptables -A INPUT -p tcp --dport 22 -j DROP
```

Ensuring the security of the Jenkins file system where the agents are installed is also vital. This includes setting correct file permissions and protecting sensitive files such as the 'config.xml' and workspace directories. The user running the Jenkins agent should have read and write access only to the necessary directories.

Proper logging and monitoring of Jenkins agents play a crucial role in early detection and response to security incidents. Logs must be constantly monitored for any suspicious activities, such as unauthorized access attempts, unusual build activity, or unexpected changes in configuration files. Implementing centralized logging can facilitate better monitoring and quicker incident response.

Moreover, it is essential to keep the agent software and any third-party plugins up-to-date. Security patches and updates should be applied promptly, as they often address vulnerabilities that could be exploited by attackers. Jenkins and its plugins frequently receive security updates, and applying these updates ensures that the installation is protected against known threats.

The use of containerized environments for Jenkins agents is gaining popularity. Tools such as Docker allow for running Jenkins agents in isolated containers, which can be quickly redeployed, ensuring a clean state. This isolation helps to contain any potential security breaches and simplifies management. Here is an example of running a Jenkins agent in a Docker container:

```
docker run -d --name jenkins-agent \
  -e JENKINS_URL=<JENKINS_MASTER_URL> \
  -e JENKINS_AGENT_NAME=<AGENT_NAME> \
  -e JENKINS_SECRET=<AGENT_SECRET> \
  jenkins/inbound-agents
```

In a containerized setup, ensure that the Docker daemon itself is secured, following best practices such as running the daemon as a non-root user and avoiding the exposure of the Docker API to untrusted networks.

Finally, regularly auditing the security configurations of Jenkins agents is essential. This involves periodically reviewing SSH configurations, file permissions, network policies, and logging setups to ensure compliance with security policies and best practices. Regular security audits help identify potential weaknesses and ensure the agents adhere to the organization's security standards.

8.7 Configuring Security Groups

Security groups in Jenkins play a pivotal role in controlling access to various parts of the Jenkins environment. These groups help segregate users based on their roles and responsibilities, thereby ensuring that access permissions are granted only to those who require them.

When configuring security groups in Jenkins, the first step involves identifying the different roles within your organization and the corresponding access levels required by each role. For example, developers may need access to job configurations, while system administrators require broader permissions to manage Jenkins nodes and security settings.

To configure security groups within Jenkins, follow these steps:

- Access the Jenkins dashboard, navigate to **Manage Jenkins**, and then select **Configure Global Security**.
- In the **Authorization** section, select the appropriate authorization strategy. If using Role-Based Access Control (RBAC), ensure that the relevant plugin is installed and configured.
- Navigate to **Manage and Assign Roles** under **Manage Jenkins**. This section allows for the creation and assignment of roles to users and groups.
- Define roles according to organizational needs. For each role, assign specific permissions that align with the required access level. Typical permissions include building jobs, configuring jobs, managing nodes, administering agents, and running system scripts.

The following example demonstrates configuring security groups using Role-Based Access Control (RBAC) with the **Role Strategy** plugin installed.

```
# Access Manage Jenkins
$ sudo jenkins-cli -s http://localhost:8080/ -auth username:api_token groovy =
# Begin script
import jenkins.model.Jenkins
import hudson.security.*

def instance = Jenkins.getInstance()

def strategy = new GlobalMatrixAuthorizationStrategy()

// Define roles and permissions
strategy.add(Jenkins.ADMINISTER, "admin")
strategy.add(Jenkins.READ, "authenticated")
strategy.add(Jenkins.READ, "anonymous")

// Set authorization strategy
instance.setAuthorizationStrategy(strategy)
instance.save()
# End script
```

This script configures an admin role with full administrative privileges, an authenticated role with basic read permissions for all logged-in users, and an anonymous role with read permissions for unauthenticated users. The **GlobalMatrixAuthorizationStrategy()** is used here to assign permissions at a granular level.

After configuring roles, the next step is to assign users to these roles:

- From the Jenkins dashboard, navigate to **Manage and Assign Roles** and select **Assign Roles**.
- Add users to the predefined roles. This step involves specifying the username and selecting the corresponding roles they should inherit permissions from.

In a scenario where Jenkins is integrated with LDAP or another directory service:

```
# Jenkins Groovy script for LDAP integration
import jenkins.model.*
import hudson.security.*

def instance = Jenkins.getInstance()

def ldapRealm = new LDAPSecurityRealm(
  "ldap://ldap.example.com",
  "dc=example,dc=com",
  "uid={0},ou=people",
  null,
  null,
  "cn=admin,dc=example,dc=com",
  "adminpassword",
  false,
  true,
  null,
  null,
  null,
  "displayName",
  "mail",
  "uid"
)

instance.setSecurityRealm(ldapRealm)
instance.save()
```

This script configures Jenkins to authenticate and manage user roles via an LDAP server. It starts by specifying the LDAP server URL and relevant search bases. The user and group search filters are adjusted to match the organization's LDAP schema.

To monitor the efficacy of security groups and roles:

- Regularly review access logs to ensure no unauthorized access.
- Use audit plugins, such as the **Audit Trail** plugin, to keep track of user activities and role changes.

```
# Sample Jenkins Audit Trail output
2023-10-01 12:00:01 user jdoe logged in
2023-10-01 12:05:45 user jdoe created job 'NewJob'
2023-10-01 12:07:30 user jdoe configured job 'NewJob'
2023-10-01 12:10:12 user admin changed permissions for role 'developer'
```

Regular audits and activity monitoring contribute to maintaining a secure Jenkins environment by ensuring that rights and roles are appropriately enforced and adjusted as per organizational requirements. This diligent approach protects against potential security breaches and enhances operational integrity.

8.8 Managing Security Settings

Effectively managing security settings in Jenkins is paramount to maintaining a secure and robust CI/CD environment. Security settings encompass a range of configurations that control access, ensure data protection, and provide auditing capabilities. In this section, we will delve into key areas of security settings including managing user accounts, configuring security realms, implementing security policies, and enabling logging and monitoring features.

The management of user accounts in Jenkins involves both local and external configurations. Local user account management is straightforward but may not be feasible in larger, more complex environments. To manage local users, navigate to **Manage Jenkins** → **Manage Users**. Here, administrators can create, update, delete, and assign roles to users. However, leveraging external identity providers such as LDAP or Active Directory is often more efficient for larger teams. Integrating with external user directories can be configured under **Manage Jenkins** → **Configure Global Security**, selecting the relevant Security Realm, and providing the necessary connection parameters and credentials.

Security realms are a pivotal aspect of Jenkins security settings. They define the method by which Jenkins authenticates users. Commonly used security realms include:

- **Jenkins' own user database** – Suitable for small teams or testing environments.
- **LDAP** – Integrates with LDAP servers for centralized user management in larger organizations.
- **Active Directory** – Allows integration with Windows-based networks.
- **GitHub or GitLab OAuth** – Uses OAuth tokens for authentication, simplifying the connection to these platforms.

Implementing these realms involves providing connection details, such as:

```
SecurityRealm ldapRealm = new LDAPSecurityRealm(
  "ldap://ldap.example.com",
  "dc=example,dc=com",
  null,
  "cn=admin,dc=example,dc=com",
  "password"
);
Jenkins.getInstance().setSecurityRealm(ldapRealm);
```

Configuring security policies includes setting password policies, configuring session timeouts, setting up CSRF protection, and defining security headers. Password policies defined in external user directories (like LDAP or Active Directory) will apply to Jenkins users authenticated through these directories. For Jenkins' own user database, custom password requirements can be enforced by using plugins such as Jenkins Password Policy Plugin.

Cross-Site Request Forgery (CSRF) protection is critical to prevent malicious commands. CSRF protection can be enabled through **Manage Jenkins → Configure Global Security → Prevent Cross Site Request Forgery exploits**. This ensures that non-authenticated requests to Jenkins require a valid crumb token.

Security headers provide an additional layer of protection by instructing browsers to adhere to certain security practices. These headers can be set using the Script Security Plugin with appropriate Groovy scripts:

```
def headers = Jenkins.instance.servletContext.request.getHttpHeaders().asMap()
headers['X-Content-Type-Options']= ['nosniff']
headers['X-Frame-Options']= ['DENY']
headers['Content-Security-Policy']= ['default-src 'self'; style-src 'self' 'unsafe-inline';']
headers['Strict-Transport-Security']= ['max-age=31536000; includeSubDomains']
```

Monitoring and logging need to be enabled to track potential security incidents. Jenkins allows configuration of various logging levels through **Manage Jenkins → System Log**. Logging captures detailed information about user activities, system events, and security incidents. To tailor logging, it is possible to define custom log recorders and assign severities:

```
import java.util.logging.Logger;

Logger logger = Logger.getLogger("jenkins.security.AuditTrail");
logger.warning("Custom security log message");
```

Security Issue Detected
User admin has attempted unauthorized access to restricted job 'Build-Proj-X'.

Security auditing is enhanced using plugins like the Audit Trail Plugin which keeps track of user operations. Once installed, navigate to **Manage Jenkins → Configure System → Audit Trail** to specify what actions to log, such as user logins, job status changes, and more.

Reviewing these security logs periodically is essential for identifying and mitigating potential security threats. Combining native Jenkins features with additional plugins provides a robust framework for monitoring and managing the security within Jenkins.

Finally, Jenkins also supports integrating with external logging and monitoring systems such as ELK stack (Elasticsearch, Logstash, and Kibana), Splunk, or even AWS CloudWatch. These integrations allow centralization of logs and provide advanced analytic capabilities to detect anomalies and respond promptly to security incidents.

8.9 Setting Up Security Auditing

Implementing security auditing within Jenkins is vital to monitor, detect, and respond to unauthorized access, configuration changes, and other security-related events. Security auditing involves configuring Jenkins to log all relevant activities and periodically reviewing these logs for signs of misuse or anomalies. This section outlines the steps to set up extensive auditing within Jenkins.

Jenkins provides various plugins and built-in functionalities that facilitate comprehensive auditing. Among them, the **Audit Trail** plugin is one of the most commonly used tools to log user actions.

```
Manage Jenkins -> Manage Plugins -> Available
Search for "Audit Trail"
Click "Install without restart"
```

Once installed, the Audit Trail plugin must be configured to specify the actions to log and the location where the logs should be stored.

```
Manage Jenkins -> Configure System
Scroll to "Audit Trail" section
Check "Log setup"
Specify a Log File (e.g., /var/log/jenkins/audit.log)
Check all appropriate logging options
```

After configuration, the Audit Trail plugin will start recording activities such as job creation and configuration changes, including user identification and timestamps.

Additionally, Jenkins has built-in support for logging at different levels, which can be configured through the **Jenkins Logger**. This helps capture more detailed system-level information, which can be invaluable for troubleshooting and forensic analysis.

```
Manage Jenkins -> System Log -> Add new log recorder
Set a name for the log recorder (e.g., Security Log)
Add logger: "jenkins.security"
Set level: ALL
Click "Save"
```

To ensure the security logs are protected and not tampered with, it's recommended to write logs to a secure, remote storage that is accessible only to authorized personnel. Tools like log management systems (e.g., ELK stack, Splunk) can be integrated to achieve this:

```
# Configuration examples might vary based on the tools being used.
# For ELK stack, Filebeat can be used to forward logs:
filebeat.inputs:
- type: log
  paths:
    - /var/log/jenkins/audit.log

output.elasticsearch:
  hosts: ["http://localhost:9200"]
  index: "jenkins-audit-%{[agent.id]}-%{+yyyy.MM.dd}"
```

Regular reviews of these logs are equally important. Implementing automated log analysis can aid in detecting suspicious activities promptly. Maintain a routine to:

- Periodically review the logs for anomalies.
- Set up alerts for critical security events or anomalies.
- Archive old logs securely to comply with retention policies.

Security auditing also mandates the usage of **Event Trigger Plugins**, which assist in running custom scripts or notifications when specific events occur. For example, the **Notification Plugin** can be configured to send an alert upon login failures:

```
# Installing Notification Plugin
Manage Jenkins -> Manage Plugins -> Available
Search for "Notification"
Click "Install without restart"

# Configuration
Manage Jenkins -> Configure System
Scroll to "Notification"
Add new Notification:
  event: "hudson.model.Hudson$LoginFailure"
  scripts: "/path/to/script.sh"
```

A sample script for sending an email notification could look like the following:

```
#!/bin/bash
TO="admin@example.com"
SUBJECT="Jenkins Login Failure Alert"
BODY="A login failure has been detected at $(date). Please review the audit logs for
    more details."

echo ${BODY} | mail -s ${SUBJECT} ${TO}
```

Ensuring regular updates to both Jenkins core and plugins is crucial, as most updates include security fixes and improvements. The periodic review of installed plugins and their configurations fortifies Jenkins' integrity.

By establishing this structured auditing framework, Jenkins administrators can maintain comprehensive oversight of their Jenkins environment, swiftly detect and respond to potential security incidents, and maintain compliance with security policies.

8.10 Best Practices for Jenkins Security

Securing Jenkins in a production environment involves a series of comprehensive measures to ensure that the continuous integration and continuous deployment (CI/CD) processes are protected from potential threats. Here, we delve into best practices for maintaining a secure Jenkins instance.

Regularly Update Jenkins and Plugins

Keeping Jenkins core and plugins up to date is crucial. Updates often contain patches for known vulnerabilities. To manage updates:

- Regularly check for updates in the *Manage Plugins* section.
- Automate the update notification process to stay informed about the latest releases.
- Test updates in a staging environment before deploying to production to ensure compatibility.

Implement Strong Authentication

Authentication verifies the identity of users. Best practices include:

- Use secure single sign-on (SSO) systems like LDAP or Active Directory.
- Enable multi-factor authentication (MFA) to add an extra layer of security.
- Periodically review and revoke access for inactive accounts.

Configure Comprehensive Authorization

Authorization ensures users have appropriate permissions based on their roles. Practices include:

- Leverage Role-Based Access Control (RBAC) to define precise permissions for different roles.
- Regularly audit user permissions to ensure they align with current organizational needs.
- Avoid granting admin privileges unless absolutely necessary.

Enforce Network Security

Protecting Jenkins from network-based attacks is paramount. Recommendations:

- Restrict network access to Jenkins using IP whitelisting.
- Use Virtual Private Networks (VPNs) for accessing Jenkins from remote locations.
- Regularly review network firewall rules to ensure they conform to security policies.

Utilize Secure Communication

All communications should be encrypted to prevent interception. Steps include:

Enable HTTPS:

```
# Generate a private key and certificate using OpenSSL
openssl req -newkey rsa:2048 -nodes -keyout jenkins.key -x509 -days 365 -out
    jenkins.cert

# Combine the key and certificate into a PKCS12 file
openssl pkcs12 -export -out jenkins.p12 -inkey jenkins.key -in jenkins.cert

# Convert the PKCS12 file to a Java Keystore (JKS) file
keytool -importkeystore -srckeystore jenkins.p12 -srcstoretype pkcs12 -
    destkeystore jenkins.jks -deststoretype JKS
```

- Use the Jenkins https.jks file in the Jenkins configuration to enable HTTPS.
- Configure agents to connect to the master using secure protocols.

Restrict Job Execution Permissions

Limiting who can execute jobs can mitigate potential risks:

- Only allow trusted users to create or modify job configurations.
- Implement restrictions on which nodes certain jobs can run.

Secure Jenkins Agents

Jenkins agents are often less secure than the primary server. To secure them:

- Ensure agents use encrypted connections (e.g., SSH, HTTPS) to communicate with the master.
- Limit the permissions of the agent's user account on the operating system.
- Regularly update agent software to the latest stable version.

Conduct Regular Security Audits

Periodic audits help detect and address vulnerabilities:

- Use Jenkins' built-in security audit features to monitor user activity.
- Review audit logs regularly for any unusual behavior.
- Conduct third-party security assessments to identify blind spots.

Backup and Recovery Planning

Having a robust backup and disaster recovery plan ensures data integrity and availability:

- Regularly backup Jenkins configurations and job data.
- Test backup restoration periodically to ensure the integrity of backups.

- Document the recovery process and ensure it is easily accessible to relevant personnel.

Compliance Adherence

Ensure Jenkins security measures comply with relevant regulations and standards:

- Implement processes to comply with regulations such as GDPR, HIPAA, or industry-specific standards.
- Regularly review and update policies to reflect changes in regulatory requirements.

Automated Security Testing

Integrating security testing into the CI/CD pipeline can identify vulnerabilities early:

- Incorporate static application security testing (SAST) tools into the build process.
- Use dynamic application security testing (DAST) tools to scan deployed applications.

By adhering to these best practices, administrators can build and maintain a secure Jenkins environment, minimizing the risk of unauthorized access and ensuring the integrity of the CI/CD pipeline.

8.11 Handling Security Incidents

Handling security incidents promptly and effectively is crucial to maintaining the security of your Jenkins environment. In this section, we will explore the systematic approach to identifying, responding to, and mitigating security incidents within Jenkins. This coverage includes incident detection methods, response protocols, root cause analysis, and post-incident recovery steps.

First, it is essential to understand the potential sources and types of security incidents that can affect Jenkins. These include unauthorized access attempts, data breaches, plugin vulnerabilities, misconfigurations, and malicious activities. Let's delve into each aspect methodically.

Incident Detection:

Early detection of security incidents can help mitigate potential damage. Employing various incident detection techniques ensures comprehensive surveillance of your Jenkins environment:

- **Log Monitoring:** Regularly review Jenkins logs for suspicious activities such as failed login attempts, unauthorized configuration changes, or unusual build activities. Configure Jenkins to send real-time alerts when certain anomalies are detected.
- **Intrusion Detection Systems (IDS):** Implement IDS tools to monitor network traffic and detect potential intrusions. IDS tools can help identify signature-based or anomaly-based threats.
- **Vulnerability Scanning:** Perform routine vulnerability scans on Jenkins and its associated infrastructure. Use tools like OWASP ZAP or Nessus to identify and address security weaknesses.
- **User Behavior Analytics (UBA):** UBA tools help analyze user behavior patterns and flag anomalies that may indicate compromised user accounts.

Incident Response:

Responding to security incidents in a structured manner is imperative to minimize impact. Establishing a well-defined incident response plan involves:

- **Incident Documentation:** Maintain a comprehensive incident response plan, documenting all steps and procedures to be followed during a security incident. This plan should be accessible to all relevant personnel.
- **Initial Response and Containment:** Upon detection of a security incident, quickly isolate the affected systems to prevent further spread. This might include disconnecting compromised Jenkins agents or disabling Jenkins services temporarily.
- **Communication Protocols:** Establish clear communication channels for notifying relevant stakeholders, including IT security teams, management, and possibly affected users. Confidentiality should be preserved to avoid unnecessary panic and information leakage.

```
#!/bin/bash
# Script to disconnect a compromised Jenkins agent

AGENT_NAME=$1

# Jenkins CLI command to disconnect the agent
JENKINS_CLI_CMD="java -jar jenkins-cli.jar -s http://jenkins.example.com
    disconnect-node $AGENT_NAME"

# Execute the command
$JENKINS_CLI_CMD
```

Root Cause Analysis:

Conduct a thorough investigation to determine the root cause of the security incident. This involves:

- **Forensic Analysis:** Analyze system logs, network traffic, and any other relevant artifacts to trace the origin of the incident. Use forensic tools like Autopsy or FTK to assist in deep analysis.
- **Identifying Vulnerabilities:** Identify the specific vulnerabilities or misconfigurations that allowed the incident to occur. This may include outdated plugins, weak passwords, or unpatched software.
- **Evaluating Impact:** Assess the extent of the damage caused by the incident, including data exfiltration, integrity violations, and service disruptions.

Post-Incident Recovery:

Once the incident has been contained and analyzed, focus on recovery and fortifying your Jenkins environment to prevent future incidents:

- **System Restoration:** Restore affected Jenkins systems from clean backups. Ensure that all systems are fully patched and updated before bringing them back online.
- **Security Enhancements:** Implement security measures identified during the root cause analysis. This may include installing security updates, enforcing stricter access controls, and enhancing monitoring mechanisms.
- **User Training and Policy Updates:** Conduct training sessions for users to educate them about security best practices and update security policies to reflect lessons learned from the incident.

```
#!/bin/bash
# Script to apply updates and security patches on a Jenkins server

# Update package lists
apt-get update

# Apply all available updates and patches
apt-get upgrade -y

# Verify Jenkins service status
systemctl status jenkins
```

Lastly, conducting a post-incident review with all stakeholders to evaluate the response effectiveness will provide valuable insights. This review should address what went well, what could be improved, and how policies or response plans should be adjusted to enhance security readiness for future incidents. By adhering to these practices, a secure and resilient Jenkins environment can be maintained against potential security threats.

8.12 Compliance and Security Policies

Compliance and security policies are essential components in the governance of an organization's IT infrastructure. They are pivotal in ensuring that Jenkins operations adhere to legal, regulatory, and internal organizational standards. This section elucidates the fundamental principles, best practices, and implementation strategies related to compliance and security policies in Jenkins.

A primary consideration when dealing with compliance in Jenkins is understanding the regulatory frameworks applicable to your industry. Common frameworks include the General Data Protection Regulation (GDPR) for EU-based data processing, the Health Insurance Portability and Accountability Act (HIPAA) for healthcare information in the U.S., and the Sarbanes-Oxley Act (SOX) for financial practices and corporate governance. Each framework has unique requirements regarding data security, audit trails, and incident reporting, which must be integrated into Jenkins' security policies.

Establishing Compliance Policies

Compliance policies should begin with a thorough risk assessment to identify potential vulnerabilities in the Jenkins environment. This includes understanding data flows, identifying sensitive data, and evaluating existing security controls. Based on the risk assessment, policies should be drafted to address the following areas:

- **Data Protection:** Enforce policies to ensure that sensitive data is encrypted at rest and in transit. Encryption practices can be implemented in Jenkins through plugins and proper configuration.
- **Access Control:** Implement strict authentication and authorization mechanisms, ensuring that access to Jenkins nodes is limited to authorized personnel only. Role-Based Access Control (RBAC) should be precisely configured.
- **Audit and Logging:** Maintain comprehensive logs of actions performed within Jenkins. This includes job executions, changes in configurations, and user activities.
- **Incident Response:** Establish a protocol for responding to security incidents, including detection, containment, eradication, and recovery activities. Regularly update and test incident response plans.

Implementing Security Policies

Security policies in Jenkins must be comprehensive and actionable. They involve defining acceptable use policies, regular audits, and implementing technical controls to enforce these policies. Key elements include:

- **Patch Management:** Ensure that Jenkins, its plugins, and dependent systems are regularly updated to the latest versions to mitigate vulnerabilities. Automated tools can assist in managing patches.
- **Network Security:** Configure firewalls and Security Groups to restrict access to Jenkins servers. Network configurations should follow the principle of least privilege.
- **Continuous Monitoring:** Implement continuous monitoring tools to detect and alert on potential security events. Integrating tools such as Prometheus and Grafana with Jenkins can provide real-time monitoring and alerting.

Integrating with Enterprise Compliance Systems

For larger organizations, it is crucial to integrate Jenkins security policies with broader enterprise compliance systems. This ensures consistency and eases audit processes. Key integration points include:

- **Single Sign-On (SSO):** Utilize enterprise SSO solutions to centrally manage authentication to Jenkins, leveraging existing identity and access management (IAM) systems.

- **Enterprise Logging Solutions:** Forward logs from Jenkins to central logging solutions like ELK Stack (Elasticsearch, Logstash, Kibana) or Splunk for consolidated log management and analysis.

- **Automated Compliance Reporting:** Develop scripts and use tools that generate compliance reports automatically, ensuring continuous compliance tracking.

Example: Configuring SSL for Data Encryption

An integral part of ensuring compliance is encrypting data in transit. This can be achieved by configuring SSL for Jenkins. Below is an example of how to generate and use an SSL certificate in a Jenkins installation:

```
# Generate a new private key
openssl genrsa -des3 -out server.key 2048

# Generate a certificate signing request (CSR)
openssl req -new -key server.key -out server.csr

# Remove passphrase from the key
cp server.key server.key.org
openssl rsa -in server.key.org -out server.key

# Generate a self-signed certificate
openssl x509 -req -days 365 -in server.csr -signkey server.key -out server.crt
```

Once the SSL certificate is created, configure Jenkins to use these certificates:

```
# Copy the certificates to Jenkins directory
cp server.crt /var/lib/jenkins/.ssl/
cp server.key /var/lib/jenkins/.ssl/

# Edit Jenkins configuration to include SSL support
nano /etc/default/jenkins

# Add or modify the arguments to include SSL
JAVA_ARGS="-Djava.awt.headless=true -Djenkins.install.runSetupWizard=false
-Dhttps.port=8443 -Dhttps.keyStore=/var/lib/jenkins/.ssl/server.key
-Dhttps.keyStorePassword=<password> -Ddeveloper.capsule.basedir=/var/lib/jenkins"
```

Restart Jenkins to apply the new configurations.

```
# Restart Jenkins
service jenkins restart
```

Verifying the SSL configuration can be done by accessing the Jenkins instance via HTTPS:

```
https://your-jenkins-server:8443
```

Security compliance in Jenkins is not static; it requires ongoing monitoring, periodic reviews, and updates to address new threats and changes in regulatory requirements. By thoughtfully applying the principles outlined here, organizations can ensure that their Jenkins environments remain secure and compliant.

Chapter 9

Integrating Jenkins with Other Tools

This chapter explores integrating Jenkins with a variety of tools to enhance its functionality. It covers integrations with version control systems, build tools, containerization platforms, testing frameworks, configuration management tools, monitoring systems, and cloud services. The chapter also discusses setting up notifications, linking with issue tracking systems, connecting artifact repositories, and leveraging Jenkins APIs for automation, ensuring seamless and efficient workflows within different technology stacks.

9.1 Introduction to Jenkins Integrations

Jenkins, an open-source automation server, significantly extends its functionalities through integrations with various tools and platforms. This capability allows Jenkins to serve as a central hub for Continuous Integration (CI) and Continuous Delivery (CD) processes. Understanding these integrations is crucial for leveraging Jenkins to its fullest potential, enhancing automation, improving collaboration, and streamlining workflows.

Integrating Jenkins with external tools involves configuring plugins or using APIs to facilitate communication and data exchange between

Jenkins and other systems. These integrations cover a wide range of functionalities, including version control, build automation, containerization, testing, monitoring, configuration management, and cloud services. Each integration brings different capabilities that enhance the overall CI/CD pipeline.

Version control systems (VCS) such as Git and Subversion (SVN) are foundational to CI/CD pipelines. Jenkins integration with VCS allows automated builds and tests to trigger on code commits, ensuring a continuous feedback loop for developers. For instance, the following configuration snippet demonstrates a generic Jenkins pipeline setup to poll a Git repository:

```
pipeline {
    agent any
    stages {
        stage('Checkout') {
            steps {
                git branch: 'main',
                    url: 'https://github.com/user/repository.git'
            }
        }
        // Further stages here
    }
}
```

Build tools such as Maven and Gradle facilitate the automation of compiling and packaging code. Integrating Jenkins with these tools enables the automatic triggering of builds, dependency management, and artifact generation. Below is an example of a Maven build step in a Jenkins pipeline:

```
pipeline {
    agent any
    stages {
        stage('Build') {
            steps {
                sh 'mvn clean install'
            }
        }
        // Further stages here
    }
}
```

Containerization platforms like Docker and orchestration tools like Kubernetes provide isolated environments for application deployment and scalability. Jenkins integration with Docker allows building container images and pushing them to repositories, while Kubernetes integration enables automated deployment and management of containerized applications. The following snippet shows a Docker build and push:

```
pipeline {
```

```
    agent any
    stages {
        stage('Build Docker Image') {
            steps {
                script {
                    dockerImage = docker.build("user/image-name:tag")
                }
            }
        }
        stage('Push Docker Image') {
            steps {
                script {
                    docker.withRegistry('https://registry.hub.docker.com', 'docker-
                          credentials-id') {
                        dockerImage.push()
                    }
                }
            }
        }
    }
}
```

Testing frameworks like JUnit and Selenium are integral for validating code correctness and functionality. Jenkins supports running these tests during the build process, aggregating results and generating reports. This integration facilitates early detection of defects and maintains high code quality. Here is an example of running JUnit tests:

```
pipeline {
    agent any
    stages {
        stage('Test') {
            steps {
                sh 'mvn test'
                junit 'target/surefire-reports/*.xml'
            }
        }
        // Further stages here
    }
}
```

Configuration management tools such as Ansible, Chef, and Puppet automate the deployment and configuration of infrastructure. Jenkins can trigger these tools as part of the deployment pipeline, ensuring that the infrastructure matches the application's needs. For example, using Ansible with Jenkins could look like this:

```
pipeline {
    agent any
    stages {
        stage('Deploy') {
            steps {
                ansiblePlaybook credentialsId: 'ansible-credentials-id',
                                playbook: 'deploy.yml',
                                inventory: 'hosts.ini'
            }
        }
```

```
    }
}
```

Monitoring tools such as Nagios and Prometheus provide critical insights into system performance and health. Integrating Jenkins with monitoring tools can trigger alerts and self-healing processes in response to system anomalies, ensuring reliability and uptime. A simple approach to integration might include calling monitoring APIs from Jenkins scripts.

Integrations with cloud services (AWS, Azure, GCP) offer scalable resources and advanced deployment capabilities. Jenkins can automate infrastructure provisioning, deployment pipelines, and resource management using cloud provider APIs. For instance, deploying an application on AWS via Jenkins might involve the following steps:

```
pipeline {
    agent any
    stages {
        stage('Deploy to AWS') {
            steps {
                withAWS(credentials: 'aws-credentials-id', region: 'us-west-2') {
                    sh 'aws s3 cp my-app.jar s3://my-bucket/'
                }
            }
        }
    }
}
```

Notification systems such as email and Slack keep the team informed about build statuses, deployment results, and other crucial events. Configuring Jenkins to send notifications ensures that stakeholders remain updated without manual intervention.

Issue tracking systems like JIRA and Redmine can be linked with Jenkins to automatically create, update, or resolve issues based on the build or deployment outcomes.

Artifact repositories such as Nexus and Artifactory store build artifacts and dependencies efficiently. Jenkins integration with these repositories streamlines artifact management and reduces build times by caching dependencies.

Jenkins APIs provide powerful tools for automation, allowing external systems to trigger builds, retrieve logs, and interact with Jenkins programmatically. This facilitates building complex CI/CD ecosystems that integrate seamlessly with various tools and services. The REST API can be accessed via:

```
import requests
```

```
url = 'http://your_jenkins_url/job/your_job_name/build'
headers = {'Content-Type': 'application/json'}
response = requests.post(url, headers=headers, auth=('user', 'api_token'))
print(response.status_code)
```

Integrating Jenkins with these tools enhances the pipeline's efficiency, accuracy, and reliability, creating a robust foundation for sophisticated CI/CD workflows.

9.2 Integrating Version Control Systems (Git, SVN)

Integrating Jenkins with version control systems (VCS) such as Git and Subversion (SVN) is a critical aspect of modern software development pipelines. Jenkins provides robust support for VCS integration, enabling automated builds, continuous integration, and continuous delivery.

Configuring Git Integration:

To integrate Jenkins with Git, the Git plugin must be installed. The Git plugin facilitates Jenkins to check out or clone repositories from a variety of Git servers, including GitHub, GitLab, and Bitbucket. To install the Git plugin:

1. Navigate to Manage Jenkins → Manage Plugins.
2. Select the Available tab.
3. Search for Git Plugin.
4. Select the checkbox and click Install without restart or Download now and install after restart.

Once installed, the next step involves configuring a Jenkins job to use a Git repository. The configuration steps are:

1. Create a new job by navigating to Jenkins Dashboard → New Item.
2. Enter a name for the job and select Freestyle project, then click OK.

3. In the new job configuration page, under the Source Code Management section, select Git.
4. Enter the repository URL in the Repository URL field. For authenticated repositories, provide credentials by clicking Add under Credentials.
5. Optionally, specify the branch to build in the Branches to build field (e.g., */main for the main branch).

To verify the integration, save the configuration, and then click Build Now from the left-hand menu. The console output should show the repository being cloned and the subsequent build steps.

Configuring SVN Integration:

Integrating Jenkins with SVN is facilitated through the Subversion Plugin. This plugin allows Jenkins to check out code from Subversion repositories. To install the Subversion Plugin:

1. Go to Manage Jenkins → Manage Plugins.
2. Navigate to the Available tab.
3. Search for Subversion Plugin.
4. Check the plugin and click Install without restart or Download now and install after restart.

After the installation, configure a Jenkins job to use an SVN repository by following these steps:

1. Create a new job by clicking on Jenkins Dashboard → New Item.
2. Provide a name for the job, select Freestyle project, and click OK.
3. In the job configuration page, under the Source Code Management section, select Subversion.
4. Enter the repository URL in the Repository URL field. For repositories requiring authentication, set up credentials by clicking Add next to Credentials.
5. Optionally, specify the SVN repository revision (e.g., HEAD, specific revision number) to be checked out in the Repository revision field.

To confirm the integration, save the configuration and click Build Now. The repository should be checked out, followed by the build execution.

Triggering Builds with VCS Changes:

Automated builds are often triggered by changes in the VCS. Both Git and SVN integrations support polling or hook-based triggers.

Git Webhooks:

To set up webhook triggers for Git:

1. Navigate to the Git repository hosting service (e.g., GitHub, GitLab).
2. Access repository settings and locate webhooks configuration.
3. Add a new webhook with the Jenkins hook URL: http://<jenkins-server-url>/github-webhook/.
4. Set the webhook events, typically push events.

SVN Polling:

For SVN, polling can be configured within Jenkins:

1. In the job configuration page, under the Build Triggers section, select Poll SCM.
2. Specify the polling frequency using cron syntax (e.g., H/5 * * * * for every 5 minutes).

The Jenkins pipeline can also be configured using declarative or scripted syntax within the Jenkinsfile to specify source code management configurations. An example Jenkinsfile for a simple build process in a Git repository might look as follows:

```
pipeline {
    agent any
    stages {
        stage('Checkout') {
            steps {
                git 'https://github.com/username/repository.git'
            }
        }
        stage('Build') {
            steps {
                sh 'make'
            }
        }
        stage('Test') {
```

```
                steps {
                    sh 'make test'
                }
            }
        }
}
```

Executed successfully, the above script checks out a Git repository, executes a build process, and runs tests. For SVN, the checkout stage would use an svn step.

```
pipeline {
    agent any
    stages {
        stage('Checkout') {
            steps {
                svn 'http://svn.example.com/repository/trunk'
            }
        }
        stage('Build') {
            steps {
                sh 'make'
            }
        }
        stage('Test') {
            steps {
                sh 'make test'
            }
        }
    }
}
```

Successful integration of Jenkins with VCS ensures automated, reliable, and repeatable build processes, forming the backbone of continuous integration and delivery pipelines.

9.3 Integration with Build Tools (Maven, Gradle)

Build tools streamline the process of building, testing, and deploying software. This section focuses on the integration of Jenkins with two predominant build tools in the industry: Maven and Gradle. Both these tools have distinct architectures and capabilities, yet Jenkins can harmonize with either to automate and enhance the build process.

Maven Integration

Jenkins natively supports Apache Maven, a powerful build automation tool primarily used for Java projects. Maven uses a Project Object Model (POM), defined in an XML file, to manage project builds, reporting, and documentation. The integration process begins with the Jenkins configuration and the subsequent setup of Maven-based Jenkins jobs.

Setting up Jenkins for Maven

Before creating a Maven-based job, ensure Maven is configured correctly in Jenkins:

- Navigate to Manage Jenkins > Global Tool Configuration.
- Under Maven, add a new Maven installation. Jenkins can install it automatically or use an existing Maven installation on the machine. Specify the Maven version and provide a name for the configuration.

Creating a Maven Job

Create a new job specifically for your Maven project:

- Select New Item from the Jenkins dashboard.
- Provide a name for your job and choose Maven project.
- In the Source Code Management section, configure the version control settings (typically Git or SVN).
- Under the Build section, specify the predefined goals and options that Maven should execute, such as clean install.

```
clean install
```

Additional configurations can include setting up specific build triggers and post-build actions such as sending notifications or archiving artifacts.

Gradle Integration

Gradle, known for its flexibility and performance, primarily utilizes a Groovy-based declarative language. Its integration with Jenkins is facilitated through Jenkins' Gradle plugin.

Installing the Gradle Plugin

First, ensure the Gradle plugin is installed in Jenkins:

- Navigate to Manage Jenkins > Manage Plugins.

- In the Available tab, search for Gradle Plugin.
- Install the plugin and restart Jenkins if required.

Configuring Gradle in Jenkins

Once the plugin is installed, configure the Gradle installation:

- Navigate to Manage Jenkins > Global Tool Configuration.
- Under Gradle, add a new Gradle installation by specifying a name and either allowing Jenkins to install Gradle automatically or pointing to a manually installed version.

Creating a Gradle Job

Create a new job for your Gradle project:

- Select New Item from the Jenkins dashboard.
- Provide a name for your job and choose Freestyle project.
- In the Source Code Management section, configure the version control settings.
- Under the Build section, add a new Invoke Gradle script build step.
- Specify the tasks that Gradle should execute, such as clean build.

```
clean build
```

Additionally, configure other job parameters like scheduling builds, managing build environments, and setting post-build actions to streamline development workflows.

Troubleshooting and Optimization

Effective integration often requires monitoring and optimizations:

- Build Logs: Inspect build logs to diagnose and resolve issues. They contain detailed records of build processes and can be accessed via the Jenkins job interface.
- Cache Management: For Maven, configure local repository settings to enhance performance. For Gradle, use the build cache to reduce redundancy.

- Pipeline as Code: Use Jenkins Pipelines (Jenkinsfile) to define and manage builds as code, providing better version control and traceability.

A sample Jenkinsfile for a Maven project:

```
pipeline {
    agent any
    tools {
        maven 'Maven_3.6.3'
    }
    stages {
        stage('Build') {
            steps {
                sh 'mvn clean install'
            }
        }
    }
    post {
        always {
            archiveArtifacts artifacts: '**/target/*.jar', allowEmptyArchive: true
        }
    }
}
```

For a Gradle project:

```
pipeline {
    agent any
    tools {
        gradle 'Gradle_6.7'
    }
    stages {
        stage('Build') {
            steps {
                sh './gradlew clean build'
            }
        }
    }
    post {
        always {
            archiveArtifacts artifacts: '**/build/libs/*.jar', allowEmptyArchive: true
        }
    }
}
```

These integrations facilitate efficient build processes, promoting continuous integration and delivery (CI/CD) practices.

Build success!

9.4 Integrating Containerization Tools (Docker, Kubernetes)

Integrating Jenkins with containerization tools such as Docker and Kubernetes significantly enhances the automation and scalability of the CI/CD pipeline. This section delves into the methodologies and practical setups for leveraging these technologies in Jenkins, ensuring seamless and efficient software deployments.

Docker Integration

Docker provides a streamlined approach to building, packaging, and distributing applications in containers, which are lightweight and portable virtual environments. Docker integration with Jenkins enables the automation of the container lifecycle from building and testing to deployment.

To integrate Docker with Jenkins, install the Docker plugin. Navigate to **Manage Jenkins** → **Manage Plugins** and search for "Docker". Install the plugin and restart Jenkins if necessary.

Next, configure Jenkins to communicate with the Docker daemon. This often involves setting up Jenkins with appropriate permissions to access the Docker socket. Ensure that the Jenkins user has the necessary permissions by either adding the user to the Docker group or setting the appropriate permissions on the Docker socket.

To demonstrate, configure a Jenkins pipeline that builds a Docker image and pushes it to Docker Hub. Write a Pipeline script using the Groovy syntax:

```
pipeline {
    agent {
        docker {
            image 'node:14'
            args '-v /var/run/docker.sock:/var/run/docker.sock'
        }
    }
    environment {
        DOCKER_IMAGE = 'my-docker-repo/my-node-app'
        DOCKER_TAG = 'latest'
    }
    stages {
        stage('Build Image') {
            steps {
                script {
                    docker.build("$DOCKER_IMAGE:$DOCKER_TAG")
                }
            }
        }
        stage('Push Image') {
```

```
            steps {
                withDockerRegistry([credentialsId: 'docker-hub-credentials', url: '']) {
                    script {
                        docker.image("$DOCKER_IMAGE:$DOCKER_TAG").push()
                    }
                }
            }
        }
    }
}
```

This Pipeline script specifies a Docker agent using the Node.js image. It binds the Docker socket from the host to the Jenkins container, enabling Docker commands within the Pipeline. The environment variables define the Docker image repository and tag. The **Build Image** stage uses the Docker build command to create a Docker image from the Dockerfile in the project. The **Push Image** stage pushes the built image to Docker Hub using Docker registry credentials.

Ensure Docker registry credentials are configured in Jenkins (Manage Jenkins → Manage Credentials).

Kubernetes Integration

Kubernetes automates the deployment, scaling, and management of containerized applications. Integrating Jenkins with Kubernetes facilitates the dynamic provisioning of Jenkins agents, scalability, and efficient resource management.

Begin by installing the Kubernetes plugin in Jenkins. Navigate to **Manage Jenkins** → **Manage Plugins** and search for "Kubernetes". Install the plugin and restart Jenkins if required.

Configure Jenkins to use Kubernetes as a cloud provider. Go to **Manage Jenkins** → **Configure System** → **Cloud** → **Kubernetes**, and provide details for Kubernetes API Server, Kubernetes Namespace, Jenkins URL, and Jenkins Tunnel. Additionally, configure Kubernetes credentials, typically a service account with appropriate permissions.

Next, define the pod templates used by Jenkins to spin up agents. Pod templates specify the configuration of containers within the pod. For example, create a pod template with a container running Node.js for building and testing applications:

```
podTemplate(label: 'nodejs', containers: [
    containerTemplate(name: 'jnlp', image: 'jenkins/inbound-agent', args: '${computer.
        jnlpmac} ${computer.name}'),
    containerTemplate(name: 'node', image: 'node:14', command: 'cat', ttyEnabled: true
        )
]) {
    node('nodejs') {
```

```
        stage('Checkout') {
            git 'https://github.com/my-repo/my-project.git'
        }
        stage('Install Dependencies') {
            container('node') {
                sh 'npm install'
            }
        }
        stage('Build') {
            container('node') {
                sh 'npm run build'
            }
        }
        stage('Test') {
            container('node') {
                sh 'npm test'
            }
        }
    }
}
```

This Pipeline script defines a pod template labeled "nodejs" with two containers: the Jenkins inbound agent and a Node.js container. The 'node' block assigns the agent, ensuring the stages are executed within the Kubernetes pod. Each stage (Checkout, Install Dependencies, Build, Test) specifies the Node.js container for executing corresponding commands.

Kubernetes facilitates dynamic scaling and efficient resource utilization by provisioning Jenkins agents on-demand. It enables distributed builds, providing robust scalability for large-scale projects.

By fully integrating Docker and Kubernetes with Jenkins, you can leverage containerization's benefits, including isolation, portability, and efficient resource management, thus enhancing your CI/CD pipeline's robustness and scalability.

9.5 Integration with Testing Tools (JUnit, Selenium)

Jenkins provides robust integration capabilities with various testing tools, notably JUnit and Selenium, to facilitate automated testing processes. This integration aids in running, monitoring, and managing test suites, thereby ensuring code quality and reliability.

JUnit Integration:

JUnit is a widely used testing framework for Java applications. Integration of JUnit with Jenkins involves several steps, which enable Jenkins to execute JUnit test cases and report the results. Below is a detailed procedure to integrate JUnit with Jenkins:

1. **Install the** JUnit **Plugin:** Jenkins typically comes with the JUnit plugin pre-installed. Verify its existence by navigating to *Manage Jenkins* → *Manage Plugins* → *Installed*. If not present, it can be installed from the *Available* tab.

2. **Configure a Jenkins Job:** Create a new job or configure an existing one. In the job configuration page, locate the *Build* section and add a *Build Step* to execute your build tool (e.g., Maven or Gradle) which includes running the JUnit tests.

3. **Publish** JUnit **Test Results:** Scroll to the *Post-Build Actions* section and select *Publish* JUnit *test result report*.

4. **Specify Test Report XMLs:** Provide the path to the JUnit XML result files. A typical pattern is ***/target/surefire-reports/*.xml* when using Maven.

Here is an example of a Jenkins pipeline configuration script that runs JUnit tests and publishes the results:

```
pipeline {
    agent any

    stages {
        stage('Build') {
            steps {
                // Checkout the code from the version control system
                checkout scm

                // Run the build script using Maven
                sh 'mvn clean install'
            }
        }
        stage('Test') {
            steps {
                // Execute JUnit tests
                sh 'mvn test'
            }
            post {
                always {
                    // Publish the JUnit test results
                    junit '**/target/surefire-reports/*.xml'
                }
            }
        }
    }
}
```

The junit '**/target/surefire-reports/*.xml' directive in the *post* block ensures that test results are collected, and reports are generated post-execution.

Selenium Integration:

Selenium is a popular framework for automating web applications. Integration with Jenkins provides a continuous feedback system through automated UI testing. Below are the steps to integrate Selenium with Jenkins:

1. **Install Selenium WebDriver:** Include Selenium libraries and WebDriver bindings in your project. These can be managed through build tools like Maven or Gradle.

2. **Configure Jenkins Job to run Selenium tests:** Similarly to JUnit, you configure a Jenkins job to run the Selenium tests. In the *Build* section, add the command to execute the test scripts, typically by invoking a build tool or a script file.

3. **Capture and Publish Test Results:** Depending on the test framework in use, capture the test results in a format that Jenkins can interpret (XML, HTML). If using a combination of JUnit and Selenium, the results can be published as JUnit reports.

Consider the following example pipeline script that runs Selenium tests and collects the results using JUnit:

```
pipeline {
    agent any

    environment {
        GECKODRIVER = '/path/to/geckodriver'
        FIREFOX_BIN = '/path/to/firefox'
    }

    stages {
        stage('Build') {
            steps {
                // Checkout the source code
                checkout scm

                // Compile the code using Maven
                sh 'mvn clean compile'
            }
        }
        stage('Test') {
            steps {
                // Execute Selenium tests
                sh 'mvn test -Dtest=*IT'
            }
            post {
```

```
                always {
                    // Publish the JUnit test results for Selenium tests
                    junit '**/target/surefire-reports/*.xml'
                }
            }
        }
    }
}
```

This script ensures that Selenium WebDriver environment variables are set, enabling Jenkins to locate the necessary browser drivers for test execution. The command sh 'mvn test -Dtest=*IT' specifies that the tests are run, and the results are processed similarly to conventional JUnit tests.

The integration of JUnit and Selenium into Jenkins pipelines enhances the efficacy of automated testing by providing a streamlined, continuous testing mechanism. This ensures that code changes are adequately verified, contributing to the overall stability and reliability of the software product.

9.6 Integrating with Configuration Management Tools (Ansible, Chef, Puppet)

Integrating Jenkins with configuration management tools such as Ansible, Chef, and Puppet enhances the automation capabilities, enabling streamlined management of infrastructure and consistent deployment processes. This section demonstrates how to configure Jenkins to work with these tools.

Ansible Integration

Ansible integration with Jenkins allows for efficient automation of complex orchestration tasks. To start, ensure that Ansible is installed on the Jenkins server.

Jenkins requires the Ansible plugin, which can be installed through the *Manage Jenkins* → *Manage Plugins* interface. Once installed, the plugin configuration involves specifying the path to the Ansible executable within the global tool configuration.

To configure, navigate to *Manage Jenkins* → *Global Tool Configuration*, scroll to *Ansible*, and enter the Ansible installation path.

```
ansible --version
```

A Jenkins job can then be set up to leverage Ansible. In the job configuration:

- Add a build step selecting *Invoke Ansible Playbook*.
- Specify the playbook path and any additional parameters like inventory file, extra variables, etc.
- Configure any additional options such as credentials for secure execution.

Here's an example of a simple Ansible playbook for installing Apache:

```
---
- hosts: webservers
  tasks:
    - name: Ensure Apache is installed
      apt:
        name: apache2
        state: present
```

During the build, Jenkins will execute the Ansible playbook, ensuring infrastructure changes are applied as specified.

Chef Integration

For integrating Chef with Jenkins, ensure that Chef Client and Knife are installed on the Jenkins server. These tools facilitate the management of infrastructure through code.

Download and install the *Knife Plugin* via the *Manage Jenkins → Manage Plugins* interface.

Within Jenkins' *Global Tool Configuration*, configure the Chef installation by specifying the paths to the Chef executable and Knife configuration:

- Navigate to *Manage Jenkins → Global Tool Configuration*.
- Scroll to *Chef*, and configure the Chef settings by providing the path to the chef-client executable and other necessary environment configurations.

To create a Jenkins job that uses Chef:

- Add a build step *Execute Shell*.
- Insert the following shell script to run Chef with a specific recipe:

```
#!/bin/bash
knife cookbook upload my_cookbook
knife bootstrap my_server -r "recipe[my_cookbook]"
```

This script uploads the specified Chef cookbook to the Chef server and bootstraps the target node to configure it.

Puppet Integration

Puppet integration with Jenkins enables the automation of application deployment and configuration management. Install the Puppet agent on the Jenkins server, followed by the Puppet Plugin from the *Manage Plugins* interface.

In *Global Tool Configuration*, configure Puppet by specifying the Puppet Master and agent details. This encompasses setting up the Puppet executable path and environment configuration necessary for Puppet commands to execute correctly.

To run Puppet scripts within a Jenkins job:

- Add a build step *Invoke Puppet*.
- Provide the necessary configurations for Puppet such as `puppet apply` command with manifests or `puppet agent` command.

Here is an example script for applying a Puppet manifest that installs Nginx:

```
node default {
  package { 'nginx':
    ensure => present,
  }
  service { 'nginx':
    ensure => running,
    enable => true,
  }
}
```

Configure the build step to invoke this manifest using:

```
puppet apply /path/to/nginx_manifest.pp
```

During build execution, Jenkins will invoke the Puppet command, applying the desired state configurations defined in the manifest.

Through these detailed configurations, integrating Ansible, Chef, and Puppet with Jenkins allows for robust continuous delivery and infrastructure automation, enabling an efficient and error-free deployment process.

9.7 Integration with Monitoring Tools (Nagios, Prometheus)

In modern CI/CD pipelines, monitoring is crucial for ensuring systems' health and performance. Integrating Jenkins with monitoring tools like Nagios and Prometheus allows continuous tracking of Jenkins' performance metrics and job statuses. This proactive approach can help in swiftly identifying and resolving issues to maintain uninterrupted delivery pipelines.

Integrating Jenkins with Nagios

Nagios is an open-source monitoring tool that provides comprehensive monitoring of systems, networks, and infrastructure. To integrate Nagios with Jenkins, follow these steps to set up a seamless interaction:

- Install NRPE on Jenkins Server: Nagios Remote Plugin Executor (NRPE) allows Nagios to execute plugins on remote hosts.

```
sudo apt-get install nagios-nrpe-server nagios-plugins
```

- Configure the NRPE daemon: Modify the NRPE configuration file located at /etc/nagios/nrpe.cfg to include the Jenkins server's IP address in the allowed_hosts parameter:

```
allowed_hosts=127.0.0.1, <Nagios_server_IP>
```

- Define Jenkins Checks: Add commands in nrpe.cfg to monitor Jenkins services. For example, to check Jenkins process:

```
command[check_jenkins_process]=/usr/lib/nagios/plugins/check_procs -c 1:1 -C java
```

- Restart NRPE Service:

```
sudo systemctl restart nagios-nrpe-server
```

- Configure Nagios Server: Add a service definition in Nagios to monitor Jenkins. Edit the relevant configuration file, typically located in the /usr/local/nagios/etc/objects directory:

```
define service{
    use                     generic-service
    host_name               Jenkins_Server
    service_description     Jenkins Process
    check_command           check_nrpe!check_jenkins_process
}
```

- Restart Nagios:

```
sudo systemctl restart nagios
```

Integrating Jenkins with Prometheus

Prometheus is an open-source monitoring and alerting toolkit designed for reliability and scalability. To integrate Jenkins with Prometheus, we use the Jenkins Prometheus plugin.

- Install the Prometheus Plugin:
  - Navigate to Manage Jenkins > Manage Plugins > Available.
  - Search for "Prometheus Metrics".
  - Select the plugin and click Install without restart.
- Configure the Prometheus Plugin:
  - Go to Manage Jenkins > Configure System.
  - Scroll to Prometheus section.
  - Enable the "Expose metrics" option.
  - Configure the appropriate endpoint (default: /prometheus).
- Set up Prometheus Server to Scrape Metrics:

```
scrape_configs:
  - job_name: 'jenkins'
    static_configs:
    - targets: ['<jenkins_server>:<prometheus_port>']
```

- Restart Prometheus Server:

```
sudo systemctl restart prometheus
```

- Verify Metrics Collection: Access the Prometheus server UI (default: http://localhost:9090) and navigate to the Targets tab. Ensure that the Jenkins target is up and metrics are being scraped successfully.

Integrating these monitoring tools with Jenkins extends monitoring capabilities to CI/CD pipelines, providing comprehensive oversight of job executions and Jenkins' health. This integration allows identification and resolution of potential issues in a timely manner, thereby maintaining workflow efficiency and system reliability.

9.8 Integrating with Cloud Services (AWS, Azure, GCP)

The integration of Jenkins with cloud services such as AWS, Azure, and GCP enables leveraging scalable infrastructure and advanced services for continuous integration and continuous deployment (CI/CD) pipelines. This section presents detailed processes for configuring Jenkins to interact with these cloud platforms, facilitating automated deployments, resource management, and environment provisioning.

Amazon Web Services (AWS)

AWS provides a comprehensive suite of cloud services that can be integrated with Jenkins, including EC2 instances for build environments, S3 for storage, and various other services like Lambda and ECS for deployment. Integration with AWS typically involves configuring the AWS CLI, setting up IAM roles, and leveraging Jenkins plugins designed to interact with AWS services.

To begin integrating Jenkins with AWS, install the AWS CLI on your Jenkins server. Ensure the necessary IAM roles and policies are configured to enable Jenkins to access AWS services.

```
# Install AWS CLI
sudo apt-get update
sudo apt-get install awscli

# Configure AWS CLI
aws configure
```

Next, install the Jenkins AWS plugins through the plugin manager available in Jenkins. Notable plugins include 'Amazon EC2 Plugin', 'AWS CodeBuild Plugin', and 'AWS Steps Plugin'. These plugins streamline the interaction between Jenkins jobs and AWS services.

Utilize the 'Amazon EC2 Plugin' to dynamically provision EC2 instances as build agents. This approach scales the Jenkins build environments based on demand.

```
node {
    // AWS credentials configuration
    withAWS(credentials: 'my-aws-credentials') {
        ec2 = amazonEC2Builder(region: 'us-west-2')

        // Provision an EC2 instance
        ec2Agent = ec2.provisionInstance(imageId: 'ami-0123456789abcdef0', type: 't2.
            micro', keyPair: 'my-key-pair')

        // Allocate as a Jenkins agent
        ec2.allocateAgent(ec2Agent)
```

```
        // Perform build steps
        // ...
    }
}
```

Microsoft Azure

Azure integration with Jenkins facilitates automated deployments and scaling of resources like virtual machines, Azure Kubernetes Service (AKS), and App Services. To start integrating Jenkins with Azure, install the Azure CLI and set up the necessary configuration.

```
# Install Azure CLI
curl -sL https://aka.ms/InstallAzureCLIDeb | sudo bash

# Login to Azure
az login
```

Install relevant Jenkins plugins such as 'Azure CLI Plugin', 'Azure VM Agents Plugin', and 'Azure App Service Plugin'. These plugins allow Jenkins to execute Azure CLI commands, provision Azure Virtual Machines, and deploy to Azure App Services.

An example of using the 'Azure VM Agents Plugin' to provision a virtual machine as a Jenkins build agent:

```
node {
    // Azure credentials configuration
    withCredentials([azureServicePrincipal(credentialsId: 'azure-sp-credentials')]) {
        // Provision a VM as a build agent
        azureVM = azureCreateVM(agentName: 'jenkins-agent',
                                image: 'Canonical:UbuntuServer:18.04-LTS:latest',
                                size: 'Standard_DS1_v2')

        // Allocate as a Jenkins agent
        azureAllocateAgent(azureVM)
        // Perform build steps
        // ...
    }
}
```

Google Cloud Platform (GCP)

Integrating Jenkins with GCP offers access to Google Compute Engine, Google Kubernetes Engine, and Cloud Storage, among other services. Start by installing the Google Cloud SDK on the Jenkins server.

```
# Install Google Cloud SDK
echo "deb [signed-by=/usr/share/keyrings/cloud.google.gpg] http://packages.cloud.
    google.com/apt cloud-sdk main" | sudo tee -a /etc/apt/sources.list.d/google-cloud
    -sdk.list
sudo apt-get install apt-transport-https ca-certificates gnupg
curl https://packages.cloud.google.com/apt/doc/apt-key.gpg | sudo apt-key --keyring /
    usr/share/keyrings/cloud.google.gpg add -
sudo apt-get update && sudo apt-get install google-cloud-sdk
```

```
# Initialize Google Cloud SDK
gcloud init
```

Install Jenkins plugins such as 'Google Kubernetes Engine Plugin', 'Google Compute Engine Plugin', and 'Google Cloud Storage Plugin'.

A typical example of using the 'Google Compute Engine Plugin' to provision a new compute instance:

```
node {
    // GCP credentials configuration
    withCredentials([file(credentialsId: 'gcp-credentials', variable: '
        GOOGLE_APPLICATION_CREDENTIALS')]) {
        // Provision a Google Compute Engine instance
        gcpInstance = googleComputeEngine(configFile: 'gce-config.yaml')

        // Allocate as a Jenkins agent
        gcpAllocateAgent(gcpInstance)
        // Perform build steps
        // ...
    }
}
```

Integrating Jenkins with AWS, Azure, and GCP enables seamless, scalable, and efficient CI/CD operations by leveraging the inherent benefits and services of these major cloud platforms.

9.9 Configuring Notification Systems (Email, Slack)

Effective notification systems are pivotal in ensuring swift communication among team members regarding build statuses, test results, and deployment progress. Jenkins provides robust integration with various notification platforms including email and Slack, which are among the most commonly used tools in professional environments.

1. Configuring Email Notifications

Jenkins facilitates email notifications through the *Email Extension Plugin*. Follow these steps to configure Jenkins to send email notifications:

1. **Install the Email Extension Plugin**:
    - Navigate to *Manage Jenkins* → *Manage Plugins* → *Available*.
    - Search for *Email Extension Plugin*.

  - Select and install the plugin.

2. **Configure Email Extension Plugin**:
   - Go to *Manage Jenkins* → *Configure System*.
   - Scroll down to *Extended E-mail Notification*.
   - Fill in the relevant SMTP server details, including *SMTP server*, *SMTP Port*, and *Authentication* credentials.
   - Specify the *Default user e-mail suffix* if necessary.

3. **Define Email Notification Triggers in Job Configuration**:
   - Open your Jenkins job configuration page.
   - In the *Post-build Actions* section, select *Editable Email Notification*.
   - Define the recipients, email subject, and body.
   - Specify the conditions under which emails should be triggered (e.g., after a build failure, always).

Here is an example configuration for sending an email in case of a build failure:

```
emailext(
    subject: "Build Failure in Job ${JOB_NAME} Build #${BUILD_NUMBER}",
    body: "Please check the Jenkins job: ${BUILD_URL}",
    recipientProviders: [[$class: 'DevelopersRecipientProvider']],
    to: 'developers@example.com'
)
```

2. Configuring Slack Notifications

Slack notifications require the installation of the *Slack Notification Plugin* and the creation of a Slack App for Jenkins:

1. **Install the Slack Notification Plugin**:
   - Go to *Manage Jenkins* → *Manage Plugins* → *Available*.
   - Search for *Slack Notification Plugin*.
   - Install the plugin.

2. **Create and Configure a Slack App**:
   - Sign in to your Slack workspace and navigate to the Slack App Directory.

- Create a new app and give it a name, choosing your development Slack workspace.
- Navigate to *OAuth & Permissions* under *Features*.
- Add the following OAuth scopes: chat:write, chat:write.customize.
- Install the app to your workspace and obtain the OAuth token.

3. **Configure Slack Plugin in Jenkins**:
   - Go to *Manage Jenkins* → *Configure System*.
   - Scroll down to *Slack* section.
   - Enter the *Workspace* (team domain), the *Channel* you wish to notify, and the *Integration Token* (OAuth access token obtained earlier).
4. **Set Up Slack Notifications in Job Configuration**:
   - In the job configuration page, add a *Post-build Action* and select *Slack Notifications*.
   - Configure the notifications for start, success, and failure as required.

Example configuration for notifying a Slack channel on build failure:

```
slackSend (
    channel: '#ci-builds',
    color: 'danger',
    message: "Build failure in ${env.JOB_NAME} #${env.BUILD_NUMBER}: ${env.
        BUILD_URL}"
)
```

These configurations enable Jenkins to send critical notifications via email or Slack, improving the overall responsiveness and effectiveness of the development process.

9.10 Integration with Issue Tracking Systems (JIRA, Redmine)

Integrating Jenkins with issue tracking systems such as JIRA and Redmine enables streamlined issue tracking, automated project management, and improved collaboration among team members. This section details the steps and configurations required to integrate Jenkins with these issue tracking systems effectively.

JIRA Integration

To integrate Jenkins with JIRA, the following prerequisites must be met:

- Jenkins should be up and running.
- A JIRA instance should be accessible and properly configured.
- The Jenkins JIRA plugin should be installed.

Step-by-Step Integration Process

1. Install the JIRA Plugin

Navigate to Manage Jenkins → Manage Plugins → Available tab. Search for JIRA Plugin, select it, and click Install without restart.

2. Configure JIRA Credentials

After installation, go to Manage Jenkins → Configure System. Locate the JIRA section and add the JIRA site configuration:

- JIRA URL: Enter the base URL of your JIRA instance.
- Username: Provide a username with sufficient permissions in JIRA.
- Password: Enter the corresponding password or API token.

3. Create a Job with JIRA Integration

Create a new Jenkins job or configure an existing one. Under the Build Environment section, select Use JIRA issue tracker. Provide the JIRA project key and issue key pattern if necessary. This setting allows Jenkins to update JIRA issues based on build results.

```
<project>
  ...
  <useJIRA>true</useJIRA>
  <jiraProjectKey>PROJECTKEY</jiraProjectKey>
  <jiraIssuePattern>JIRA-\\d+</jiraIssuePattern>
  ...
</project>
```

4. Post-build Actions

Configuring post-build actions enhances the integration further by updating JIRA issues based on the build status. Under Post-build Actions, select Post to JIRA and configure the desired actions:

- Link build information to JIRA issues.
- Transition JIRA issues based on build status (e.g., move issues to Done if the build is successful).

```
Build successful: Transition issue to Done
Build failed: Leave comment with failure details
```

Redmine Integration

Redmine can be integrated with Jenkins using similar steps, although the specifics differ due to Redmine's unique API and settings.

1. Install the Redmine Plugin

Start by navigating to Manage Jenkins → Manage Plugins → Available tab. Search for Redmine Plugin, select it, and click Install without restart.

2. Configure Redmine Credentials

After installing the plugin, go to Manage Jenkins → Configure System. Find the Redmine section and add the Redmine site configuration:

- Redmine URL: Enter the base URL of the Redmine instance.
- API Key: Provide an API key generated from the Redmine user's account.

```
# Example configuration
Redmine URL: http://redmine.example.com
API Key: 12345abcde67890fghij
```

3. Create a Job with Redmine Integration

Creating or configuring a Jenkins job involves adding Redmine-related features under the Build Environment section. Check Enable Redmine integration and configure the related settings, including project identifiers and issue ID patterns.

4. Post-build Actions

As with JIRA, configure post-build actions to update Redmine issues based on build outcomes. Under Post-build Actions, select Post to Redmine and specify the required actions:

- Update issue statuses.
- Add comments to Redmine issues.

Post to Redmine options could include:

- Success: Mark the issue as resolved.
- Failure: Add a failure comment.

By following these steps, Jenkins can effectively interact with JIRA and Redmine, facilitating automated issue tracking and project management improvements. The integration supports a smoother workflow and better coordination among development, operations, and project management teams.

9.11 Integrating with Artifact Repositories (Nexus, Artifactory)

Artifact repositories play a crucial role in managing binary artifacts produced by builds and ensuring that these artifacts can be reused consistently across different environments. This section delves into integrating Jenkins with two widely-used artifact repositories: Nexus and Artifactory.

Nexus Repository Integration

Nexus is a popular artifact repository manager from Sonatype. Its seamless integration with Jenkins allows for efficient storage, retrieval, and management of build artifacts. To integrate Jenkins with Nexus, follow these detailed steps:

1. **Installing the Nexus Platform Plugin**

Begin by installing the Nexus Platform Plugin in Jenkins. Navigate to **Jenkins Dashboard** → **Manage Jenkins** → **Manage Plugins** → **Available** tab, then search for **Nexus Platform Plugin** and install it.

2. **Configuring Nexus Server Details**

Post installation, configure the Nexus server details in Jenkins:

- Go to **Jenkins Dashboard** → **Manage Jenkins** → **Configure System**.
- Locate the section **Nexus Repository Manager Servers**.
- Click on **Add Nexus Repository Manager Server**.
- Fill in the **Server ID**, **Server URL**, and **Credentials**.

- Save the configuration.

3. **Uploading Artifacts to Nexus**

To upload artifacts, configure Jenkins jobs to interact with Nexus. Modify the job configuration as follows:

- In the build configuration of the job, add a post-build action.
- Select **Nexus Repository Manager Publisher**.
- Choose the configured Nexus server, specify the repository name, and define the artifact details (group, artifact ID, version, packaging type, etc.).
- Execute the build to upload the artifacts seamlessly to Nexus.

4. **Example Configuration in Jenkins Pipeline**

For Jenkins Pipeline (Declarative or Scripted), use the 'nexusArtifactUploader' plugin within the pipeline script. Example for a Declarative Pipeline:

```
pipeline {
    agent any
    stages {
        stage('Build') {
            steps {
                // your build steps here
            }
        }
        stage('Upload to Nexus') {
            steps {
                nexusArtifactUploader(
                    nexusVersion: 'nexus3',
                    protocol: 'http',
                    nexusUrl: 'http://your-nexus-repo:8081',
                    groupId: 'com.yourcompany',
                    version: '1.0.0',
                    repository: 'maven-releases',
                    credentialsId: 'nexus-credentials',
                    artifacts: [
                        [artifactId: 'your-artifact', classifier: '', file: 'target/your-artifact
                            -1.0.0.jar', type: 'jar']
                    ]
                )
            }
        }
    }
}
```

Artifactory Integration

Artifactory from JFrog is another extensively used artifact repository manager, providing robust integrations with CI/CD tools, including Jenkins. To integrate Jenkins with Artifactory, perform the following steps:

1. **Installing the JFrog Artifactory Plugin**

First, install the JFrog Artifactory Plugin for Jenkins. This can be done via **Jenkins Dashboard** → **Manage Jenkins** → **Manage Plugins** → **Available** tab. Search for **JFrog Artifactory Plugin** and proceed with the installation.

2. **Configuring Artifactory Server in Jenkins**

Post plugin installation, configure Artifactory server details:

- Navigate to **Jenkins Dashboard** → **Manage Jenkins** → **Configure System**.
- Find the section **JFrog Artifactory**.
- Add an **Artifactory Server**.
- Provide the **Server ID**, **Artifactory URL**, **Username**, Password/API Key and save the details.

3. **Uploading Artifacts to Artifactory**

Configure Jenkins jobs to upload artifacts to Artifactory:

- In the job configuration, add a post-build action.
- Select **Deploy artifacts to Artifactory**.
- Choose the configured Artifactory server and specify the target repository, deployer credentials, etc.
- Specify the artifacts to be deployed.
- Run the build to upload the artifacts to Artifactory.

4. **Example Configuration in Jenkins Pipeline**

For Jenkins Pipeline (Declarative or Scripted), use the 'rtUpload' step provided by the JFrog Pipeline API. Example for a Declarative Pipeline:

```
pipeline {
    agent any
    environment {
        ARTIFACTORY_SERVER = 'your-artifactory-server'
        CREDS_ID = 'artifactory-credentials'
```

```
    }
    stages {
        stage('Build') {
            steps {
                // your build steps here
            }
        }
        stage('Upload to Artifactory') {
            steps {
                script {
                    def server = Artifactory.server(ARTIFACTORY_SERVER)
                    def uploadSpec = """{
                        "files": [
                            {
                                "pattern": "target/your-artifact-1.0.0.jar",
                                "target": "libs-release-local/com/yourcompany/your-
                                    artifact/1.0.0/"
                            }
                        ]
                    }"""
                    server.upload(uploadSpec)
                }
            }
        }
    }
}
```

By integrating Jenkins with artifact repositories like Nexus and Artifactory, you ensure reliable management of your build artifacts, support for various build frameworks, and maintain consistency across different deployment environments. This integration is pivotal in a well-structured CI/CD pipeline, allowing for seamless artifact handling and automated deployment processes.

9.12 Using Jenkins APIs for Automation

Jenkins APIs provide a powerful way to interact programmatically with Jenkins. This enables the creation, configuration, and management of jobs, nodes, and various Jenkins components through automated scripts and applications. The API can be accessed in multiple ways, primarily through REST API calls, Python, and Groovy scripting within Jenkins pipelines or external scripts. Here, we delve deeper into each of these approaches to harness the full potential of Jenkins for automation.

Jenkins' REST API is perhaps the most versatile method and supports a wide array of operations. REST calls to Jenkins can be authenticated using HTTP Basic authentication, API tokens, or with CSRF protection tokens. Below is an example of a REST call to create a new Jenkins job:

```
# Creating a new Jenkins Job using REST API
curl -X POST 'http://<jenkins_url>/createItem?name=NewJob' \
--data-binary '@config.xml' \
--header 'Content-Type: application/xml' \
--user 'username:api_token'
```

In this example, config.xml contains the job configuration. Using this method, automation scripts can dynamically create new jobs, update configurations, or delete existing jobs.

Jenkins pipelines support embedded Groovy scripting, leveraging the Pipeline Domain Specific Language (DSL). The following Groovy script demonstrates how to use the Jenkins API in a pipeline to create a new job:

```
def jenkins = Jenkins.instance

// Creating a new job configuration (use Job DSL or a template)
def configXml = '''
<project>
  <actions/>
  <description/>
  <keepDependencies>false</keepDependencies>
  <properties/>
  <scm class="hudson.scm.NullSCM"/>
  <canRoam>true</canRoam>
  <disabled>false</disabled>
  <blockBuildWhenDownstreamBuilding>false</blockBuildWhenDownstreamBuilding
      >
  <blockBuildWhenUpstreamBuilding>false</blockBuildWhenUpstreamBuilding>
  <triggers/>
  <concurrentBuild>false</concurrentBuild>
  <builders/>
  <publishers/>
  <buildWrappers/>
</project>
'''

def newItem = jenkins.createProjectFromXML("NewJob", new ByteArrayInputStream(
      configXml.bytes))
println("Created new job: ${newItem.fullDisplayName}")
```

This script programmatically creates a new job named NewJob using the provided XML configuration. Such pipelines can include extensive logic to configure job parameters, add triggers, or integrate steps dynamically during the pipeline execution.

External automation scripts using Python can interact with Jenkins' REST API through libraries such as python-jenkins. The following Python snippet showcases how to use this library to manage Jenkins jobs:

```
import jenkins
```

```
server = jenkins.Jenkins('http://<jenkins_url>', username='user', password='
    password')

# Creating a new Jenkins job
job_name = 'example_job'
job_config = '''<project>
  <actions/>
  <description/>
  <keepDependencies>false</keepDependencies>
  <properties/>
  <scm class="hudson.scm.NullSCM"/>
  <canRoam>true</canRoam>
  <disabled>false</disabled>
  <blockBuildWhenDownstreamBuilding>false</blockBuildWhenDownstreamBuilding
      >
  <blockBuildWhenUpstreamBuilding>false</blockBuildWhenUpstreamBuilding>
  <triggers/>
  <concurrentBuild>false</concurrentBuild>
  <builders/>
  <publishers/>
  <buildWrappers/>
</project>'''

server.create_job(job_name, job_config)
print(f'Created job: {job_name}')
```

This Python script connects to a Jenkins instance, creates a job named example_job with the specified configuration, and then verifies the creation. Automating Jenkins job management with Python can significantly streamline CI/CD processes, particularly within environments that heavily utilize Python for automation tasks.

For more advanced use cases, invoking Jenkins APIs from scripted pipelines or external applications provides robust solutions. By leveraging these APIs, teams can automate repetitive tasks, handle complex workflows, and seamlessly integrate Jenkins with other systems. Integrating APIs into Jenkins pipelines enhances the ability to create, configure, and orchestrate resources dynamically, fostering efficient and flexible CI/CD environments.

Using Jenkins APIs for automation transforms the way teams interact with the platform, allowing for sophisticated and efficient continuous integration and deployment pipelines.

Chapter 10

Advanced Jenkins Features

This chapter delves into the advanced features of Jenkins, including the use of Jenkins DSL, advanced pipeline functionality, and implementing shared libraries. It covers distributed builds, master-agent configurations, multi-branch pipelines, and the concept of Pipeline as Code with Jenkinsfile. Additionally, the chapter addresses creating custom plugins, customizing the Jenkins UI, remote access API, and performance optimization and scaling strategies to handle complex and large-scale CI/CD requirements.

10.1 Introduction to Advanced Jenkins Features

As software development practices evolve, continuous integration and continuous delivery (CI/CD) requirements become increasingly sophisticated. To effectively manage these complexities, Jenkins offers a suite of advanced features that extend its core capabilities. This section provides an overview of these advanced functionalities, setting the stage for an in-depth exploration in subsequent sections.

Central to advanced Jenkins usage is the Jenkins Domain Specific Language (DSL), designed to give users more expressive power when defining jobs and pipelines. Unlike the declarative syntax used in basic

Jenkins pipelines, the Jenkins DSL offers a more flexible, script-based approach. This allows for dynamic configurations and more complex workflows.

Furthermore, Jenkins accommodates intricate build processes through advanced pipeline features. This includes the use of sequential and parallel execution stages, conditional execution, and complex post-build actions. By leveraging these features, users can design sophisticated CI/CD pipelines that cater to diverse project requirements.

Shared libraries represent another critical aspect of advanced Jenkins usage. Implementing shared libraries enables the reuse of common code across multiple pipelines, fostering modularity and reducing duplication. This not only enhances maintainability but also promotes standardization across projects.

Distributed builds and master-agent configurations are pivotal when scaling Jenkins to handle larger workloads. In a distributed build environment, multiple agents are configured to offload tasks from the master node. This setup optimizes resource utilization and enhances build performance. Understanding the nuances of configuring and managing such environments is crucial for successfully implementing scaled Jenkins solutions.

Another powerful capability provided by Jenkins is the multi-branch pipeline. This feature supports the automatic creation of pipelines for each branch of a repository, facilitating consistent CI/CD processes across branches. It significantly improves version control integration and enhances the overall efficiency of development workflows.

Pipeline as Code is a paradigm shift in how Jenkins pipelines are defined and managed. By encapsulating pipeline definitions within a Jenkinsfile, projects gain versioned, easily replicable CI/CD configurations. This practice aligns with Infrastructure as Code (IaC) principles, promoting transparency, traceability, and consistency.

The flexibility of Jenkins is further extended by parameterized builds. By allowing parameters to be passed into builds, users can trigger customizable build processes, catering to various scenarios and requirements without altering the core job definitions.

To integrate Jenkins with other systems and automate external interactions, the Jenkins Remote Access API provides a comprehensive interface. This API enables the execution of Jenkins operations programmatically, supporting diverse use cases such as automated job triggering, status monitoring, and result retrieval.

Customization is also a key feature in advanced Jenkins usage. Through custom UI elements and customized views, users can tailor the Jenkins interface to better fit their workflow needs and preferences. Custom views, dashboards, and widgets can be configured to display relevant information succinctly and intuitively.

Creating custom plugins is another avenue to extend Jenkins functionality. Jenkins supports a robust plugin architecture that allows developers to create and integrate bespoke plugins to address specific requirements not met by existing plugins. This involves understanding Jenkins' plugin development framework and APIs.

Performance optimization and scaling strategies are paramount for organizations dealing with complex and large-scale CI/CD environments. Optimizing Jenkins involves tuning various parameters, such as executor configurations, garbage collection settings, and plugin selection. Scaling strategies, on the other hand, might include setting up multiple Jenkins masters, utilizing Kubernetes for orchestration, and employing high-availability configurations.

The subsequent sections of this chapter will delve deeper into each of these advanced features. Through detailed explanations, code examples, and practical tips, readers will gain a comprehensive understanding of how to harness the full potential of Jenkins to meet modern CI/CD challenges.

10.2 Using Jenkins DSL (Domain Specific Language)

The Jenkins Domain Specific Language (DSL) provides a powerful mechanism to define and manage Jenkins jobs programmatically. Utilizing Groovy-based syntax, Jenkins DSL allows for the automation and version control of Jenkins jobs, enabling users to script Jenkins job configurations as code. This concept works harmoniously with the principles of Infrastructure as Code (IaC), enhancing reproducibility, scalability, and maintainability of the CI/CD pipeline infrastructure.

Getting Started with Jenkins DSL

To utilize Jenkins DSL, the Job DSL plugin must be installed. This plugin allows you to define Jenkins jobs in a programmatic way using Groovy scripts. Once the plugin is installed, the definition and management of jobs can be facilitated by writing DSL scripts, which can then be executed via Jenkins' Script Console or through dedicated DSL Job configurations.

Basic Structure of a DSL Script

A Jenkins DSL script typically starts by defining a job using the job keyword followed by the job's name. Within the job configuration block, various facets of the job, such as triggers, source control management (SCM), and build steps, are defined. Below is an example of a basic DSL script defining a simple job:

```
job('example-job') {
    description('A sample Jenkins job created via DSL script')

    scm {
        git('https://github.com/your/repo.git')
    }

    triggers {
        scm('H/15 * * * *') // Poll SCM every 15 minutes
    }

    steps {
        shell('echo "Building project..."')
    }
}
```

Loading and Running DSL Scripts

DSL scripts can be loaded and executed in Jenkins through a variety of methods. The most common approach is to create a freestyle job or a pipeline job with a build step that runs the DSL script. For a freestyle job, you can add a Process Job DSLs job step, and for a pipeline, you can use the jobDsl function.

```
pipeline {
    agent any
    stages {
        stage('Generate Jobs') {
            steps {
                jobDsl target: 'jobs/*.groovy', // Specify the path to DSL scripts
                       removedJobAction: 'DELETE',
                       removedViewAction: 'DELETE',
                       ignoreMissingFiles: true
            }
        }
    }
}
```

Job Templates and Reusability

One of the strengths of Jenkins DSL is its ability to create reusable job templates. This allows for the definition of a base configuration that can be extended or customized for various jobs, dramatically reducing redundancy and effort. This can be achieved using the job method in combination with the using keyword.

```
job('template-job') {
    description('Template job to be used as a base')

    scm {
        git('https://github.com/your/repo.git', 'main')
    }

    steps {
        shell('echo "Base build step"')
    }
}

job('actual-job') {
    using('template-job') // Inherit configuration from template-job
    steps {
        shell('echo "Additional build step for actual-job"')
    }
}
```

Handling Complex Configurations

Jenkins DSL supports complex job configurations such as parameters, post-build actions, and advanced SCM options. Here's an example that contains parameterized builds and multiple build steps:

```
job('complex-job') {
    parameters {
        stringParam('Branch', 'main', 'Branch to build')
        choiceParam('Environment', ['dev', 'staging', 'prod'], 'Deployment Environment'
            )
    }

    scm {
        git {
            remote {
                url('https://github.com/your/repo.git')
            }
            branch('$Branch')
        }
    }

    triggers {
        cron('H H * * *')
    }

    steps {
        shell('echo "Starting build..."')
        shell('echo "Building branch: $Branch"')
    }

    publishers {
        archiveArtifacts('**/target/*.jar')
        mailer('notify@example.com', false, false)
    }
}
```

Integrating with Pipelines

An essential aspect of harnessing Jenkins DSL is its seamless integration with Jenkins Pipelines. Within a Jenkinsfile, you can invoke DSL scripts to generate and manage jobs dynamically, promoting highly modular and maintainable pipeline definitions.

```
pipeline {
    agent any
    stages {
        stage('Setup') {
            steps {
                script {
                    def dslScript = '''
                    job('dynamic-job') {
                        scm {
                            git('https://github.com/your/repo.git')
                        }
                        steps {
                            shell('echo "This is a dynamically created job"')
                        }
                    }
                    '''
                    jobDsl scriptText: dslScript
                }
            }
        }

        stage('Build') {
            steps {
                build job: 'dynamic-job'
            }
        }
    }
}
```

Jenkins DSL's docility to Groovy syntax, coupled with its robust configurability, makes it an indispensable tool for engineers aiming for efficient CI/CD pipeline management. Properly leveraging DSL can lead to noticeably enhanced project maintainability, consistency, and scalability.

10.3 Advanced Pipeline Features

Jenkins pipelines are a set of plugins that support the implementation and integration of continuous delivery pipelines into Jenkins. Building on the basic knowledge of Jenkins pipelines, this section explores advanced features which provide powerful capabilities to define and optimize continuous delivery workflows. We will examine scripted and declarative pipelines, the use of parallel execution blocks, and the integration of external libraries to enhance and distribute tasks.

Scripted vs Declarative Pipelines:

A scripting language like Groovy allows the creation of scripted pipelines, while declarative pipelines come with a more structured format. Understanding the distinctions and use-cases for each enables developers to choose the appropriate style for their specific needs:

```
node {
    stage('Build') {
        // Code for building the project
    }
    stage('Test') {
        // Code for running tests
    }
    stage('Deploy') {
        // Code for deployment
    }
}
```

```
pipeline {
    agent any
    stages {
        stage('Build') {
            steps {
                // Code for building the project
            }
        }
        stage('Test') {
            steps {
                // Code for running tests
            }
        }
        stage('Deploy') {
            steps {
                // Code for deployment
            }
        }
    }
}
```

The declarative syntax simplifies the creation of pipelines by offering a more straightforward, YAML-like format. This structure is enhanced by built-in functionalities such as post conditions and options for better error handling and control:

```
pipeline {
    agent any
    stages {
        stage('Build') {
            steps {
                // Code for building the project
            }
        }
        stage('Test') {
            steps {
                // Code for running tests
```

```
            }
        }
        stage('Deploy') {
            steps {
                // Code for deployment
            }
        }
    }
    post {
        success {
            echo 'Pipeline succeeded!'
        }
        failure {
            echo 'Pipeline failed!'
        }
    }
}
```

Parallel Execution:

Advanced pipelines leverage parallel execution to reduce build times and optimize resource utilization. Parallel execution can be implemented in both scripted and declarative pipelines. Here is an example in a declarative pipeline:

```
pipeline {
    agent any
    stages {
        stage('Build') {
            steps {
                // Code for building the project
            }
        }
        stage('Test') {
            parallel {
                stage('Unit Tests') {
                    steps {
                        // Code for running unit tests
                    }
                }
                stage('Integration Tests') {
                    steps {
                        // Code for running integration tests
                    }
                }
            }
        }
        stage('Deploy') {
            steps {
                // Code for deployment
            }
        }
    }
}
```

For more granular control over parallel tasks in a scripted pipeline:

```
node {
    stage('Build') {
```

```
        // Code for building the project
    }
    stage('Test') {
        parallel (
            'Unit Tests': {
                // Code for running unit tests
            },
            'Integration Tests': {
                // Code for running integration tests
            }
        )
    }
    stage('Deploy') {
        // Code for deployment
    }
}
```

Using External Libraries:

Integrating external libraries can modularize and reuse functions across multiple Jenkins pipelines, promoting consistency and reducing redundancy. Shared libraries in Jenkins are typically Groovy scripts maintained in a Version Control System. Here is an example of how a shared library might be utilized:

In the repository, you might have a structure like:

```
(root)
+- vars
|   +- callAnotherJob.groovy
```

callAnotherJob.groovy:

```
def callAnotherJob(String jobName) {
    build job: jobName
}
```

In the pipeline, the shared library can be employed as follows:

```
@Library('my-shared-library') _
pipeline {
    agent any
    stages {
        stage('Build') {
            steps {
                // Code for building the project
            }
        }
        stage('Test') {
            steps {
                // Code for running tests
            }
        }
        stage('Call Another Job') {
            steps {
                callAnotherJob('downstream-job')
            }
        }
    }
```

```
}
```

By integrating shared libraries, complex build processes are streamlined, reducing script maintenance overhead and encouraging code reuse across different projects.

Advanced pipeline features in Jenkins offer comprehensive tools to optimize and scale continuous delivery workflows. Detailed understanding and application of these concepts enable more efficient and maintainable CI/CD processes, contributing to enhanced DevOps practices.

10.4 Implementing Jenkins Shared Libraries

Shared libraries in Jenkins provide a powerful means of abstracting and reusing common code across different pipelines. Leveraging shared libraries enables developers and DevOps engineers to maintain a consistent, modular, and scalable approach to Continuous Integration/Continuous Deployment (CI/CD) processes, enhancing maintainability and reducing redundancy.

A shared library is a collection of reusable, version-controlled Groovy scripts packaged in a directory structure. These scripts can be invoked from different Jenkinsfiles, allowing teams to centralize common logic. Introducing shared libraries promotes the DRY (Don't Repeat Yourself) principle and simplifies pipeline definitions by offloading complex logic.

To implement shared libraries, follow these steps:

- **Structuring the Library:** Organize the library files within a specific directory structure.
- **Defining Library Methods:** Write Groovy scripts in the appropriate directory.
- **Configuring Jenkins:** Integrate the shared library with Jenkins by configuring it within Jenkins' configuration settings.
- **Using the Library:** Utilize the shared library within Jenkinsfiles to call reusable functions.

Structuring the Library

The first step is to organize the library into a structure that Jenkins can recognize. A typical shared library has the following directory layout:

```
(root)
+- src                     # Groovy source files (Optional)
|   +- org
|       +- foo
|           +- Bar.groovy      # e.g. src/org/foo/Bar.groovy
+- vars                    # Global shared library scripts
|   +- foo.groovy            # e.g. vars/foo.groovy
+- resources               # Resource files (Optional)
|   +- org
|       +- foo
|           +- Bar.txt       # e.g. resources/org/foo/Bar.txt
```

In this structure, vars/ contains global Groovy scripts that provide reusable methods. The src/ directory includes additional Groovy classes, and resources/ holds static resources required by the scripts.

Defining Library Methods

Scripts within the vars/ directory must define a single method named call, enabling them to be invoked like a function in the Jenkinsfile.

An example script, vars/helloWorld.groovy, might look like this:

```
def call(name = 'world') {
    echo "Hello, ${name}!"
}
```

This simple script takes a parameter name and prints a greeting message to the Jenkins console.

Configuring Jenkins

Once the library is structured and includes the necessary scripts, configure Jenkins to utilize the shared library:

- Navigate to **Manage Jenkins** > **Configure System**.
- Scroll down to **Global Pipeline Libraries**.
- Add a new library by clicking **Add**.
- Provide a name, e.g., **my-shared-library**.
- Specify the repository source and branch information.
- Save the configuration.

Jenkins will then be aware of the shared library and can retrieve it from the configured repository.

Using the Library

To utilize the shared library in a Jenkinsfile, use the @Library annotation followed by the library name. Call the defined methods as needed.

An example Jenkinsfile using the previously defined helloWorld method:

```
@Library('my-shared-library') _
pipeline {
    agent any
    stages {
        stage('Example') {
            steps {
                helloWorld('Jenkins') // Call the shared library method
            }
        }
    }
}
```

This Jenkinsfile imports the shared library named my-shared-library, which contains the helloWorld.groovy script. In the stages block, it invokes the helloWorld method with the parameter 'Jenkins'.

Advanced Library Usage

Beyond basic scripts, shared libraries support advanced use cases such as custom classes and static resources. Classes in the src/ directory are structured hierarchically according to their package names and can be utilized for more complex logic.

For instance, a class src/org/foo/Bar.groovy:

```
package org.foo

class Bar {
    static void printMessage(String message) {
        echo message
    }
}
```

This class method can be invoked in the Jenkinsfile by referring to the class and method explicitly:

```
@Library('my-shared-library') _
import org.foo.Bar

pipeline {
    agent any
    stages {
        stage('Example') {
            steps {
                script {
                    Bar.printMessage('Hello from Bar class!')
                }
            }
        }
    }
}
```

Resource File Utilization

Resource files can be included in shared libraries to support operations such as templating or configuration management. Place these files in the resources/ directory and access them within the Groovy scripts.

For example, a script reading a resource file:

```
def call() {
    def resourceContent = libraryResource 'org/foo/Bar.txt'
    echo resourceContent
}
```

Incorporate this script within the Jenkinsfile:

```
@Library('my-shared-library') _
pipeline {
    agent any
    stages {
        stage('Example') {
            steps {
                readResourceFile() // Method to read and print resource content
            }
        }
    }
}
```

Implementing shared libraries in Jenkins enhances pipeline reusability, reduces complexity, and ensures consistent pipeline behavior across projects. Properly structured and effectively utilized shared libraries streamline the CI/CD process, supporting robust and maintainable software development workflows.

10.5 Distributed Builds and Master-Agent Configuration

In large-scale Continuous Integration/Continuous Deployment (CI/CD) environments, running all build and test jobs on a single Jenkins server may lead to bottlenecks due to resource constraints. To alleviate this, Jenkins offers a distributed build architecture that leverages a Master-Agent configuration. This allows the workload to be distributed across multiple machines, balancing the load and improving performance and reliability. The Jenkins master is responsible for managing the build process, while agents (also referred to as nodes or slaves) execute jobs as directed by the master.

Master-Agent Architecture Overview: The master node orchestrates the entire Jenkins environment, including scheduling build jobs, dispatching builds to agents for execution, monitoring agents' status, and collecting build results. Agents run the jobs dispatched to them by the master. This architecture effectively separates the management tasks from the actual build and test executions, optimizing resource usage.

- **Master Node:** Handles user requests, manages job scheduling, monitors and manages agents, aggregates build results, and handles plugin interactions. The master node should typically have sufficient resources to handle these tasks but does not need the heavy computational power required for running all build jobs.
- **Agent Nodes:** These execute individual build jobs. Agents can be provisioned dynamically, and they can run on different operating systems, enabling a diverse build and test environment. Resources on the agents should be scaled according to the expected load for builds and tests.

Setting Up Agent Nodes:

To set up an agent node, follow these steps:

1. **Navigate to the Jenkins Dashboard:** Click on 'Manage Jenkins', then 'Manage Nodes and Clouds'. 2. **Add a New Node:** Click on 'New Node', provide a name for the node, and select 'Permanent Agent' or 'Dynamically Provisioned Node' depending on your setup. 3. **Configure the Node:** Fill out the required fields such as the number of executors (the number of jobs this node can run concurrently), remote root directory (the directory on the agent where Jenkins will store files), and launch method (e.g., via SSH, command line execution).

Example configuration using SSH to connect to a Linux-based agent:

```
Host *jenkinsagent*
  Hostname agent.example.com
  User jenkins
  IdentityFile /path/to/private_key
```

4. **Launch the Node:** Once configured, launch the agent using the chosen method. Under the agent configuration, select 'Launch agent via SSH'. Upon successful connection, Jenkins will be able to dispatch jobs to this node.

Configuring Labels and Node Usage:

Labels allow jobs to be targeted to specific nodes. For instance, you can label nodes based on their capacity, operating system, or any other characteristic. This can be particularly useful when certain jobs require specialized environments.

1. **Assign Labels to Nodes:** In the node configuration, use the 'Labels' field to specify relevant labels, separated by spaces.

Example labels for a Windows OS agent with high memory:

```
windows high-memory
```

2. **Target Jobs to Labeled Nodes:** In the job configuration, specify the required labels under the 'Restrict where this project can be run' section. Jenkins will ensure that the job runs only on agents matching the specified labels.

Pipeline Configuration for Master-Agent Setup:

In a Jenkins pipeline, you can specify particular agents for job execution using the 'agent' directive. This directive instructs Jenkins to allocate the job to a suitable agent node for execution.

```
pipeline {
    agent any
    stages {
        stage('Build') {
            agent { label 'linux' }
            steps {
                sh 'make'
            }
        }
        stage('Test') {
            agent { label 'high-memory' }
            steps {
                sh 'make test'
            }
        }
    }
}
```

Master-Agent Security Considerations:

Ensuring secure communication between Jenkins master and agents is imperative. Jenkins supports several security mechanisms:

1. **Using SSH Keys:** For agents connected via SSH, use strong SSH keys instead of passwords. Configure the SSH key pair on both the master and the agent nodes. 2. **Enabling Agent-to-Master Access Control:** Jenkins provides an "Agent-to-Master Access Control" mechanism, which restricts what agents can do, enhancing security. 3. **Securing the Jenkins Master URL:** Always use HTTPS for the Jenkins master URL, and ensure that certificates are properly configured to prevent man-in-the-middle attacks.

Monitoring and Managing Agents:

Jenkins provides tools to monitor and manage agents:

1. **Node Status:** The 'Manage Nodes and Clouds' section displays the status of each node, including whether it is online or offline. 2. **Load Statistics:** Jenkins can provide load statistics, indicating the number of jobs and resource usage, which helps in scaling resources efficiently. 3. **Log Management:** Each agent maintains logs which can be accessed from the 'Nodes' section for troubleshooting and performance tuning.

Scaling Considerations:

As Jenkins usage grows, it's crucial to scale the infrastructure to match. Considerations include:

1. **Dynamic Provisioning:** Use cloud-based solutions and container technologies (e.g., Kubernetes, Docker) for elastic scaling. Jenkins can provision and de-provision agents based on demand. 2. **Resource Allocation:** Monitor resource usage and allocate more CPU, memory, or storage to prevent bottlenecks. 3. **High Availability:** Implement high availability for the Jenkins master to prevent single points of failure. This can be achieved using master clustering solutions.

The distributed build and master-agent configuration in Jenkins is designed to maximize efficiency, improve performance, and ensure scalability. Adhering to these best practices allows for robust CI/CD pipelines capable of handling complex and large-scale software projects.

10.6 Setting Up Multi-Branch Pipelines

Multi-branch pipelines in Jenkins offer a powerful way to handle multiple branches within a single repository, facilitating automated building and testing for each branch. This capability is crucial for maintaining consistency across various stages of development and ensures that all branches remain functional and up-to-date. By leveraging multi-branch pipelines, Jenkins can automatically discover, manage, and execute jobs for all branches, making continuous integration and continuous deployment (CI/CD) processes more efficient.

To set up a multi-branch pipeline, follow these detailed steps:

- **Install the Required Plugins:** Ensure that you have the necessary plugins installed, namely the Pipeline and Multi-branch Pipeline plugins. Navigate to Manage Jenkins → Manage Plugins, and install these plugins if they are not already present.
- **Create a New Item:** In the Jenkins dashboard, click on New Item.

Provide a name indicative of the project and select Multibranch Pipeline as the project type. Click OK to proceed.

- **Configure Branch Sources:** Once the multi-branch pipeline project is created, you need to configure the branch sources. Click on Branch Sources → Add Source and select the appropriate source type (e.g., Git, GitHub, Bitbucket).
  - **Repository URL:** Enter the repository URL where the source code resides. Ensure that Jenkins has the necessary access permissions to this repository.
  - **Credentials:** If the repository requires authentication, add the corresponding credentials.
- **Configure Build Triggers:** You can configure how Jenkins triggers builds for branches. Under Build Strategies, configure the desired options such as building whenever there is a change in the branch (e.g., Periodically if not otherwise run or Build when a change is pushed to GitHub).
- **Pipeline Configuration:** Jenkins requires a Jenkinsfile at the root of each branch in the repository. The Jenkinsfile contains the pipeline script which defines the build, test, and deployment stages. The presence of this file enables Jenkins to automatically scan branches and initiate jobs.

```
pipeline {
    agent any

    stages {
        stage('Build') {
            steps {
                echo 'Building...'
                // Insert build commands here
            }
        }
        stage('Test') {
            steps {
                echo 'Testing...'
                // Insert test commands here
            }
        }
        stage('Deploy') {
            steps {
                echo 'Deploying...'
                // Insert deploy commands here
            }
        }
    }
}
```

- **Branch Indexing:** Jenkins will scan the repository for branches containing a Jenkinsfile and automatically create pipeline jobs for those branches. This process is known as branch indexing. You can configure how frequently Jenkins performs this scan by setting the appropriate schedule under the Scan Repository Triggers.

```
triggers {
  periodic(1) // Scan every 1 minute
}
```

- **Build Strategy Configuration:** Jenkins allows configuring additional strategies to handle branches, such as excluding branches by name or regex, or customizing the handling of pull requests.

  - **Branch Discovery:** Select specific branch discovery strategies, such as discovering branches that are not pull requests or excluding branches that are filed as pull requests.
  - **Property Strategy:** Define property strategies to handle different branch properties, such as retention policies, environment variables, or specific build behaviors.

- **Manage Build History and Clean Up:** Configuring retention policies ensures the build history does not consume excessive resources. Under Orphan Item Strategy, specify how to handle branches that no longer exist in the repository.

```
orphanedItemStrategy {
    discardOldItems {
        numToKeep(5) // Keep the last 5 builds
    }
}
```

- **Save Configuration:** Once all the configurations are complete, click on Save. Jenkins will then initialize the branch indexing process, scan the repository, and generate appropriate jobs for each branch.

By adhering to these steps, multi-branch pipelines in Jenkins can effectively manage and automate CI/CD workflows for each branch in a repository. This setup not only streamlines development processes but also ensures that all branches, whether for feature development or quick fixes, are consistently tested and deployed, ultimately enhancing the integrity and quality of the software product.

10.7 Pipeline as Code with Jenkinsfile

The concept of Pipeline as Code involves defining the entire build process through code, which is stored in a text file known as a Jenkinsfile. This allows for versioning and testing of pipelines the same way as any other software code, ensuring transparency, traceability, and collaboration on CI/CD processes.

A Jenkinsfile can be written using Declarative Pipeline syntax or Scripted Pipeline syntax. The Declarative Pipeline syntax provides a simplified and more structured format while the Scripted Pipeline syntax offers more flexibility and detailed control using Groovy code. Below, we will explore both syntaxes in detail, starting with the more approachable Declarative Pipeline.

A basic Declarative Pipeline example in a Jenkinsfile:

```
pipeline {
    agent any
    stages {
        stage('Build') {
            steps {
                echo 'Building...'
                // Insert build-related steps here
            }
        }
        stage('Test') {
            steps {
                echo 'Testing...'
                // Insert test-related steps here
            }
        }
        stage('Deploy') {
            steps {
                echo 'Deploying...'
                // Insert deployment-related steps here
            }
        }
    }
}
```

In this example, the pipeline block defines the start of the pipeline in Declarative syntax. The agent any directive declares that Jenkins can run the pipeline on any available agent. The stages block contains multiple stage blocks, each representing a distinct part of the CI/CD process. Within each stage, the steps block specifies the steps to be executed.

The Scripted Pipeline syntax offers a more granular level of control. Here is a simple example of a Scripted Pipeline in a Jenkinsfile:

```
node {
    stage('Build') {
```

```
        echo 'Building...'
        // Insert build-related steps here
    }
    stage('Test') {
        echo 'Testing...'
        // Insert test-related steps here
    }
    stage('Deploy') {
        echo 'Deploying...'
        // Insert deployment-related steps here
    }
}
```

In this example, the node block defines the start of the pipeline and specifies that it should run on a Jenkins node. Each stage block is similar to those in the Declarative example, containing the steps to be executed.

Beyond these basic structures, one can leverage various features such as parallel execution, post-processing steps, and the use of environment variables to create sophisticated pipelines.

For example, to run multiple stages in parallel, you can extend the Declarative Pipeline syntax as follows:

```
pipeline {
    agent any
    stages {
        stage('Build and Test') {
            parallel {
                stage('Build') {
                    steps {
                        echo 'Building...'
                        // Insert build-related steps here
                    }
                }
                stage('Test') {
                    steps {
                        echo 'Testing...'
                        // Insert test-related steps here
                    }
                }
            }
        }
        stage('Deploy') {
            steps {
                echo 'Deploying...'
                // Insert deployment-related steps here
            }
        }
    }
}
```

In this pipeline configuration, the parallel block is used to run the Build and Test stages concurrently, potentially reducing the overall execution time.

The post section in a Declarative Pipeline is used to define steps that should run at the end of the pipeline, or following a specific stage, regardless of the pipeline's success or failure:

```
pipeline {
    agent any
    stages {
        stage('Build') {
            steps {
                echo 'Building...'
            }
        }
    }
    post {
        always {
            echo 'This will always run'
        }
        success {
            echo 'This will run only if the build succeeds'
        }
        failure {
            echo 'This will run only if the build fails'
        }
    }
}
```

The always, success, and failure blocks specify what should happen after the pipeline execution, providing a flexible mechanism to manage post-build actions such as cleanup, notifications, or logging.

Environment variables play a crucial role in Jenkins Pipelines, allowing for dynamic and parameterized builds. Within a Declarative Pipeline, environment variables can be set and accessed as follows:

```
pipeline {
    agent any
    environment {
        MY_VAR = 'Some value'
    }
    stages {
        stage('Build') {
            steps {
                echo "Building with MY_VAR=\${MY_VAR}"
            }
        }
    }
}
```

The environment block defines the variable MY_VAR, which is then accessed in the echo step. The ability to use environment variables flexibly enables greater configurability of pipelines without requiring modification of the Jenkinsfile.

By encapsulating the entire pipeline process within a Jenkinsfile, Jenkins facilitates the management of complex build, test, and deployment workflows through code. This approach not only enhances visibility and traceability across the development lifecycle but also aligns with modern practices in continuous integration and continuous deployment, fostering a more robust and automated pipeline architecture.

10.8 Parameterized Builds

Parameterized builds in Jenkins allow for dynamic and flexible execution of jobs, enabling users to provide input parameters at the time of triggering a build. This feature significantly enhances the usability and utility of Jenkins for complex, real-world applications where build configurations may vary. Parameters can include strings, booleans, choice lists, files, credentials, and other custom types.

To configure a job to accept parameters, navigate to the job configuration page and check the box labeled This project is parameterized. This reveals a button labeled Add Parameter, providing a dropdown list of parameter types to add. Each type of parameter offers a specific input method designed to facilitate particular kinds of data from the user.

- **String Parameter**: Allows the user to input a simple string. This is useful for generic text information, such as environment names or version numbers.
- **Boolean Parameter**: Provides a checkbox, enabling a true/false option. This is suitable for toggling features on or off during the build process.
- **Choice Parameter**: Creates a dropdown list of predefined values. This helps standardize the input choices and ensures users select from an approved list of options.
- **File Parameter**: Lets the user upload a file to be used in the build process. This is particularly useful for builds that require configuration files or other external resources.
- **Credentials Parameter**: Facilitates the secure input of credentials, such as usernames and passwords. This type is critical for maintaining secure access to external systems.
- **Run Parameter**: Allows selection of a build from another project, referencing the specific results or artifacts needed for the current build.

- **Password Parameter**: Handles sensitive text input, masking the characters to secure sensitive information.

Once parameters are defined, they can be referenced within the build process. Jenkins provides various methods to access these parameters, such as using them within build steps, Groovy scripts, or shell commands.

```
#!/bin/bash

echo "Building for environment: $ENVIRONMENT"
echo "Deploy version: $VERSION"

if [ "$DEBUG_MODE" = "true" ]; then
    echo "Debugging mode enabled."
fi

# Further build steps...
```

In the above example, ENVIRONMENT, VERSION, and DEBUG_-MODE are parameters defined in the job configuration. When the build is triggered, users can specify the values of these parameters, which the shell script then accesses and utilizes.

Pipeline jobs can also leverage parameters, adding dynamic capability to the Jenkinsfile definition. Parameters within pipeline jobs are defined using the parameters directive at the beginning of the pipeline script.

```
pipeline {
    agent any

    parameters {
        string(name: 'ENVIRONMENT', defaultValue: 'staging', description: 'Target
            environment')
        booleanParam(name: 'DEBUG_MODE', defaultValue: true, description: 'Enable
            or disable debugging')
    }

    stages {
        stage('Build') {
            steps {
                script {
                    echo "Building for environment: ${params.ENVIRONMENT}"
                    echo "Debug mode: ${params.DEBUG_MODE}"
                }
            }
        }

        stage('Deploy') {
            steps {
                script {
                    if (params.DEBUG_MODE) {
                        echo "Deploying in debug mode."
                    } else {
                        echo "Deploying in normal mode."
                    }
```

```
            }
          }
        }
      }
}
```

In the pipeline script above, the parameters block declares two parameters: ENVIRONMENT and DEBUG_MODE. The build stages then access these parameters using the params object, allowing the pipeline script to adapt based on the specified values.

Parameterized builds in Jenkins can also be triggered via API calls, facilitating automation and integration with other systems. The URL query string method allows parameters to be appended to the Jenkins job URL, enabling remote triggering with specific values.

```
curl -X POST "http://jenkins-server/job/my-job/buildWithParameters?
    ENVIRONMENT=production&DEBUG_MODE=false" --user username:
    api_token
```

The above curl command triggers a Jenkins job named my-job with parameters ENVIRONMENT set to production and DEBUG_MODE set to false. The –user flag authenticates the request, ensuring secure access to the Jenkins server.

Understanding and utilizing parameterized builds in Jenkins allows for a more adaptable, user-responsive CI/CD process. Employing parameters in job configurations and pipelines delivers flexible and tailored build automation, integral for sophisticated and scalable development workflows.

10.9 Jenkins Remote Access API

The Jenkins Remote Access API enables you to interact with Jenkins programmatically and retrieve information about Jenkins jobs, builds, and configurations. This API supports both REST and XML-RPC services, allowing developers to integrate Jenkins with other systems and automate tasks without manual intervention. Let's delve into the details of using the Jenkins REST API, providing comprehensive examples for various operations.

The Jenkins REST API is designed to work seamlessly with numerous HTTP requests, where the following operations are the most commonly used:

- **GET** - Retrieve information from Jenkins.
- **POST** - Create or update resources.
- **HEAD** - Retrieve metadata without the response body.
- **DELETE** - Remove resources.

To utilize the Jenkins REST API, ensure you have the appropriate user permissions. API tokens are used for authentication, which can be created in the Jenkins user profile section.

Example 1: Retrieving Jenkins Job Information

The following example shows how to retrieve information about a specific job, including its configurations and the latest build status:

```
curl -X GET http://jenkins-server/job/job_name/api/json --user username:apitoken
```

The output will be a JSON-formatted response containing details about the specified job. Here is an example of the output:

```
{
  "description" : "A sample job",
  "displayName" : "Example-Job",
  "fullDisplayName" : "Example-Job",
  "buildable" : true,
  "inQueue" : false,
  "lastBuild": {
    "number": 23,
    "url": "http://jenkins-server/job/job_name/23/"
  },
  ...
}
```

Example 2: Triggering a Jenkins Job

Assume the need to trigger a specific job remotely. This can be accomplished using a **POST** request. Below is an example using cURL to trigger a job:

```
curl -X POST http://jenkins-server/job/job_name/build --user username:apitoken
```

If the job has parameters, include them in the POST request as follows:

```
curl -X POST http://jenkins-server/job/job_name/buildWithParameters \
    --data "PARAMETER1=value1&PARAMETER2=value2" \
    --user username:apitoken
```

Example 3: Accessing Build Artifacts

To retrieve build artifacts from a completed build, send a GET request to the appropriate URL, including the build number:

```
curl -X GET http://jenkins-server/job/job_name/23/artifact/artifact_name \
    --user username:apitoken
```

This command downloads the specified artifact for inspection or further processing.

Example 4: Deleting a Job

To delete a job from Jenkins remotely, use the following **POST** request:

```
curl -X POST http://jenkins-server/job/job_name/doDelete --user username:apitoken
```

API Rate Limits and Best Practices

It is crucial to be aware of rate limits when utilizing the Jenkins API, as too many requests in a short period may result in being temporarily blocked. Here are best practices for efficient use:

- Limit the frequency of API calls.
- Cache responses locally to avoid redundant calls.
- Rate limit your script to avoid overwhelming the Jenkins server.

Authenticating API Requests

While basic authentication (username and token) is often used as demonstrated in the examples above, it is recommended to switch to more secure methods such as API tokens or OAuth tokens, particularly for production systems.

Example 5: Authenticating with an API Token

Create a token from the Jenkins user profile page, then use it for API requests, commonly achieved by replacing **username:password** with **username:apitoken**.

An API token request for retrieving system information would look like this:

```
curl -X GET http://jenkins-server/api/json --user username:apitoken
```

The Jenkins Remote Access API provides an extensive and flexible toolset for interacting with Jenkins, offering numerous capabilities to enhance and automate continuous integration and delivery pipelines. It not only empowers developers and administrators to improve their workflow efficiency but also facilitates integration with other systems and services seamlessly.

10.10 Customizing Jenkins UI

Customizing the Jenkins user interface (UI) allows users to tailor the look and feel of their Jenkins instances to meet specific needs and preferences. This section outlines the steps involved in achieving this, focusing on the practical aspects of UI customization and extending Jenkins functionality through custom themes, views, and dashboard configurations.

At its core, Jenkins provides a web-based UI that can be modified using configuration settings, custom CSS/JavaScript, and plugins. These customizations improve user experience and enhance the efficiency of CI/CD processes. The primary customization methods discussed here will include using the Jenkins Configuration as Code (JCasC) plugin, applying themes, modifying views, and creating custom dashboards.

Jenkins Configuration as Code (JCasC)

The JCasC plugin enables administrators to define the entirety of Jenkins configurations as code. This includes UI settings. To install this plugin:

```
# Open Jenkins Dashboard
# Navigate to "Manage Jenkins" -> "Manage Plugins"
# Search for "Configuration as Code" under the "Available" tab
# Install the plugin and restart Jenkins

# To configure JCasC, create a configuration file (e.g., jenkins.yaml) with the desired
    settings

jenkins:
  systemMessage: "Welcome to the Custom Jenkins UI"
  numExecutors: 4
  scmCheckoutRetryCount: 3

# Apply the configuration by specifying the path to the 'jenkins.yaml' file
```

Applying Themes

The Jenkins Simple Theme Plugin allows users to customize the Jenkins UI via custom CSS and JavaScript files. After installing the plugin through the Jenkins Plugin Manager, navigate to the configuration page:

```
# Open Jenkins Dashboard
# Navigate to "Manage Jenkins" -> "Configure System"
# Find the "Theme" section and enter the URLs for custom CSS and JavaScript files

simple-theme-plugin:
  theme: "https://path-to-your-css-file.css"

# Save the configuration and refresh the Jenkins page to apply the new theme
```

Consider creating a style.css that changes the background color and font styles:

```
/* style.css */
body {
    background-color: #f0f0f0;
}

h1, h2, h3, h4, h5, h6 {
    font-family: 'Arial', sans-serif;
    color: #333;
}
```

Modifying Views

Jenkins views provide a method to organize and display jobs and build results. The Extended View Plugin offers additional customization options for creating and managing views. Install this plugin and then configure it as follows:

```
# Open Jenkins Dashboard
# Click on the "New View" link in the sidebar
# Select "List View" or "My Views" and provide a name for the view
# Configure the view by selecting jobs or applying filters

# Using the 'List View', users can manage job displays and set up columns
listView:
  columns:
    - status
    - weather
    - name
    - lastSuccess
    - lastFailure
    - lastDuration

# Save and access the newly created view from the Jenkins Dashboard
```

Creating Custom Dashboards

Custom dashboards in Jenkins can be created using the Dashboard View Plugin. It allows users to combine various portlets such as job status, build statistics, and pipeline views into a single cohesive dashboard. To set up a custom dashboard:

```
# Open Jenkins Dashboard
# Click on the "New View" link in the sidebar
# Select "Dashboard" and provide a name for the dashboard
# Add different portlets to the dashboard, such as:
# - Jobs Grid
# - Build Statistics
# - Disk Usage
# - Pipeline Graph

dashboardView:
```

```
columns:
  - jobColumn:
      width: Half
      showJobHealth: true
  - buildStatisticsColumn:
      width: Half

# Save and view the customized dashboard from the Jenkins Dashboard
```

These portlets can be arranged according to preferences and organizational requirements. Portlets like build statistics and pipeline graphs help in monitoring system health and project progress at a glance.

By leveraging these UI customization techniques and tools, administrators can create a more user-friendly and efficient Jenkins environment tailored to their specific CI/CD workflows.

10.11 Creating Custom Plugins

Creating custom plugins in Jenkins allows you to extend and customize the functionality beyond the built-in capabilities. This becomes essential when your CI/CD workflows demand unique requirements or when integrating with specialized tools and services. Crafting a plugin involves understanding the Jenkins Plugin API, which provides the necessary architecture to build, distribute, and manage Jenkins plugins.

The first step involves setting up the development environment. Jenkins plugins are primarily written in Java, and the Maven build tool is used to manage dependencies and the build lifecycle. Ensure that you have Java Development Kit (JDK) and Apache Maven installed.

To create a new plugin, follow these steps:

- **Setup Maven Archetype**: Jenkins provides a Maven archetype that simplifies plugin creation. Run the following command to generate a new plugin project:

```
mvn archetype:generate -Dfilter=io.jenkins.archetypes:plugin
```

- **Configure the Project**: After running the archetype command, you will be prompted to provide some information like groupId, artifactId, version, and package. Once the project structure is created, navigate to the project directory.

```
cd your-plugin-directory
```

- **Define Plugin Metadata**: Plugin metadata, such as its name, version, and developer details, is defined in the pom.xml file. Modify the pom.xml to include a unique artifactId, appropriate dependencies, and the required Jenkins version.
- **Implement Plugin Functionality**: Write the Java classes that implement your plugin's functionality. At a minimum, create an entry point for the plugin by extending appropriate Jenkins classes such as Builder, Notifier, or Publisher.

  For instance, to create a simple HelloWorldBuilder, you might define a class like this:

```
package io.jenkins.plugins.sample;

import hudson.Launcher;
import hudson.model.BuildListener;
import hudson.model.AbstractBuild;
import hudson.tasks.Builder;
import hudson.tasks.BuildStepDescriptor;
import hudson.tasks.BuildStepMonitor;
import hudson.tasks.Publisher;
import net.sf.json.JSONObject;
import org.kohsuke.stapler.StaplerRequest;

import java.io.IOException;

public class HelloWorldBuilder extends Builder {

    @Override
    public boolean perform(AbstractBuild build, Launcher launcher,
          BuildListener listener)
            throws InterruptedException, IOException {
        listener.getLogger().println("Hello, Jenkins!");
        return true;
    }

    @Extension
    public static final class DescriptorImpl extends BuildStepDescriptor<Builder
          > {
        public boolean isApplicable(Class<? extends AbstractProject> aClass) {
            return true;
        }

        public String getDisplayName() {
            return "Say Hello World";
        }
    }
}
```

- **Extension Points**: Use Jenkins' Extension Points to integrate your plugin with the Jenkins ecosystem. The @Extension annotation in the example above automatically registers the DescriptorImpl class as a Jenkins extension, making it available to users.
- **Testing Plugins**: Write unit tests to ensure the plugin behaves as

expected. Jenkins provides the Jenkins Test Harness, a testing framework which simplifies plugin testing:

```
package io.jenkins.plugins.sample;

import hudson.model.FreeStyleProject;
import org.junit.Rule;
import org.junit.Test;
import org.jvnet.hudson.test.JenkinsRule;

public class HelloWorldBuilderTest {

    @Rule
    public JenkinsRule jenkins = new JenkinsRule();

    @Test
    public void testPerform() throws Exception {
        FreeStyleProject project = jenkins.createFreeStyleProject();
        HelloWorldBuilder builder = new HelloWorldBuilder();
        project.getBuildersList().add(builder);
        jenkins.buildAndAssertSuccess(project);
    }
}
```

- **Building and Packaging**: Use Maven to build and package your plugin. The following Maven goals will compile the code, run the tests, and package the plugin into a .hpi file:

```
mvn clean package
```

- **Installing the Plugin**: To install your plugin into Jenkins, copy the generated .hpi file to the $JENKINS_HOME/plugins directory and restart Jenkins. Alternatively, you can upload it through the Jenkins UI under Manage Jenkins → Manage Plugins → Advanced → Upload Plugin.

- **Using the Plugin**: Once installed, your HelloWorldBuilder should appear in the Jenkins job configuration page under the Build section.

- **Distributing the Plugin**: If you wish to share your plugin with the community, you can host it on a public repository like GitHub and submit it to the Jenkins Plugin Index. Follow the guidelines provided by the Jenkins community for submitting plugins.

Creating custom plugins empowers developers to tailor Jenkins to their specific workflows, ensuring a more seamless and efficient CI/CD environment. With a thorough understanding of the Jenkins Plugin API and the steps outlined above, you can enhance Jenkins capabilities and contribute to the broader Jenkins ecosystem.

10.12 Performance Optimization and Scaling

Performance optimization and scaling are critical aspects of maintaining an efficient and reliable Jenkins instance, especially in large-scale Continuous Integration and Continuous Deployment (CI/CD) environments. Effective management of these aspects can significantly enhance build performance, minimize downtime, and ensure smooth operation across multiple builds and projects. This section explores several strategies and techniques to optimize Jenkins performance and scale it to meet growing demands.

One of the primary methods to optimize performance is through resource allocation and hardware scaling. The following guidelines ensure the efficient use of available resources:

- **CPU and Memory:** Allocate sufficient CPU and memory to both the Jenkins master and agent nodes. It's advisable to monitor the CPU and memory usage regularly and adjust the allocation as needed. Jenkins operations such as fetching the source code, running builds, and archiving artifacts can be resource-intensive, necessitating ample resources for smooth execution.
- **Disk I/O:** High disk I/O performance is crucial for Jenkins, as it frequently reads and writes large volumes of data. Using Solid State Drives (SSD) can improve I/O performance significantly over traditional Hard Disk Drives (HDD). Additionally, separating the Jenkins home directory from the workspace directories can improve disk performance.
- **Network Bandwidth:** Ensure that the network infrastructure is capable of handling the traffic generated by Jenkins, particularly in a distributed setup. Adequate bandwidth and low latency between the master and agent nodes are essential for quick data transfer and efficient execution of distributed builds.

Jenkins can be optimized at the software configuration level by tweaking various settings:

- **Garbage Collection:** Adjusting the Java garbage collection settings can help manage memory usage more effectively. Use the G1 garbage collector for better performance with large heaps, and configure JVM options such as -Xms and -Xmx to set the initial and maximum heap size respectively.

- **Thread Management:** Jenkins executes multiple tasks concurrently using threads. Tuning thread parameters, such as -Dhudson.remoting.Engine.maxThreads, can sometimes resolve performance bottlenecks.
- **Build Queue Management:** Jenkins uses a build queue to manage job execution. Configuring executors properly and balancing the load across multiple agents can prevent job queue build-up, ensuring timely job execution.

Caching mechanisms can play a crucial role in improving Jenkins performance. Common techniques include:

- **Repository Caching:** Utilize local mirrors or caches for dependency management systems like Maven, Gradle, or npm. This reduces the time spent fetching dependencies from remote servers.
- **Build Artifact Caching:** Storing build artifacts on faster storage solutions or using external artifact repositories can reduce the time required for artifact management.
- **Workspace Caching:** Reuse workspaces for recurring builds to avoid redundant operations, such as checkout or dependency installation.

Optimizing Jenkins performance also involves efficient use of plugins and proper configuration:

- **Plugin Management:** Regularly update plugins to their latest versions to benefit from performance improvements and bug fixes. Additionally, remove or disable any unnecessary plugins to reduce resource consumption.
- **System Logs and Monitoring:** Enable logging and set up monitoring for JVM performance, build history, and system health. Plugins like Monitoring and Metrics provide insights into Jenkins performance metrics and help identify bottlenecks.

Implementing an effective scaling strategy is vital as the Jenkins workload grows:

- **Horizontal Scaling:** Add more agent nodes to distribute the load. Configure Jenkins to use cloud-based agents or dynamically provisioned agents for elastic scaling based on current workload.
- **Master-Agent Configuration:** Separate the build execution from the Jenkins master by offloading builds to dedicated agent nodes. This frees up the master for administrative tasks, making the system more responsive.
- **Load Balancing:** Distribute builds evenly across multiple agents to prevent overloading individual nodes. Utilize plugins such as Least Load Plugin to manage load distribution effectively.

An example of setting up a Jenkins agent dynamically on the cloud using the AWS EC2 plugin is given below:

```
<clouds>
  <hudson.plugins.ec2.EC2Cloud>
    <name>aws</name>
    <region>us-east-1</region>
    <instanceCap>10</instanceCap>
    <templates>
      <hudson.plugins.ec2.SlaveTemplate>
        <ami>ami-0abcdef1234567890</ami>
        <type>t2.medium</type>
        <initScript>#!/bin/bash
          sudo yum update -y
          sudo yum install -y java-1.8.0-openjdk
        </initScript>
        <numExecutors>2</numExecutors>
        <remoteFSRoot>/home/ec2-user/jenkins</remoteFSRoot>
        <labels>aws-ec2</labels>
        <mode>NORMAL</mode>
      </hudson.plugins.ec2.SlaveTemplate>
    </templates>
  </hudson.plugins.ec2.EC2Cloud>
</clouds>
```

Executing properly optimized and scaled Jenkins environments produces outputs indicating more efficient resource utilization and enhanced build performance:

```
[Worker 1] Build succeeded in 2m 14s
[Worker 2] Build succeeded in 2m 11s
[Metrics] CPU Usage: 60%, Memory Usage: 70%, Disk I/O: Minimal
```

Scaling Jenkins efficiently ensures it remains capable of handling increased loads, providing a stable and high-performing CI/CD solution. Techniques discussed here align with the fundamental goals of maintaining efficient resource use, minimizing bottlenecks, and enabling robust, scalable Jenkins operations.